The Oxfordian Shakespeare Series

William Shakespeare

HAMLET

Fully Annotated from an Oxfordian Perspective

With an Introduction to the Play

By Richard F. Whalen

The Oxfordian Shakespeare Series

HAMLET

First edition published 2018

ISBN: 978-1-62550-563-7 PB
978-1-62550-559-0 EB

LOC: 2018954328

Printed in the United States of America.

Horatio Editions
Santa Fe NM
RichardFWhalen@Gmail.com

Design by Breezeway Books
Distribution by CreateSpace

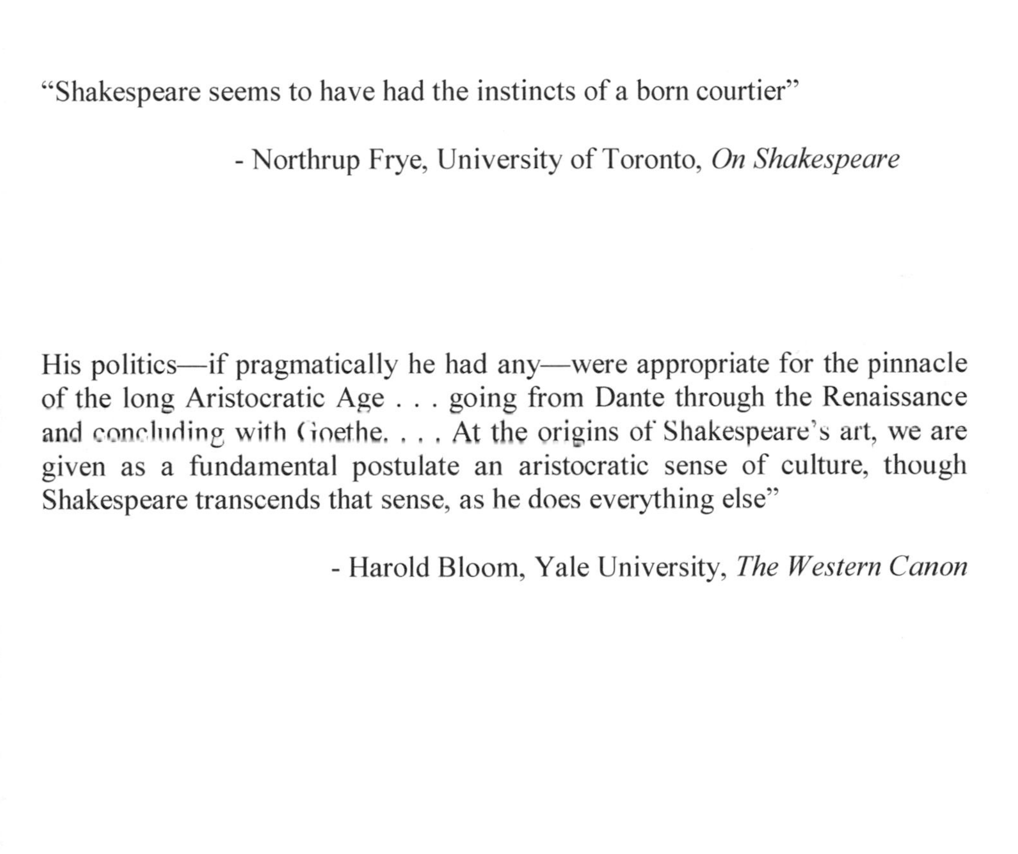

"Shakespeare seems to have had the instincts of a born courtier"

- Northrup Frye, University of Toronto, *On Shakespeare*

His politics—if pragmatically he had any—were appropriate for the pinnacle of the long Aristocratic Age . . . going from Dante through the Renaissance and concluding with Goethe. . . . At the origins of Shakespeare's art, we are given as a fundamental postulate an aristocratic sense of culture, though Shakespeare transcends that sense, as he does everything else"

- Harold Bloom, Yale University, *The Western Canon*

Contents

Preface

These Oxfordian editions of Shakespeare plays offer a frankly different view of them and their author. It takes the view that the great poet-dramatist was Edward de Vere, the seventeenth Earl of Oxford, writing under the pen name "William Shakespeare," and was not the commoner from Stratford-on-Avon, known there as Shakspere. Supporting this view are the many correspondences in the plays to Oxford's life and times. The case that Oxford wrote Shakespeare becomes more compelling as these correspondences, clear allusions and direct references multiply in many of the plays, especially in *Hamlet, Othello, Macbeth, Anthony and Cleopatra, The Merchant of Venice*, and *All's Well That Ends Well.*

For almost a century, Oxfordian scholars have been researching Oxford's life and the Shakespeare works. Their efforts have turned up a wealth of evidence for his authorship of them and many insights that inform the plays and give them a new and deeper meaning. The editors of the plays in this series have drawn on their scholarship and also on the scholarship of "Stratfordian" scholars, whose discoveries and observations sometimes support the case for Oxford. For readers and theatergoers, the result is a much better understanding of the author's intention and design and a greatly enhanced understanding and appreciation of the plays as literary masterpieces.

In recent decades, support for Oxford as Shakespeare has been growing rapidly. Eminent writers, actors, directors, lawyers and judges are among those who have become persuaded that Oxford was the true author. In a breakthrough that augurs well for "Oxfordians," a fair number of university professors have also seen merit in the case for Oxford. Several hundred have expressed their doubts that Will Shakspere of Stratford wrote the Shakespeare works, and more than a few have become convinced that Oxford was Shakespeare.

Knowing how Oxford drew on his life experience, wide reading, travels and his deepest concerns can greatly enrich the reader's appreciation of his literary accomplishment and open new avenues for study and research for students and professors. Theater directors and actors will find new and intriguing ways to interpret the plays, which take on new meanings. The plot lines have more nuances. The characters have more depth and complexity, and the interactions among them are more dramatic. Audiences who accept Oxford as the dramatist will find richer meanings in the plays and enjoy a greater appreciation of the interactions among the characters.

Preface

The introductions and line notes to the play text call attention to the allusions and direct references to Oxford's life experience as a ranking courtier in Queen Elizabeth's court and a traveler in Italy, France and Scotland. The line notes also clarify words, phrases and constructions that may be obsolete or unfamiliar but that are important to an understanding of a passage. They explain words and phrases that had quite different meanings four centuries ago. Some of the word play, puns and unusual metaphors require translation for today's reader and theatergoer. As in all modern-day editions of the Shakespeare plays, the play-text orthography has been modernized for easier reading and understanding.

In the five years since publication of the second Oxfordian edition of *Macbeth* Oxfordian research and scholarship have brought to light significant additional evidence for Oxford's authorship of the Shakespeare plays, which has been incorporated in the Overview, especially in the section on "The Controversy over the Dramatist's Identity."

Overview

He was one of the "best for comedy" in the Elizabethan Age. Among Queen Elizabeth's courtiers, he was "most excellent...in the rare devices of poetry." He excelled "in letters...many Latin verses...yea, even more English verses." He was among those "who honored poesie with their pens and practice." And tellingly, he was listed first among courtier writers "who have written excellently well, as it would appear if their doings could be found out and made public." *

This praise by Elizabethan literary critics all referred to Edward de Vere, the seventeenth Earl of Oxford (1550-1604), who, in the view of many who have studied his life story as well as the Shakespeare plays and poems, was Elizabeth's chief poet-playwright, whose identity was not made public and whose plays appeared under the pseudonym "William Shakespeare,"

His authorship of the Shakespeare poems and plays, although not identified in historical documents, was likely an open secret. It was known in court and theater circles, but it was not a fact to be published and for two reasons: The plays commented on court figures and affairs, often satirically; and writing plays performed in the "vulgar" public theaters and publishing them were considered far beneath the dignity of a nobleman in a highly class-conscious society. And so Oxford used the pen name William Shakespeare, which has become the most famous name in world literature.

The Shakespeare plays were written perceptively and authoritatively from the point of view of a nobleman and courtier at the center of political power in England, Queen Elizabeth's court. They are almost exclusively about the ambitions, crimes, loves, foolishness, cowardice and bravery of monarchs, the nobility, aristocrats and political leaders, including the way they use and mis-use political power. All the principal characters in the plays are kings, queens, dukes, duchesses, earls, countesses and other members of the nobility. The single exception is *The Merry Wives of Windsor*, but the castle at Windsor is where young Oxford spent several weeks recuperating from an illness; and in the play the suitor who finally wins the hand of Anne Page is the only nobleman in the play. He is a man "too great of birth . . . who capers, dances, writes verse and speaks merrily"—an apt self-description of Oxford.

Like all great writers of genius, Oxford drew on his life experience and deepest concerns. His rich, turbulent, controversial life in London and Elizabeth's court and his travels in France, Italy and Scotland fit the profile of a man who would have written the works of Shakespeare. The point of view of the Shakespeare plays is that of an aristocrat, not a commoner such as Shakspere of Stratford. Characters from the ranks of commoners are buffoons, dolts and figures of fun; they are to be appreciated as comical characters, often sarcastically as comic relief and occasionally for their earthy, unsophisticated folk wisdom.

Even some leading Stratfordian scholars have sensed the aristocratic character of the dramatist. "Shakespeare," says Northrup Frye of the University of Toronto, "seems to have had the instincts of a born courtier." Harold Bloom of Yale finds in Shakespeare "an aristocratic sense of culture." He puts the dramatist's political views at the pinnacle of the long Aristocratic Age" of literature from Dante to Goethe. Oxford of course was a born courtier and was immersed in the aristocratic culture of Elizabethan England and Renaissance Italy. (Will Shakspere of Stratford was not.)

The plays demonstrate a profound understanding of history and literature by a writer who had ready access to private libraries and their rare and expensive books and who read widely, including works in Italian, French and ancient Greek that had not yet been translated into English but are recognized as important sources for Shakespeare plays. Two hundred books have been identified as sources for and influences on Shakespeare plays. The dramatist had a deep understanding of English, Continental, medieval and classical history and literature, as well as the latest developments in theology, medicine, astronomy and the law. From his youth onward, Oxford had ready access to private libraries.

As a ranking nobleman in Queen Elizabeth's court, Oxford could observe the maneuvering and power politics of courtiers such as the Earl of Leicester, the inspiration for the murderous Claudius in *Hamlet*. The Queen and her court were the primary audience for whom he wrote his Shakespeare plays. They were a knowing audience that would appreciate the intricate plots, sophisticated language, double meanings, allusions to the Queen and the thinly veiled satire of court figures, such as the lampoon of Lord Burghley, the Queen's chief minister and Oxford's father-in-law, in the character of Polonius in *Hamlet*. Such was the power of Oxford's genius that his plays, written to be performed for an aristocratic audience in Elizabeth's court, were popular with commoners in the Globe Theater and proved to have universal appeal that has struck the minds and hearts of readers and spectators everywhere for all time.

As Oxford in the person of Hamlet instructs the visiting troupe of players: "The purpose of playing, whose end, both at the first and now, was and is, to hold, as 'twere, the mirror up to nature; to show virtue her own feature, scorn her own image, and the very age and body of the time his form and pressure."

* Quoted in the first paragraph are Francis Meres, *Palladis Tamia* (1589); Gabriel Harvey, "Gratulariones Valdinensis" address to Oxford before Queen Elizabeth (1578); Henry Peacham, *The Complete Gentleman* (1622); and George Puttenham, *The Art of English Poesie* (1589).

The Dramatist's Life

Edward de Vere saw his first theatrical performances as a youngster at Hedingham Castle, where he was born in 1550, eight years before Elizabeth became queen. His father, the sixteenth Earl of Oxford, maintained a troupe of actors. When Edward was eleven, Queen Elizabeth and her entourage stayed at Hedingham almost a week, and plays were among the usual entertainments for the queen when noblemen such as his father were called upon to host the royal entourage visiting their castles during the queen's "progresses" around England.

When his father died in 1562, young Edward inherited the earldom of Oxford with its vast properties. Even though his mother was living, under feudal law Edward became a ward of the Crown to protect his patrimony and for his education until he reached the age of twenty-one. As a ward of the Crown, he was sent to London to live at the mansion of William Cecil, later Lord Burghley, master of the court of wards, minister of state and the queen's chief counselor throughout most of her reign. In *Hamlet*, Burghley is lampooned as Polonius, the King's chief counselor.

Oxford's education was no doubt largely self-directed with the guidance of various tutors and mentors. It began early in his pre-teens when he was sent as a boarding pupil to live with Sir Thomas Smith, a renowned scholar and diplomat, who owned one of the largest libraries in England. After his father died and Oxford moved to Cecil House as a ward of the Crown, a period of formal education in his early teens was reported as Latin, French, cosmography (probably including astronomy), and "exercises with his pen," writing and drawing. (See Ward, Anderson.) Still in his early teens, he received degrees from Cambridge and Oxford, probably honorary in recognition of his precocious learning, although he may also have done some studying at Oxford.

When Oxford was living at Cecil House, William Cecil was amassing one of the largest libraries in England, including many volumes procured from printers on the Continent. Many of the books are known to have been sources for the Shakespeare plays and poems. In the manuscript collection was the only extant copy of the Anglo-Saxon *Beowulf*, which had a significant influence on *Hamlet.* His tutors at Cecil House would testify to Oxford's dedication to study and his intellectual accomplishments. He enrolled at Gray's Inn, the most prestigious of London's four Inns of Court, where young men studied law and produced plays in which they also acted. Law scholars and judges find a profound knowledge of law throughout Shakespeare's works. (See Regnier.)

One of Cecil's retainers was Oxford's uncle, Arthur Golding, a scholar-translator who helped manage Oxford's estates and probably oversaw his education. When Oxford was in his mid-teens, the first translation into English of Ovid's *Metamorphoses* was published, with Golding listed as the putative author. All scholars agree that the translation (even today considered the best) was, along with the Geneva edition of the Bible, the most important influence on the works of Shakespeare. The racy translation, however, is very different from and far superior to Golding's other writings, which were mostly translations of pious, religious books. It is likely that Golding's brilliant nephew may have done most, if not all, of the translating. Cecil's gardener, too, was a published scholar whom Oxford would have known; he was the most noted English horticulturist of the time, and Shakespeare's works are full of detailed, accurate references to a wide range of plants and flowers, cultivated and wild, the kind of information that would transcend the knowledge of a casual observer but would proceed from one learned in botany.

Oxford was a published poet, but the only verse found under his name, initials, or a recognized pseudonym is a handful of songs and poems, most of them from his early teenage years. They are, nevertheless, considered to be some of the best poems and song lyrics by an early Elizabethan courtier-writer. Although he was hailed during his lifetime as an excellent playwright, no plays published under his name, have been found. They would appear under his Shakespeare pseudonym, as would the Sonnets.

When Oxford turned twenty-one, he and Cecil's daughter, Anne, were married. Queen Elizabeth attended the ceremony in Westminster Abbey. In his early twenties, he traveled on the Continent for about fifteen months, and the Shakespeare plays that are set principally in Italy and France exhibit first-hand knowledge of their geography and landmarks, especially in the cities of northern Italy–Venice, Milan, Padua, Florence, Sienna and Verona. He served with the military in Scotland, and *Macbeth* shows first-hand knowledge of Scotland--its geography, clans, mores, laws and even its unusual weather. (There is no evidence that Shakspere of Stratford traveled on the Continent or to Scotland.)

When he was in his late twenties, court records list eleven plays that were performed for Queen Elizabeth, but the records do not name the author of the plays, and none of them have been found. Many of the titles, however, suggest Shakespeare plays that appeared later. For example, "The Historie of Error" may well have been an early *Comedy of Errors*; "The Historie of the Solitarie Knight" could have been *Timon of Athens*; and "The Historie of the Rape of the Second Helene" may have been an early version of *All's Well That Ends Well*. In *All's Well,* the heroine, Helena, tricks her recalcitrant husband into bedding her in the dark thinking she is another woman. Published rumors had it that Oxford was a victim of this same bizarre bed trick when he was twenty-four years old and had been married for three years.

Oxford was immersed in the world of the theater, not just as a playwright but also as a patron of acting companies, employer of playwrights and at least once as a performer, in a court entertainment called a "masque." He was the patron of at least two acting companies that appeared regularly in Queen Elizabeth's court. John Lyly and Anthony Munday, both playwrights, served as his secretaries. Scholars see many resemblances between their plays and the Shakespeare plays.

While writing poems and plays, Oxford was living a full, even tumultuous, life. Besides traveling on the Continent and going on military expeditions, he produced pageants and extravaganzas for the queen and won jousting tournaments held in her honor. He exhibited an eccentric and mercurial temperament, spent extravagantly, got into rancorous disputes with other courtiers and fought with his enemies in the streets of London (shades of *Romeo and Juliet*). After a long estrangement from his first wife, whom he suspected of infidelity, he fathered five children with her and an illegitimate child with one of the queen's Ladies in Waiting, much to Elizabeth's displeasure. She sent both Oxford and his mistress to the Tower of London for their transgressions. Although Elizabeth was quick to banish him from her court when he dared to disobey or displease her, it was never for long. Banishment and reconciliation are recurring themes in the Shakespeare plays.

When Oxford was in favor, he delighted the queen with his dancing, his wit and his theatricals. In 1586, she awarded him an extraordinary grant of a thousand pounds a year for life, the equivalent of hundreds of thousands of dollars annually in today's money. She gave no reason for it and required no accounting. One explanation is that she did this because she had managed when he was her ward to appropriate for her treasury much of his wealth and estates and then decided he needed the cash to maintain a lifestyle suitable for a leading nobleman. She also loved theatrical entertainments and, although notoriously tight-fisted, she may well have been backing Oxford as her court playwright and theatrical impresario. The queen's successor, King James, whose wife also loved plays and theatricals, would continue the grant until Oxford's death.

The Earl of Oxford was not the stereotypical aristocrat of dignity, decorum and rectitude. Far from it. By all accounts, he was a difficult, improvident, eccentric aristocrat of many contradictions. He could clown in processions in the London streets to make the people laugh. While some heaped scurrilous abuse on him, others gave him lavish praise. His contemporaries, including King James, referred to him as "Great Oxford" and "great-souled." He was called "peerless in England" by the scholar Gabriel Harvey in a speech made before the queen, but Harvey also called him "a passing singular odd man." His mercurial temperament may be understood in the light of findings by modern-day psychologists who hold that many writers of genius experience moods of both despair and euphoria that seem to have characterized Oxford's personality–and the personalities of many of the conflicted leading characters in the Shakespeare plays, especially Hamlet.

Remarried after the death of his first wife, Oxford lived his last years in Hackney near the market town of Stratford-at-Bow on the outskirts of London. During the last eight years of his life (1597-1604), a surge of twelve Shakespeare plays poured from the presses–five in one year alone. The first edition of *Hamlet* appeared in 1603 and the second, a much-improved edition, in 1604, the year Oxford died. It was as if the author, perhaps sensing that death was near, were making final revisions to his plays before releasing them for publication.

Oxford died at age fifty-four, probably a suicide, a year after the death of Queen Elizabeth. (See Detobel.) Through his improvident spending and the Queen's manipulations of his finances, he had lost almost all of his income-producing estates, upon which rested the reputation and power of a titled aristocrat. He was interred in St. Augustine's church at Hackney. A nephew reported that his body was later removed to Westminster Abbey in London, but records at the Abbey were not maintained until 1616. The church at Hackney was torn down two centuries later, and the whereabouts of Oxford's remains is unknown. "Though I once gone to all the world must die." (Sonnet 81) After his death, no new Shakespeare plays were published with signs of being authorized releases until 1623, when thirty-six plays were published in a volume now called the First Folio, which was dedicated to Oxford's son-in-law and that man's brother. Half the plays had never before been in print.

His Stage and His Audience

Playwrights write for their audiences and the premier audience for the best playwrights during the reign of Elizabeth I was the Queen herself, her court and England's aristocrats. She loved music and dancing and theatrical entertainments, which were performed in the great halls of her palaces. Early in her reign, she granted a nobleman a license to produce "comedies, tragedies, interludes, [and] stage plays" for the entertainment of her subjects as well as for her "solace and pleasure." E. K. Chambers, one of the most eminent Shakespeare scholars, considers that the success of the theater during her reign was largely due to her appreciation and support. At the beginning of his four-volume work, *The Elizabethan Stage*, he states that she and her court had "a profound effect in helping to determine the character of the Elizabethan play," including of course Oxford's Shakespeare plays. As Professor Alvin Kernan of Princeton University put it: "Shakespeare had the court and its interests very much in mind when he wrote."

While the Globe and the other public theaters get most of the attention today as the stage for the Shakespeare plays, there are more than twice as many records of performances of Shakespeare plays at the royal court, the indoor Blackfriars theater, universities, the Inns of Court and at manor houses of aristocrats than at the outdoor public theaters. For a city of around 150,000 people, London offered many opportunities for acting companies to perform plays before all levels of society, from the royal court to the tavern yard.

Blackfriars was the most important of the indoor, "private" theaters, so called because they were located in private precincts of London. Blackfriars was a walled precinct that had once been a sizable monastery complex. Its great hall was much smaller than the public theaters, but it provided protection from rain and snow. The price of admission was much higher than that of the public theaters. Performances were in the evening and were lighted by torches. The fashionable, well-to-do audience watched performances by visiting acting companies, and companies of choir boys presented previews of plays before performing them at court. For a short time, Oxford held the lease to the Blackfriars theater, where his troupe of young actors performed. Blackfriars was so popular that the theatergoers' carriages sometimes caused traffic jams in the narrow, winding streets.

Plays were also performed at the Inns of Court, legal societies where students and acting companies staged entertainments. Shakespeare's *Comedy of Errors* and, notably, *Twelfth Night* with its legal jesting, were performed by visiting troupes of actors at two of the four Inns of Court.

Noblemen sponsored acting companies to shelter them from laws that branded itinerant actors as "rogues and vagabonds" and made them subject to arrest if they offended anyone in power. The most prominent companies were the Lord Chamberlain's Men and the Lord Admiral's Men. Oxford was the patron of two acting companies and probably a third. (Records for all the acting companies are scant and fragmentary.) In the 1580s, when he was in his thirties, Oxford's Men performed at court and possibly at the first public theater, called quite simply The Theatre. They also went on tour in the provinces, as did other acting companies from time to time. More than a decade later, another record mentions that plays were performed by Oxford's Men, which may have been reorganized from the 1580s company. Oxford also had a troupe of boy actors who performed at court and at Blackfriars. Two years before he died, Oxford secured the Queen's special permission for his company to perform in the yard of a tavern called the Boar's Head. In the *Henry the Fourth* plays, the Boar's Head Tavern is where Falstaff and Prince Hal drink sherry and indulge in verbal jousting. As it happens, the boar was Oxford's heraldic emblem.

Another nobleman who sponsored acting companies was the Earl of Sussex. During one Christmas season at court, Sussex's Men staged five of the eleven anonymous plays, now lost, some of which bear titles that sound intriguingly like early versions of Shakespeare plays. Sussex was one of Oxford's close friends at court and, in the opinion of some, almost a surrogate father.

Acting companies also performed Shakespeare plays at the huge public theaters, which regularly drew thousands of commoners. Oxford was twenty-six when the first two public theaters were built, the Theatre and the Curtain. The Rose, the Swan and other theaters followed. Though many do not realize it, the famous Globe Theater was not built until 1599, just five years before Oxford died.

The largest of these partially roofed, open-air theaters could hold two thousand spectators or more for the afternoon performances. "Groundlings" paid a penny to stand on the ground, which was open to the sky. The more prosperous spectators sat on benches in three covered balconies where the seats were two or three times more expensive. The public theaters were so big and the performances so frequent that seeing plays must have been an enormously popular entertainment, and playwrights produced many hundreds of plays. Almost all of them are now lost. The courtyards of taverns like the Boar's Head were also used for theatrical entertainments, but not much is known about them.

The repertory of the acting companies was enormous. At the height of a theater season, an acting company might give a hundred and fifty performances of thirty different plays. There were no long runs of a play on successive days. A leading actor might perform as many as seventy roles, playing different roles day after day. How plays were staged and how the actors managed to memorize so many different roles continues to be a subject of study by scholars of Elizabethan theater.

The Composition and Publication of the Plays

When it was that Oxford wrote each of his Shakespeare plays and in what sequence and how often he revised a play are also subjects of continuing study and debate by Stratfordian and Oxfordian scholars. No author's notes or other records exist to indicate a year of composition or revision for any play. No authors' manuscripts, which might have been dated, have survived.

An approximate chronology of composition dates for some of the Shakespeare plays can be derived from dates of first performance, first publication, or first mention of a play in various records. For example, an early version of *Hamlet* was performed by 1589, the first record of its existence, when Thomas Nashe mentioned in passing "whole *Hamlets*, I should say handfuls of tragical speeches."

Stratfordian scholarship dates the composition of a dozen or so plays after Oxford's death in 1604. Their dating, however, is based on especially meager and questionable evidence. As the eminent Stratfordian scholar, E. K. Chambers, wrote about trying to date the plays in his chapter on "The Problem of Chronology": "There is much of conjecture, even as regards the order [of the plays], and still more as regards the ascriptions to particular years." His observation applies to the allegedly post-1604 plays, which are dated based on apparent references or allusions in the plays to contemporary events to make them fit the lifespan of Shakspere of Stratford, who died in 1616. The post-1604 dating scheme fails because none of those references and allusions is unique to writings or events that occurred after 1604. Oxford could have written the allegedly post-1604 plays before his death, even many years before he died. Posthumous publication or first performance is not at all unusual for playwrights then or now. (See Whalen "A Dozen Shakespeare Plays.")

The first collection of Shakespeare plays, the principal authority for the canon, was published in London in 1623, two decades after Oxford died (and almost a decade after the death of Shakspere of Stratford.) The big, expensive book contained thirty-six plays and was entitled *Mr. William Shakespeares Comedies, Histories, & Tragedies*. Later on, editors began to call it the "First Folio," a nickname derived from the size of the pages.

Half of the plays in the First Folio were seeing print for the first time. Four of them had never before been published or even mentioned in the records. Where these eighteen plays had been or who possessed the manuscripts of them prior to their publication is a subject of continuing study and debate. The other eighteen plays had appeared earlier in individual editions called quartos, nearly all of them during Oxford's lifetime.

The full extent of the Shakespeare canon also remains a subject of study and debate. For example, scholars have generally accepted the quarto edition of *Pericles* as canonical, even though it was not included in the First Folio. Opinion is divided about whether *The Two Noble Kinsmen* should be included; it was published in 1634 as by John Fletcher and William Shakespeare. *Locrine* is not generally accepted into the canon, although the title page of its quarto edition says it was "newly set forth, overseen and corrected by W.S." Later in the 1600s, editions of Shakespeare plays included a half dozen plays that scholars now exclude from the canon, although *Edward the Third* has recently been accepted by many as a Shakespeare play.

Over the past three centuries, editors of successive editions have modernized the spelling and punctuation, corrected what seem to be printers' errors and offered interpretations of puzzling words and passages. They have also tried to reconcile the considerable differences between the quarto and First Folio texts of some of the plays. These textual problems have created an enormous industry in the world of Shakespeare scholarship.

Overview

The Controversy over the Dramatist's Identity

For Stratfordians it is simple. William Shakespeare was born and raised in Stratford-on-Avon. "William Shakespeare" is the name on the plays and poems. Therefore, William Shakespeare of Stratford-on-Avon was the author of them.

But it is not that simple. The name of the Stratford man was "Shakspere" or a close variant in all eight official church records from his baptism in 1564 in Stratford to his death there in 1616—not "Shakespeare". And "Shakspere" was the name of his father, his siblings and his children two dozen times in church records of baptisms, marriages and deaths.

"Shakspere" was the spelling of the six extant signatures, supposedly by him, including three times on his mundane will, which is notable for not being the will of a literary figure. Whether Shakspere himself penned the signatures is doubtful. The former curator of wills at the Public Record Office noted that a clerk would often sign for a deponent who could not sign his name but whose identity was verified by witnesses. Finally, it's hard to accept that if Shakspere of Stratford were the great poet-dramatist who penned nearly a million words published in London as by "Shakespeare" he would at the end of his life have left a will with his name spelled "Shakspere" or a close variant of it five times and not "Shakespeare."

Variants of the Stratford man's name included "Shaxpere," "Shagspere," and "Schackspere" but not "Shakespeare." (The Stratford spellings seemed to reflect a flat "a," as in "shack spur", although how spoken words sounded is debated.) Spelling his name in so many different ways was not at all unusual. Elizabethan spelling in general was chaotic, even of surnames, so it is all the more significant that in London the name on the poems and plays was uniformly "Shakespeare." The two names were similar but not the same. They were different names designating two different men. The Will Shakspere of Stratford was not the William Shakespeare of London, where it was the pen name of the Earl of Oxford. (See Pointon, and Whalen "Shakspere/Shakespeare.)

In a curious twist of literary history, for a time in the late 1800s and early 1900s, Stratfordian scholars, editors and critics who no doubt believed Shakespeare to be the man from Stratford used the "Shakspere" spelling in Stratford to designate the poet-dramatist. Even among them were Keats, Coleridge and Carlyle. Then the Stratfordians apparently began to realize that this would not do since the plays and poems had been published as by "William Shakespeare." So around 1915, they did an about face and in their writings began to use "Shakespeare" to designate the Stratford man despite the historical evidence to the contrary. They made the great poet-dramatist

Shakespeare into Shakspere of Stratford, for whom there is no evidence that he could write anything at all.

Nothing is known about what Will Shakspere of Stratford was doing until he reached his late twenties, except that he married and had three children by age twenty-one. Growing up in Stratford, he would have spoken the Warwickshire dialect of his illiterate parents, relatives and neighbors. The dialect was much different from the English of London and that of the Shakespeare poems and plays. No attendance records or curriculum for the one-room school in Stratford survive for the years he was of school age. Similar grammar schools in England taught the Latin language, not written English as such.

During his twenties, when young men begin to make their way in the world (and publishing if they are writers), what Shakspere was doing and where he was living, is unknown. When he was in his late twenties, he began to turn up in business and theater records in London—but not as a writer.

No letters written or received by him have been found. No records from his lifetime connect him with writing of any kind, much less the Shakespeare plays and poems. No one in Stratford, including his family and others who must have known him, left any word that he was an author. If he owned any books during his lifetime, no records of them have been found, whereas the Arden *Dictionary of Shakespeare Sources* has nearly two hundred entries, including rare and expensive volumes typically found only in the libraries of the wealthy.

His three-page will was the will of a businessman; it contains no mention of books or manuscripts or anything literary. He was supposedly buried under a slab that does not even carry his name. The short, enigmatic inscription on the Stratford monument on the wall nearby says nothing about plays, poems or the theater; and the effigy of a writer in the monument is a fraud. No one wrote anything about him at the time of his death, even though the Shakespeare plays and poems were the most successful in London.

Will Shakspere's life is grossly unfit for the life of a writer, much less that of the great poet-dramatist whose works demonstrate exceptional learning, travels in Scotland, France and Italy, eloquent fluency in the English of London plus knowledge of several other vernacular languages, especially French and Italian, and an insider's knowledge of life in royal court circles.

To support their claim for Will Shakspere of Stratford-on-Avon, Stratfordians cite mentions of Avon and Stratford in the prefatory matter to First Folio of 1623 and today's effigy of a writer in the monument to "Shakspeare" in the Stratford church. In the First Folio, Ben Jonson, a master of deliberate ambiguity and the creator of the prefatory matter, contributed a long poem to the memory of the dramatist in which he called him "Sweet Swan of Avon." But although Stratford is on the Avon River, Jonson's "of Avon" could as easily refer to Hampton Court, one of the royal palaces most frequently used for theatrical performances. "Hampton," as the author and Oxfordian Alexander Waugh explains, was a corruption of the Celtic-Roman name "Avondunum" for the palace that was then shortened to "Avon." He found five writers who mentioned that early on Hampton Court, which was on the Thames River, had been called Avon (Welch for "river.") Educated readers of the First Folio could recognize and appreciate Jonson's ambiguity, alluding either to the Avon River of the obscure town of Stratford or to the Avon meaning the famous Hampton Court with its great hall for theatrical performances, including many Shakespeare plays.

Five pages later, Leonard Digges in his short poem referred to "thy Stratford moniment." Readers of the First Folio would think first of the London suburb, Stratford-at-Bow, the marketplace for London, not the small town of Stratford-on-Avon that was a three-day journey from the capital. And Oxford lived the last years of his life in a mansion close by Stratford-at-Bow where he may well have been rewriting plays before publication. Digges's "moniment" is also ambiguous. "Moniment" in the usage of those times could mean someone's accomplishment, such as a writer's creative works, not necessarily a monument of stone.

This minimal biographical information is poetically allusive and no doubt deliberately ambiguous. Nothing in the First Folio of Shakespeare plays directly and unambiguously states that Will Shakspere of Stratford-on-Avon wrote them, although it would have been quite natural and easy to do so, if it were true. The name of his hometown, "Stratford-on-Avon," does not appear in the First Folio. The First Folio's prefatory matter, which is contradictory and sometimes deliberately ambiguous or false, cannot be taken at face value and is not reliable evidence for Shakspere as the poet-dramatist. (See Whalen "Ambiguity First Folio.)

In fact, the First Folio's publication and dedication arguably on balance are better evidence for the Earl of Oxford as the dramatist. The big, expensive volume of thirty-six Shakespeare plays was dedicated to Oxford's son-in-law, the Earl of Montgomery, and to that man's brother, the wealthy and powerful Earl of Pembroke, who at one time had been engaged to another of Oxford's daughters. Pembroke, the preeminent patron of the arts and as Lord Chamberlain an influential leader of the Protestant faction, probably financed publication of the First Folio. Ben Jonson, who had published his own *Works* in a large, folio volume in 1616, was eminently qualified to see the Shakespeare First Folio through the presses and was already benefitting from Pembroke's generous patronage.

The timing of the First Folio's publication, seven years after Shakspere died and nineteen years after Oxford died, and its dedication to the two brothers might well have been influenced by political considerations. Sponsored writings were often political. At the time, King James of England was trying to negotiate a controversial marital liaison with Catholic Spain.

Many of the Shakespeare plays in the First Folio implicitly supported a Protestant monarchy for England. A shift in England's power structure toward a Catholic faction would have jeopardized the power and fortunes of many Protestant noblemen and courtiers, including Montgomery and Pembroke. As it happens, Pembroke not only was a leading patron of writers but as Lord Chamberlain had oversight power over theater performances and the publication of plays. Significantly, the First Folio was not dedicated to King James even though he was the reigning monarch, the patron of the King's Men acting company and a fan of the Shakespeare plays. Politics trumped protocol. And modern-day Stratfordian politics dictate that the dedication to Montgomery, Oxford's son-in-law, and Pembroke pass without mention. It shrinks to insignificance the brief, allusive and ambiguous mentions of "Avon" and "Stratford," supposed evidence for Shakspere.

More eye-catching and commanding for the Stratfordian argument is today's monument to "Shakspeare" (no first name) in Holy Trinity Church at Stratford-on-Avon. The large monument on the wall depicts a man holding a quill pen and poised to write on a sheet of paper on of all things a pillow. (There's a reason for that.) Seemingly, it is a memorial to the Stratford man as a writer, even though no historical evidence even suggests, much less proves, that he wrote anything at all.

Today's effigy of a writer, however, is not the original. It depicted a sack-holder and was erected sometime before 1623, perhaps many years earlier. In 1634, the antiquarian-historian William Dugdale visited Stratford and made a sketch of the original monument for the engraver's illustration of it in Dugdale's massive volume on Warwickshire County. Dugdale's sketch and the engraving of it show a man with a drooping moustache, arms akimbo, grasping a sack of wool—no paper, pen or writing surface. For almost a century, this sack-holder was the image used in editions of Shakespeare to depict the Stratford man. Over the next centuries, however, the effigy in the monument was taken down several times by Stratford church and civic leaders for repair and "beautification," transforming it into today's effigy of a man with a goatee and upturned moustache and with pen and paper. The rough shape of the historical woolsack survives as a neat pillow for a writing surface. Some Oxfordians suggest that the dour effigy with a wool sack was erected for Shakspere's father, a leading citizen of Stratford and a dealer in wool. Today's effigy of a writer in the church would become a major attraction for tourists, leaving for many an unforgettable but false impression that the Stratford man was a writer. The original effigy, however, did not depict a writer. Today's is a fraud. (See Whalen "Stratford Bust.")

As scholars and theater people in the 1700s and 1800s realized that Shakespeare's works were the greatest literary achievement in Western civilization, they raised an imagined profile of Will Shakspere and deified him as the immortal Bard of Avon, the divine Shakespeare. The town of

Stratford became the most popular tourist attraction in England outside of London and a commercial shrine to him. The idea of a small-town commoner writing such stupendous creations was appealing to many who espoused new, democratic ideals. Given the woefully inadequate historical evidence for the Stratford man as Shakespeare, what remained was the similarity of name, the weight of centuries of tradition, and for many the attractive belief that the great poet-dramatist was an ordinary, unassuming man of no special education or worldly experience but a truly incredible genius.

No one seriously began to question Will Shakspere's credentials until the mid-1800s when biographers began to notice the lack of anything literary in the life of Will Shakspere and proposed Sir Francis Bacon, the philosopher, essayist and statesman, as someone more qualified to have written the works of Shakespeare. As the search intensified for the true author, Christopher Marlowe, William Stanley the sixth Earl of Derby (Oxford's son-in-law), and many others were also put forward as candidates. Then, in 1920, J. Thomas Looney, an inquisitive and methodical English schoolmaster, published his pioneering book identifying Edward de Vere, the seventeenth Earl of Oxford, as the true author of Shakespeare's works. Since then, more than a score of books and hundreds of articles have expanded on the evidence for Oxford. Today, his candidacy has by far the most support among non-Stratfordians.

The evidence against Shakspere as Shakespeare has led many well-known figures in literature, the theater and the law to express their doubts about the Stratford man. They include Walt Whitman, Mark Twain, Henry James, William James, John Galsworthy, Ralph Waldo Emerson, Sigmund Freud; university professors William Y. Elliott of Harvard, Mortimer Adler of the University of Chicago, Hugh R. Trevor-Roper of Oxford; Shakespearean actors Derek Jacobi, Mark Rylance, Jeremy Irons, Michael York; and over the years five justices of the U.S. Supreme Court. Three of them became convinced that Oxford was Shakespeare: Justices John Paul Stevens, Antonin Scalia and Harry Blackmun. The justices often quote from Shakespeare in their decisions and some have engaged in moot courts on the law in the plays, such as, whether Hamlet was guilty of murder. Also among the Oxfordians are Freud, Derek Jacobi, David McCullough and Ambassador Paul Nitze.

More than four thousand men and women, including several hundred academics, have signed the on-line declaration of reasonable doubt about the identity of William Shakespeare, and their number continues to increase. (See www. DoubtAboutWill.org)

Suggested Readings

The following books are a selected few from the wide range of scholarship on the seventeenth Earl of Oxford as the author of the plays that appeared under his pseudonym, William Shakespeare. Citations and bibliographies in these works lead to many other works about Oxford and the authorship controversy, including two by Stratfordian scholars.

Anderson, Mark. *Shakespeare by Another Name:A Biography of Edward de Vere, Earl of Oxford, the Man Who Was Shakespeare*. New York: Gotham, 2004. A major work of 600 pages including extensive end notes, and probably the most comprehensive, authoritative and influential biography after Ogburn's.

Clark, Eva Turner. *Hidden Allusions in Shakespeare's Plays: A Study of the Early Court Revels and the Personalities of the Times.* London: Palmer, 1930. 3d ed. Jennings LA: Minos, 1974. Edited with additional material by Ruth Loyd Miller.

Farina, William. *De Vere As Shakespeare: An Oxfordian Reading of the Canon*. Jefferson NC: McFarland, 2006.

Garber, Marjorie. *Shakespeare's Ghost Writers: Literature as Uncanny Causality*. New York: Methuen, 1987. New York: Routledge, 2010 with a new Preface. Including a balanced assessment of the case for Oxford as Shakespeare by a Harvard English professor and a Stratfordian (so far).

Looney, J. Thomas. *"Shakespeare" Identified in Edward de Vere, the Seventeenth Earl of Oxford*. London: Palmer, 1920. The book that launched Oxford as Shakespeare.

Miller, Ruth Loyd, ed. *Oxfordian Vistas*. Jennings LA: Minos, 1975. A collection of scores of research articles, many by Miller.

Ogburn, Charlton. *The Mysterious William Shakespeare: The Myth and the Reality*. McLean VA: EPM, 1984. After Looney's, probably the most influential book on Oxford as Shakespeare.

Ogburn, Dorothy and Charlton. *This Star of England: William Shakespeare, Man of the Renaissance*. New York: Coward-McCann, 1952. By the parents of Charlton. The two lengthy books by parents and by their son are thorough assessments of the evidence against Shakspere and for Oxford.

Poynton, A. J. *The Man Who Was Never Shakespeare.* Tunbridge Weslls, Kent: 2011. For the evidence that Will Shakspere of Stratford was not the author of the Shakespeare works; see esp. pp. 24, 268-73.

Suggested Reading

Price, Diana. *Shakespeare's Unorthodox Biography.* Westport CT: Greenwood Press, 2001. With a valuable appendix on the paper trails for two dozen contemporary writers and the lack of any for Shakspere (but a Stratfordian defense of today's Stratford monument of a writer as the original).

Shahan, John M. and Alexander Waugh, eds. *Shakespeare Beyond Doubt? Exposing an Industry in Denial*. The Shakespeare Authorship Coalition, 2013, 2016. A collection of essays rebutting the Stratfordian *Shakespeare Beyond Doubt* (no question mark), edited by Paul Edmondson and Stanley Wells of The Shakespeare Birthplace Trust in Stratford. Cambridge UP, 2013. Shahan created the DoubtAboutWill web site and has waged a campaign against the Stratford establishment.

Shapiro, James. *Contested Will: Who Wrote Shakespeare?* New York: Simon & Schuster, 2010. The first book-length history of the authorship controversy by a university English professor, including the case for Oxford as Shakespeare.

Ward, B. M. *The Seventeenth Earl of Oxford (1550-1604) from Contemporary Documents*. London: Murray, 1928. The first book-length biography of Oxford, based on archival research by an Oxfordian, who chose not to include the evidence for him as Shakespeare.

Warren, James, ed. *An Index to Oxfordian Publications.* 4th ed. Somerville MA: Forever Press, 2017. A list and cross-index of thousands of articles and hundreds of books.

Whalen, Richard F. *Shakespeare–Who Was He? The Oxford Challenge to the Bard of Avon*. Westport CT: Greenwood-Praeger, 1994. A short introduction to the Oxfordian proposition.

Whittemore, Hank. *100 Reasons Shake-speare Was the Earl of Oxford.* Somerville MA: Forever Press, 2016. A popular, even breezy, listing and description of the "100 reasons," based the biographical and historical evidence.

Introduction to *Hamlet*

Something is rotten in the state of Denmark.
(1.4.94)

The most personal and "autobiographical" of his Shakespeare plays, *Hamlet* is set in the court of Denmark, standing for the court of Queen Elizabeth of England; and Hamlet, the Prince of Denmark, is the voice of the dramatist, Edward de Vere, the seventeenth Earl of Oxford, a prominent member of her court. The best writers write best about what they know best, their own life and deepest concerns; and the parallels between Oxford's life and concerns and Hamlet's are many and striking.

Not recognizing Oxford as the dramatist, Stratfordian commentators have struggled to make sense of the play but give up. They are driven to conclude that *Hamlet*, the creation of the world's greatest playwright, is enigmatic. But with Oxford as the dramatist, the play that he finished just before he died makes perfect sense as the agonized, artistic expression of his deepest concerns,

The most striking and compelling feature of Hamlet's personality is what he calls his "antic disposition," his episodes of manic high spirits, sometimes verging on hilarity, that make great theater. At other times he falls into a deep depression in soliloquies about the meaning and purpose of life, to the point of considering suicide. The manic highs of his "antic disposition" are sometimes real and sometimes deliberately put on to throw his adversaries off balance, and they mirror what can be discerned about Oxford's personality.

Throughout the play, Hamlet's manic highs are taken by those around him to be some kind of wild madness, a fine frenzy that seems to them to convey something of his thinking that is beyond their understanding. At times, Hamlet deliberately turns on an antic disposition to serve his purpose while at other times he appears to feel and act as if actually experiencing a manic high. In stark contrast, when his mood swings to deep depression in his soliloquies he despairs about life to the point of considering suicide. Commentators on the play debate whether this is a real disturbance of Hamlet's mind or a feigned and artful craziness, designed to deceive and discombobulate while subtly conveying truth to a knowledgeable audience. Arguably, Oxford may well have meant it to be both.

Only someone who was very much like Hamlet, someone with his own periodic manic highs and deep depressions could have written so convincingly about them in *Hamlet*. There is evidence from Oxford's life that he experienced this mood disorder. He could be mercurial and unpredictable but most of the time seemingly quite normal, although somewhat eccentric by society's standards. William Cecil, his guardian, who knew him as well as anyone did, wrote that "there is much more in him of understanding than any stranger would think." (See Ward.)

His contemporaries were puzzled and disturbed by his behavior, while recognizing his admirable traits. In a letter to his father in 1573, Gilbert Talbot mentioned the twenty-three-year-old Oxford's unpredictable mood swings: "My Lord of Oxford is lately grown into great credit, for the Queen's Majesty delighteth more in his personage and his dancing and valiantness than any other. . . . I think Sussex doth back him all that he can. If it were not for his fickle head, he would pass any of them shortly."

In an extravagant, satirical sketch of Oxford, the scholar and mercurial literary figure Gabriel Harvey summed up Oxford as "a passing singular odd man." He ended his fevered poem, however, by citing Oxford's wisdom, wit and gallant virtues, which he had praised extravagantly in an earlier address to him.

George Chapman, also a contemporary of Oxford, had the lead character in *The Revenge of Bussy d'Ambois* (1613) depict Oxford as "the most goodly fashioned man I ever saw. . . . of spirit passing great . . . . Spoke and writ sweetly . . , valiant and learned." But then he adds that Oxford was strangely haughty and disdainful of lesser men who tried to make themselves appear to be more important. He thought Oxford was proud, wary, passionate, insulting and raging (much like Hamlet). (See Whalen *On Looking*.)

More recently, Charlton Ogburn concluded in a section on Oxford's character in his 900-page biography (1984, 1992) of Oxford as Shakespeare that on the records of his life he was "arrogant, unstable and erratic."

Two Stratfordian scholars also described Oxford's eccentric and difficult personality. Back in 1899, Sidney Lee, editor of the original *Dictionary of National Biography,* summed up the prevailing view of Oxford's personality before he was identified as Shakespeare. In his three-page entry for Oxford he wrote that William Cecil, the Queen's chief minister and Oxford's guardian during his teenage years "found his perverse humor a source of grave embarrassment." He added that "Oxford's eccentricities and irregularities of temper grew with his years . . . . [and] despite his violent and perverse temper, his eccentric taste in dress, and his extravagant waste of his substance, [Oxford] evinced a genuine interest in music and wrote verse of much lyric beauty."

In his 500-page biography of Oxford (2003), Alan Nelson of UC-Berkeley, a Stratfordian, assumes that Oxford was not Shakespeare and takes every opportunity to denigrate him. He puts the most negative possible spin on the evidence for Oxford's character and career, even entitling his book, *Monstrous Adversary*. ("Monstrous," however, might also apply to Hamlet's character when he was being his most difficult for those around him, particularly those for whom he had little respect.) In Nelson's opinion, Oxford's character disqualifies him as the poet-dramatist, despite the biographies of great writers and the scholarship attesting to their eccentricities and difficult personalities. If, however, his book is used as a research tool with the understanding that Oxford was Shakespeare, it provides valuable evidence for Oxford's character and personality, despite Nelson's biased interpretations of his extensive archival research,

An eccentric, erratic and sometimes irritating temperament that quite unaccountably drops at times from normal behavior into a deep depression and at other times soars into manic, high-energy, rapid-thinking behavior has been identified in many great writers, artists and composers. The intensity of their manic-depressive disorder can vary among them from the mild to the extreme. They experience these episodes of mood swings while most of the time leading a mostly normal, if still eccentric, life. That is when they can re-organize, edit and improve their creative work. Psychologists and psychiatrists today call it a bi-polar disorder and consider it a mental illness that can be treated with medications such as lithium when it leads to seriously disruptive, anti-social behavior such as irresponsible spending splurges when manic or thoughts of suicide when depressed.

Research psychologist Kay Redfield Jamison of Johns Hopkins University documents in *Touched with Fire* (1993) the biographical, autobiographical and medical evidence for manic-depressive behavior in dozens of writers, artists and composers of genius. She concludes that compared to the general population a "vastly disproportionate number" of them were manic-depressive. They include writers Lord Byron, Coleridge, Poe, Melville, Keats, Shelley, Blake, Woolf, Twain, O'Neill and Robert Lowell. Also artists Leonardo da Vinci, Vincent Van Gogh and Edvard Munch; composers Schumann, Berlioz and Mahler; and the nineteenth-century philosopher-psychologist William James. She did not include Oxford, but he fits the profile of a manic-depressive. Nothing in Will Shakspere's documented biography suggests a manic-depressive temperament like Oxford's and Hamlet's, much less the temperament of a creative writer of genius.

Establishment Shakespeare scholars, not accepting Oxford as its author, have struggled to understand *Hamlet* but have given up. For them, *Hamlet* and its hero are enigmatic or problematic, a puzzling mystery. Stephen Greenblatt of Harvard says in the first paragraph of his introduction to the play in the Norton collected Shakespeare works (1997) that "*Hamlet* is an enigma. Mountains of feverish speculation have only deepened the interlocking mysteries." In the Riverside collected Shakespeare (1974) Frank Kermode says in the opening paragraphs of his introduction to the play: "Certainly *Hamlet* is problematic."

In the Folger Shakespeare Library edition of *Hamlet* (1992, 2012), contributor Michael Neill says that it has a reputation as "the most intellectually puzzling" Shakespeare play, and the one that has drawn "the most bafflingly different readings." For Philip Edwards, editor of the New Cambridge edition (1985, 2003), *Hamlet* is "perplexing and problematic for the critic." In the introduction to his Arden 1982 edition Harold Jenkins endorses the view of Harry Levin of Harvard, the lead contributor to the Riverside Shakespeare, who called *Hamlet* "the most problematic play ever written by Shakespeare or any other playwright," citing its proliferation of "unanswerable questions." In the first sentence of his Norton Critical Edition (1963), Cyrus Hoy says, "Everything about *The Tragedy of Hamlet* is problematic."

In their Arden 2006 edition of *Hamlet* the editors describe in the first page of their introduction what they see as the difficulty of developing a "theory of *Hamlet*" to explain what the play is all about. They cite Horace Howard Furness, editor of the Variorum *Hamlet,* who wrote in 1908 that so much had been much written about *Hamlet* even by then that he would let his best friend die if to save him he would be forced to hear his friend's theory of *Hamlet.* Then in the concluding section of their introduction, entitled "The Continuing Mystery of *Hamlet,*" the editors refer to the "ongoing need to explain the play . . . to resolve its ambiguities and mysteries." The editors also find that Horatio is "enigmatic throughout" and Queen Gertrude "baffling."

The hero Hamlet in particular has puzzled Stratfordian commentators. In the first paragraph of her introduction to the Longman Cultural Edition of *Hamlet*, Constance Jordan asks, "What do we really know of Shakespeare's most enigmatic character?" In his Norton Critical Edition (2011), Robert S. Miola says Hamlet "has evoked widely different critical responses," from being "a good and moral man trapped in a predicament he cannot handle" to a hero who is "immoral, insane or incoherent." The editor of *The Reader's Encyclopedia of Shakespeare* says that Hamlet is a "profoundly puzzling hero;" and the associate editor says Hamlet "has inspired more speculation and comment than any other figure in Western literature," citing the "famous problem" of Hamlet's delay: why he seems to procrastinate and delay avenging the murder of his father. There are, however, good reasons why Hamlet does not act immediately to exact revenge by killing Claudius.

One leading Stratfordian scholar did sense that in some way and for some reason the hero Hamlet reflected the author of the play. On the first page of the introduction to his Oxford University Press edition (1987), G. R. Hibbard says that *Hamlet* is "for many the most personal of the plays conveying, as does no other, a sense of the playwright's involvement with his own creation." He does not expand on this "involvement" but does speculate cautiously, and perceptively, that the play was written "at the compulsive urging of his *daemon* for his own satisfaction."

T. S. Eliot also sensed the author's personal involvement in the troubles of Hamlet, and came perilously close to solving the mystery of the critics' enigmatic *Hamlet*. He too found the play "puzzling and disquieting" and went further, famously calling it "most certainly an artistic failure." Explaining why he called it a failure, however, he unwittingly provided support for Oxford as its author. In his essay "Hamlet and His Problems" (1921), Eliot agrees with the minority view that "the supposed identity of Hamlet with his author is genuine" and suggests that something in the author's life experience must have inspired him to write the play.

Eliot confidently attributes the play to an unknown "period of crisis" in the life of its author, whom he implicitly accepts to have been Will Shakspere. The play, he says, is "full of some stuff that the writer [Shakspere] could not drag to light." Significantly, he concludes that this unknown "stuff" of his life experience can never be known because "we need a great many facts in his [Shakspere's] biography" and more facts about his personal experience. Unsaid, but implied, is that it's very unlikely that any more biographical facts about Shakspere will be discovered, much less facts of such great significance.

With Oxford as the dramatist, we do know the "stuff," the facts of his life story that inspired him to write *Hamlet*. The play makes perfect sense as the agonized, poetic expression of Oxford's deepest concerns toward the end of his life, as much for himself as for his audience and readers.

For those in court audiences and for readers of *Hamlet* who knew Oxford personally or by reputation, *Hamlet* was not Eliot's "artistic failure." It would have been an entertaining and disturbing work of genius about thinly veiled real people, principally Oxford as Hamlet, Oxford's mother as Gertrude, Robert Dudley Earl of Leicester as Claudius, William Cecil as Polonius, and Anne Cecil as Ophelia. The play was not performed or printed in its final form until after all the principal characters had died. For modern-day readers and spectators who know Oxford wrote it, *Hamlet* on its own merits can be an entertaining, even sensational play about corruption in high places and the problems it makes for someone who feels responsible to do something about it.

Stratfordian editors and commentators also find *Hamlet* puzzling and enigmatic because they fail to recognize the deliberate ambiguity for dramatic purpose in the play. *Hamlet* challenges the audience and the reader to grasp and appreciate how its principal characters are conflicted in their motives and actions and how unsure they are about what is happening to them and around them and what they really want to do. This deliberate ambiguity, which reflects the ambiguities of life, particularly for men and women in positions of power, reaches its climax at the end of the play.

In Oxford's *Hamlet* the resemblances of Hamlet to Oxford and of the other leading characters to important persons and events in Oxford's life are many and striking. The evidence for them is covered in this introduction, as well as in the line notes to the play.

Hamlet

When Edward de Vere, the only son and heir of the sixteenth Earl of Oxford, was twelve, his father died, and he became a ward of the Crown, ostensibly to continue his education and protect his inheritance, one of the richest in England, until he reached his majority at age twenty-one. He was sent to London to live in the household of William Cecil, the Queen's chief minister and her Master of the Court of Wards, effectively his guardian. At the time, Cecil's daughter, Anne, was six and she and Oxford would grow up together in the Cecil household almost as sister and brother into their teenage years. When Oxford turned twenty-one and Anne fifteen, they were wed in what was undoubtedly a marriage arranged by Cecil, who reportedly promised Oxford an enormous dowry. By then, Oxford would have realized that he was deep in debt. (See Anderson.)

In the play, Hamlet is the only son and the underage heir of the late King Hamlet. He's living in Elsinore Castle with Polonius, the King's chief minister, and his daughter Ophelia, almost as brother and sister. Polonius, who is a caricature of William Cecil, is concerned that the teenage Lord Hamlet may take advantage of young Ophelia, who, like her parents, is a commoner. At one point he uses Ophelia as bait to try to learn Hamlet's intentions not only toward her but also toward King Claudius, who suspects that Hamlet suspects that Claudius assassinated his father to gain the throne. No one knows that Claudius secretly poisoned King Hamlet.

As a privileged aristocrat in his early teens and living away from his family, Oxford no doubt took little notice that Robert Dudley, later the Earl of Leicester, who had positioned himself to be an administrator of the estate of Oxford's father, was acquiring control of his inheritance and its revenues. Leicester would have a lifelong reputation for satisfying a ruthless ambition for power, money and women by arranging for the deaths by poison or "accident" of anyone standing in his way. He was said to have been "a rare artist" in poisoning by Sir Robert Naunton, an Elizabethan courtier who would become secretary of state for King James. Naunton compared Leicester's reputation to that of the infamous Italian poisoner Cesare Borgia. Leicester, however, was never formally accused of any crimes; the rumor mill assumed that he used hired assassins to conceal his murderous treachery. Leicester's notorious reputation as a poisoner and using henchmen to carry out his murderous poisonings are fundamental to the plot of *Hamlet*.

Reported rumors would have it that Leicester's victims by poison included John Sheffield, a baron and the husband of the beautiful Douglass Howard, whom Leicester then married in secret, a marriage he would later repudiate as illegal; Sir Nicholas Throckmorton, who died suddenly after dining at Leicester's house; the first Earl of Essex, whose wife was having an affair with Leicester and who married him after her husband's death; and the Countess of Lennox, a powerful political intriguer, who had a claim to the English throne and who became ill and died unexpectedly a few days after dining with Leicester.

Oxfordian archival scholar Nina Green gives a detailed, documented account of the suspicious circumstances of the death of Oxford's father, the sixteenth Earl of Oxford, the significance of details in his will and Leicester's role in the plundering of Oxford's estates for himself and the Queen, which would lead to the loss of most of Oxford's inheritance, the basis of a nobleman's prestige and power. In her article "The Fall of the House of Oxford," she concludes:

> Did Sir Robert Dudley [later the Earl of Leicester], almost before the ink was dry on the sixteenth Earl's will, arrange to have the sixteenth Earl "poisoned in the garden for his estate," as Hamlet remarks in the play-within-the play? . . . . The primary beneficiary—in fact almost the only real beneficiary—of the sixteenth Earl's death was Sir Robert Dudley. Four hundred years have passed, and the truth will never be known. However, the facts revealed in the historical documents alluded to in the foregoing paragraphs [of her article] suggest that it would not have been unreasonable for de Vere [the Earl of Oxford] to have entertained suspicions of foul play in the death of his father, nor, as Shakespeare, to have written a play about his suspicions, casting Dudley in the part of the usurper, King Claudius.

Robert Dudley was one of the Protestant "new men" (as was William Cecil), who climbed to preference and power in the court of the Protestant Queen Elizabeth. She rewarded them with titles of nobility and grants of estates as they helped her rule England while enriching themselves. They initially came to her court untitled and competed for political power and its wealth with each other and with the Catholic old nobility, such as the earls of Oxford and Sussex and the Duke of Norfolk, who inherited their ancient titles. (See Read.)

Biographers depict the Earl of Leicester as tall and handsome, self-important and reserved, charming when it suited his ambitions and adept at making a show of friendship to his adversaries and targets of opportunity. Ruthless in his ambition, he was a man of considerable intelligence and ability, who had "princely tastes" and "a very ingratiating manner." (*Encyclopedia Britannica* 1911). The Claudius character in Oxford's play fits that description almost perfectly, especially his ambition and ingratiating manner.

Queen Elizabeth not only made Dudley the Earl of Leicester but also her favorite companion and virtually her king consort. Biographer Martin A. S. Hume cited Leicester's "unprincipled influence" on Elizabeth to serve his purpose of dominating her. The historian Conyers Read says that "one of the most amazing things about this amazing woman was her blind faith in

Leicester," adding that for the Elizabethan mind-set and given Leicester's evil reputation, her attraction to him must have seemed to be the result of " a malignant spell cast upon her." So close was their relationship that Leicester was even rumored to have secretly married her and to have had children with her. Elizabeth never married and died without leaving an heir.

Throughout their careers, Oxford found Leicester competing with him by using his newly gained revenue from Oxford's inherited estates and large grants by the Queen of properties and commercial monopolies to finance his expensive lifestyle. (See Rye.) The wealth of the gifts and grants that the Queen awarded to Leicester was probably unprecedented, vastly exceeding what Oxford received. He staged lavish theatrical spectacles for the Queen and made himself into a leading patron of Elizabethan art and literature.

He also competed with Oxford for prestigious assignments in the military, notably when Leicester had him relegated to a lesser role when the Spanish Armada threatened England. His rivalry extended to the theater. In the early 1580s, he and Oxford were both patrons of acting companies that performed for Queen Elizabeth, and something about the way they competed for her attention and for the prestige of being invited to perform at court so disturbed her and/or her counselors that in an extraordinary move she took the leading players from their companies and that of the Earl of Sussex to form a new acting company, the Queen's Men under her direct patronage. (See Gurr.)

Although Leicester completely charmed Elizabeth, almost everyone else who had any dealings with Leicester hated him. In a list of pros and cons for Leicester as a possible husband for Queen Elizabeth, Burghley wrote laconically that he was "hated of many." The Venetian ambassador to London reported home that Burghley and Leicester had the most influence on Elizabeth and that Leicester "has given offense to many persons and is generally detested." (See Cavalli.) Given his evil reputation but his extraordinary success with Queen Elizabeth, Leicester is one of the most controversial figures in British history.

Oxford also had reason to believe rumors that the Earl of Sussex, his good friend and probably his mentor and surrogate father, was one of Leicester's victims. Oxford was just twenty when he served as an adjutant to Sussex, who commanded the English army in the conflict with rebels on the border with Scotland. Sussex, who would become the Queen's Lord Chamberlain, was a leader of the political opposition to Leicester. With his dying words, as reported by Naunton, he issued a warning about Leicester: "Beware of the gypsy [his nickname at court], for he will be too hard on you all. You know not the beast as well as I do." Sussex's death removed a powerful rival to Leicester in Queen Elizabeth's court. In *Hamlet,* Claudius schemes to have Hamlet killed to remove his popular rival for the throne of Denmark.

Leicester himself died unexpectedly in his mid-fifties. A spy reported to the Spanish government that Leicester became violently ill after dining at the house of an unidentified acquaintance where he had stopped on his way to the mineral springs at Buxton. He forced himself to vomit (suspecting poison?) and became feverish. Continuing on his way, he stopped three days later at his hunting lodge at Cornbury, where he died. The spy, Marco Antonio Messia, added that he had seen Leicester in the weeks before his death and that Leicester "had showed every appearance of perfect health as if he would have lived for years." Messia no doubt suspected poison.

There was no state funeral for Leicester, no official mourning, no eulogies by members of Elizabeth's court, nor by Elizabeth, who went into seclusion for several days of mourning. His funeral and burial were private. Conyers Read concluded that "England, indeed, was well rid of him." Given Leicester's reputation, the rumor mill immediately found reasons to suspect that he had been poisoned by his wife. Just six months later she married her late husband's gentleman of the horse, a man of much lower social status, much poorer and much younger than she. (See Elizabeth Jenkins, Gristwood, Read, Derek Wilson.)

Leicester's malevolent reputation was confirmed for many of his contemporaries by an anonymous, political tract, published during his lifetime, that accused him arranging for the murder over the years of almost a dozen men and women who had all died under questionable circumstances, most often by what appeared to be poison. Its author(s) are presumed to have been English Catholics exiled in France who hated Leicester and who hoped to restore Catholicism and themselves to power in England. Although condemned and banned by Queen Elizabeth, manuscript copies of what would be nicknamed *Leicester's Commonwealth* circulated among aristocrats. It was not printed in England until several years later. (Conceivably, the nickname may refer sarcastically to Leicester's seeming control of the Queen's England.)

The sensational polemic reflects an in-depth knowledge of the corruption in Queen Elizabeth's court and the plotting and counterplotting by the new Protestant factions and the old Catholic nobility as they maneuvered to gain power and wealth. At one point the Catholics reportedly were sure that Leicester had treacherously betrayed the Duke of Norfolk, Oxford's friend and fellow member of the old nobility, which led to the duke's execution for his alleged role in a plot to have the Protestant Queen Elizabeth assassinated and the Catholic Mary Queen of Scots put on the English throne.

In his scholarly edition of *Leicester's Commonwealth* (1985), D. C. Peck calls it "something of an artistic masterpiece" and "one of the most entertaining pieces of defamatory writing ever seen in English." He found complex political positions in the booklet, including "a veneration of Sussex . . . and most of all a virulent hatred for Leicester."

The identity of its author(s) has been much debated. Peck and others attribute it to Charles Arundell and disaffected Catholics in exile in France.

Arundell, however, was not a published writer, so there's little evidence for his writing talent. The well-written, entertaining, booklet might well be attributed to Oxford. It's written in the form of a conversation among a gentleman-statesman, an elderly lawyer and a young scholar that resembles a play script. The dialogue is lively and sometimes humorous. It demonstrates an intimate knowledge of court intrigues and reflects Oxford's friendship with the Earl of Sussex, his dalliance for a time with the Catholic old nobility faction, and especially a personal enmity for Leicester. Oxford was thirty-four and an accomplished dramatist in 1584 when it appeared. Oxfordian scholar Nina Green was the first to suggest him as the author.

All in all, it would seem clear that Oxford would have hated Leicester for his rumored murder by poison of his father and his plundering of his estate, as well as for Leicester's lifelong success with Queen Elizabeth in the competition with Oxford and other courtiers for her favor and gifts. Oxford could get some measure of revenge and perhaps some relief from his rage by writing *Leicester's Commonwealth* and at the end of his life depicting Leicester as the villainous poisoner Claudius in *Hamlet*.

The first Shakespeare scholar to see Leicester as the inspiration for Claudius was Georg Brandes, an influential Danish critic and university professor. In 1898, he published his most important work, *William Shakespeare, a Critical Study*, in which he noted perceptively: "There is much in the character of King Claudius to suggest that Shakespeare has here taken Leicester as his model. The two have in common sensuality, an ingratiating, conciliatory manner, astute dissimulation, and complete unscrupulousness." Stratfordian editors of *Hamlet* have overlooked or chosen to ignore the likely influence of Leicester on the creation of Claudius in *Hamlet*. Contemporary court audiences and readers could hardly have missed the parallels.

Early on, Oxfordian scholars saw Leicester in Claudius. The first was Eva Turner Clark in her *Hidden Allusions in Shakespeare's Plays* (1930) just a decade after J. Thomas Looney first identified Oxford as the author of the Shakespeare works. Since then, many leading Oxfordian scholars, including Mark Anderson in 2005, have also seen Claudius as Leicester.

The many parallels between the Earl of Oxford and Prince Hamlet naturally are also quite remarkable.

Both are only sons and their fathers' natural heirs: Oxford the heir to the estate of his father, the sixteenth Earl of Oxford, Hamlet the heir of his father, King Hamlet of Denmark. Because they have not reached their majority, Oxford could not have control of his inheritance, and Hamlet cannot assume the Crown of Denmark. Death by poison figures in the deaths of both their fathers. Oxford's father died suddenly and unexpectedly as if by poison; Hamlet's father was poisoned before the play begins.

In their vulnerable youth both Oxford and Hamlet are victimized by crafty villains. Robert Dudley, later the Earl of Leicester and England's most notorious poisoner, contrived to gain control of most of Oxford's inheritance. Before the play begins, Claudius, brother of King Hamlet, has poisoned the king and contrived to assume the Crown of Denmark. Contested inheritance is a major preoccupation in Oxford's life and the Hamlet story.

Revenge figures prominently for both Oxford and Hamlet. Oxford would naturally have wanted some form of revenge and/or retribution for the death of his father and loss of most of his inheritance to Leicester. The revenge instinct is a universal instinct of human nature. The Ghost of Hamlet's father reveals to him that he was poisoned by his brother Claudius and enjoins him to avenge his assassination.

Oxford's mother re-married soon after the death of her husband, the sixteenth Earl of Oxford, and in the play Hamlet's mother quickly marries Claudius soon after he poisons her husband, King Hamlet.

Perhaps most significantly, both Oxford and Hamlet exhibit the personality traits of manic-depression.

While Oxford's own life was the primary source for the story of Hamlet, he also found a literary source for the plot of *Hamlet* (if anyone asked) in the ancient legend of Amlcthus/Amlcth. Stratfordian commentators take it to be the primary source. Amleth ("Hamlet" is an anagram of it) was a Prince of Denmark and heir to the throne, who feigned madness until he could avenge the murder of his father the King by his uncle, who seized the throne and then married his widow. Amleth feigned madness to avoid the same fate until he could get his revenge. In addition, the most important influence (and perhaps a source) for Oxford was the similar Greek story of Orestes. This important influence is overlooked by Stratfordian commentators. (See "*Hamlet*'s Sources and Influences—and Its Forerunners by Oxford" in this edition.)

In act 1 scene 2, Oxford sets up for an unusual plot twist that only makes sense as reflecting circumstances of his father's death, which did not at first appear to be suspicious. When his father died in 1562, Robert Dudley was thirty and had not yet been widely suspected of the rumored poisonings for personal and political gain. Oxford was twelve, and it's likely that it was years later—and only in retrospect—that he would begin to suspect that Dudley had his father murdered by poison.

This delay in realization is mirrored in *Hamlet* when Claudius makes his first appearance in the play and addresses his assembled court as King of Denmark. He expresses at length his grief over the death of his brother, King Hamlet, and adds slyly that he (and the court) must keep in mind that he is now King of Denmark. Gertrude is sitting beside him, and he says that he married her with both joy (if he can be believed) and sorrow at his brother's death (a hypocritical lie). His expressions of joy and sorrow, nevertheless, could sound and read, superficially altogether sincere and legitimate. No one knows or suspects that he poisoned Hamlet's father, the King, and had prepared to quickly marry his widow, Gertrude.

Just as Oxford only years later would realize how his father died, only later in the play, when the Ghost tells Hamlet how his father died will the first-time audience and readers of *Hamlet* realize in retrospect how Claudius revealed himself in his first speech in the play to be a hypocritical, ingratiating politician and disarming villain. It's an unexpected, reverse plot twist that is perhaps puzzling but is explained by the circumstances of the death of Oxford's father and his delayed realization of them.

Claudius also notes slyly that Gertrude as King Hamlet's widow became the "imperial jointress" of Denmark. "Jointress" was an arcane legal term for a widow's complex rights of inheritance in various circumstances, such as a pre-marital property settlement and jointure agreement. In this case, her marriage to Claudius gave him a certain claim to the late King Hamlet's lands that she had inherited. (See Regnier.) "Imperial," in this context an exaggeration, could imply ruling or governing rights, in addition to property rights.

This is the first of many references and allusions in the play to civil, criminal and ecclesiastical law. They also include the law governing Hamlet's intent when he kills Polonius in act 3 scene 4, Hamlet's inheritance rights under Elizabethan civil law, ecclesiastical law concerning the funeral and burial rites for Ophelia, and clever parodies of the law by both the Gravedigger and Hamlet.

One of the parodies (at 5.1.7-15) satirizes defense counsel's argument and the judge's ruling in the Hales v. Pettit lawsuit, filed in 1558. The lawsuit was one of many included in a lawyer's volume of reports and commentaries on "divers cases," published in 1571 in Law French, a specialized, technical, legal language, soon to be obsolete, that was used by lawyers and judges, a volume that Oxford (but not Shakspere) could have seen at the Gray's Inn law school where he was a student.

When he was sixteen, Oxford matriculated at Gray's Inn where he could attend lectures and moot courts in Law French and peruse the law library. Gray's Inn was also noted for the students' rowdy parties and especially for the plays they produced and performed. In the same year (1566) students performed *The Supposes*, a loose translation from the Italian by George Gascoigne, unless by young Oxford under Gascoigne's name, as some Oxfordians argue. The play is considered an important source for Oxford's *The Taming of the Shrew*, which appeared as by William Shakespeare. Queen Elizabeth was the Patron Lady of Gray's Inn, and students occasionally performed plays for her.

In his journal article, "The Law in *Hamlet*" (2011), the Oxfordian Thomas Regnier, an appellate court attorney, has demonstrated the extent, subtlety and accuracy of the law that is integral to the plot line of *Hamlet* and also how legal issues in the play "parallel watershed events in Oxford's life, particularly events that concerned homicide and property law."

King Claudius, having assumed the throne of Denmark and hypocritically expressed his joy and sorrow, boldly thanks his assembled court for their collective "wisdoms" that have "freely" gone along with his taking the throne. It's a masterful piece of smoothly wicked oratory that co-opts the tacit agreement of the assembled court. In Claudius's first appearance in the play, Oxford has him displaying character traits of the Earl of Leicester, described by Brandes as ingratiating, conciliatory, dissimulating and unscrupulous.

No one can express any objection to Claudius's assumption of the Crown, except Hamlet, and then only obliquely. He is sitting below the King, and is the only one still dressed in mourning black. As the only son of King Hamlet, he is the most direct, natural heir to the throne, but he is still a minor, not yet twenty-one. Until he reaches his majority, he cannot under Elizabethan law and practice take control of his inheritance. He expresses his objection in the first of his riddling speeches in the play. When Claudius addresses him as "my cousin Hamlet and my son," Hamlet interrupts him, objecting, "A little more than kin and less than kind." (1.2.67)

Later in scene 2, Hamlet in soliloquy agonizes over his mother marrying Claudius so soon after the death of her husband, King Hamlet, when Hamlet was in his teens and away at the university in Wittenberg. He laments, "That it should come thus: not two months dead—nay not so much, not two—So excellent a king . . . . And yet within a month. . . . a little month." (1.2.137-145) Moreover, three scenes later, Hamlet will learn from the Ghost that Claudius with the consummate charm of "witchcraft" seduced Gertrude into committing adultery with him before marrying her. John Updike imagined this adulterous love affair in his historical novel *Gertrude and Claudius* (2000).

The parallels to the re-marriage of Oxford's mother probably only a few months after of the death of her husband, the sixteenth Earl of Oxford, are quite clear. Oxford's mother, Margery Golding de Vere, Countess of Oxford, married Charles Tyrell, a man of no distinction and far below her in social standing, when Oxford was thirteen and living in the Cecil household in London away from his mother in Essex. No records indicate that he returned home for the wedding or communicated with her about her re-marriage.

Although no record of Margery's marriage to Tyrell has been found, a letter from her to William Cecil strongly suggests that it was very soon after the death of Oxford's father. It mentions for the first time "Mr. Tyrell" and "we both," indicating that they were married and living together, seemingly for some time, and that Cecil naturally would know about it. Tyrell's name appears only incidentally in her letter, which asks Cecil's help in securing grain that her tenant farmers had agreed to give her. She writes that Tyrell would go in person to see Cecil on the matter except for the difficulties and dangers of traveling to London and apparently because he might not be welcome at court, which might well be regretted by "us both."

The letter is dated 11 October 1563, fourteen months after the death of her husband, the sixteenth Earl of Oxford, and it's probably a fair inference that she and Tyrell had been married at least several months before she wrote her letter and had been romantically involved several months before marrying. That would put their "engagement" and marriage quite soon after her husband died, an over-hasty and apparently very private marriage of a countess who had been a lady-in-waiting to Queen Elizabeth, to a man who was not a member of the nobility—a marriage that Oxford no doubt found objectionable.

Her letter also shows that she knew about the predatory tactics of the Earl of Leicester, who had gained control over Oxford's inherited estates. She says she heard that a servant of Robert Christmas, an associate/henchman of Leicester, ordered her farmers not to deliver any of her grain to her. Although Tyrell had been master of the horse, a kind of super-groom, for the Earl of Leicester, apparently that counted for little when it came to the ownership of grain harvested on her land, which was among the estates that had come under Leicester's control. She closes by asking Cecil to extend her compliments to his wife and to "my son with God's blessing and mine, & well to do to his life's end." (See Golding, Margery; Ward.)

In act 3 scene 4, Hamlet's strained relations with his mother come to a head. In a wild scene in her "closet," a small room adjoining her bedroom, he accuses her of marrying "with wicked speed" her husband's murderer, who stole the crown of Denmark, and even of having been complicit in the murder; and then making love to Claudius in a sweat-soaked bed, "stewed in corruption." (3.4.100) Hamlet is so disgusted and angry that she fears for her life.

In this scene, Oxford is no doubt venting his anger at his mother for her over-hasty marriage to Tyrell. There is nothing in the extant records to indicate that Oxford had anything to do with his mother. No correspondence between mother and son. No mention in the surviving records or letters by others linking them. They may well have been estranged. When she died in Essex, Oxford was eighteen and living at Cecil house in London, but the records have nothing about Oxford at his mother's death and burial. Tyrell died two years later. Oxford's first biographer, B. M. Ward, says that Tyrell "seems to have been an insignificant character" and that Oxford never mentioned Tyrell "other than contemptuously," probably taking their marriage as a slight to the memory of his father and to the noble Oxford heritage.

While Leicester as the inspiration for Claudius has been ignored by Stratfordian editors and commentators, Polonius as a lampoon of William Cecil Lord Burghley was recognized in the past by many leading Stratfordian scholars. Unaccountably, however, it is not even mentioned in modern-day editions of *Hamlet*, perhaps because it is such strong evidence that Oxford was its author. The many resemblances of Polonius to Cecil, Oxford's guardian during his teenage years, are quite striking. Just as William Cecil Lord Burghley was a commoner who became chief minister to Queen Elizabeth, Polonius is a commoner and chief minister to King Claudius. Both, despite their shortcomings, are respected, or at least tolerated, by their monarch.

Burghley had a reputation for being verbose in his communications and cautiously circumlocutory in his statecraft. His surviving letters include memos to himself that ruminate on some problem or another with run-on sentences that seem to never end. His memos on political problems typically expatiate on pros and cons, and alternative causes and effects at great length. An unpublished, political pamphlet he wrote was described by his biographer Conyers Read as such "a tedious, long-winded affair" that even Burghley himself might have become bored with it. Polonius is long-winded to the point of tediousness, often rambling so as to seem to be an authority while avoiding having to take a position on a difficult matter, and exasperating his listeners. At one point, Queen Gertrude chides him: "More matter, less art."

Burghley was also well-known for his network of spies and informers at home and abroad. The historian Martin Hume says that "Burghley's network of secret intelligence . . . was extremely extensive." Burghley's informers reported to him on Oxford, who complained three times in letters to him about "backfriends," that is, false friends, and about Oxford's servants who were making what he called false reports about him to Burghley. (See Oxford, *Letters and Poems.*)

In *Hamlet*, Polonius spies on his own daughter, Ophelia, arranging a meeting for her with Hamlet so that he and the King can eavesdrop to try to learn Hamlet's intentions. He sends a servant, Reynaldo, to Paris to inform him of the behavior of his son Laertes, just as Burghley had informers reporting on the behavior of his wayward son, Thomas, in Paris. Polonius hides behind an arras, a wall-hanging, in Gertrude's room to spy on Hamlet who is angrily upbraiding her for marrying Claudius. Hamlet detects someone eavesdropping from behind the arras, with fatal consequences for Polonius.

Burghley is also mocked at several other points in the play. In act 2 scene 2, Hamlet in one of his antic moods and for no obvious reason calls Polonius a "fishmonger." Burghley had sponsored a law that made Wednesday a day to eat fish, in addition to Friday and Saturday and during Lent. Although the law would help fishmongers sell more fish locally and for export, its primary purpose was to increase the demand for fish and thus encourage the building of more and larger fishing ships and ultimately increase England's ship-building capability as a naval power. In Parliament, it became known as "Cecil's fast," requiring fish at meals and fasting from meat. A royal proclamation drafted by Cecil spelled out enforcement details and punishments for the law, which applied principally to London and its environs. Living in Cecil's household for a decade, Oxford would have been well aware of "Cecil's fast." When the law expired in 1583, Cecil urged that the Wednesday fish-day be continued, but Parliament refused. A court audience would not have missed the allusion to Lord Burghley as "fishmonger" Polonius.

Later in the scene, still in his antic mood, Hamlet calls Polonius "Jephthah," a Biblical warrior who rashly vowed that if he was successful in his campaign against the Ammonites he would sacrifice the first thing he meets when he returns home. His virgin daughter, the first to welcome him, became his sacrificial victim. This probably alludes to William Cecil, a commoner, "sacrificing" his daughter, fourteen-year-old Anne, in an arranged marriage to the seventeenth Earl of Oxford, to make it more likely that the Queen would elevate him to the nobility as Baron Burghley so that his descendants would be nobility.

In act 4 scene 3, again in an antic mood, Hamlet tells the King that Polonius, whose body he has hidden, is at supper, not where he eats but where he is eaten by "a certain convocation of politic worms. . . . Your worm is your only emperor for diet." In December 1520 the Holy Roman Emperor convoked an assembly, or "diet," of Roman Catholic Church officials at Worms, a town in Germany, to hear Martin Luther defend his demands for church reform. The Diet of Worms, which began in January 1521, marked the beginning of Protestantism, and Burghley, a patriotic Protestant, reportedly liked it to be known that he was born when the assembly was being convoked.

Burghley's motto was "Cor unum, via una," that is "one heart, one way," and "Corambis" was the name of the Polonius character in the first quarto (1603) of *Hamlet*. The suffix "bis" means "again, twice" implying double-hearted, with echoes of double-cross, double-dealing. For whatever reason, in the second quarto (1604) Oxford used the more anodyne "Polonius," probably from "Polus" and "Pondus," nicknames for Burghley. (See Miller.)

Several leading Stratfordian scholars have recognized the resemblance of Polonius to Burghley. As early as 1869 G. R. French had suggested that Polonius, Laertes and Ophelia were supposed to stand for Burghley, Robert Cecil and Anne Cecil. In 1930, the eminent scholar E. K. Chambers noted in his two-volume *William Shakespeare: A Study of Facts and Problems* that "it has often been thought that Polonius may glance Lord Burghley." In his *Essential Shakespeare* (1937) J. Dover Wilson wrote that "Polonius is almost without doubt intended as a lampoon of Burghley." *The Reader's*

Encyclopedia of Shakespeare (1966) concurred: "Many scholars have argued that Burghley is being satirized as Polonius in *Hamlet*."

Historian Joel Hurstfield wrote in *The Queen's Wards* (1958) that Burghley's *Ten Precepts* is "the authentic voice of Polonius" in his advice to his son, Laertes on how to comport himself in Paris. (1.3.55-80) Burghley's *Ten Precepts* was not printed until two years after Will Shakspere died, and Chambers and other Shakespeare scholars do not address the question of how he could possibly have seen the manuscript. It's also most unlikely that Shakspere could have known about Burghley's verbosity satirized in Polonius or his reputation for supporting fishmongers or his being born when the Diet of Worms was convoked.

In his introduction to *Hamlet* in the Norton collected Shakespeare works, Stephen Greenblatt of Harvard not only ignores claims by his fellow Stratfordian scholars that Polonius resembles Burghley he has almost nothing at all to say about Polonius, a major character in the play. Greenblatt and other *Hamlet* editors have chosen to ignore the long, scholarly tradition of Polonius as Burghley, no doubt because it risks their having to consider that Oxford wrote the play and the rest of the Shakespeare canon.

Modern-day readers of *Hamlet* in Stratfordian editions will find nothing about Polonius as Burghley, with one dismissive exception. Despite the opinions of his predecessors, Harold Jenkins in his edition (1982) of the play rejects as "sheer conjecture" the "notion" that Polonius was a caricature of Burghley, asserting that Polonius's precepts to his son "derive from a long literary tradition." He makes a good case but does not address the likelihood that a court audience and readers knowing Burghley's propensity for verbosity and giving such advice would recognize the satire.

If it is granted that William Cecil Lord Burghley is lampooned in Polonius, then it should follow that Cecil's only daughter, Anne, inspired Ophelia, the only daughter of Polonius. Like Anne, the daughter of the chief minister to Queen Elizabeth, Ophelia is a teenage girl under the sway of her father, the chief minister to King Claudius. And like Anne, Ophelia is a commoner living in a household with an older teenage boy who was a member of the nobility, Prince Hamlet, representing the dramatist, the Earl of Oxford, who lived his teenage years in the Cecil household with his guardian, in effect a surrogate father.

The politically powerful commoner Cecil, who would naturally want a marriage for his daughter that would advance his family's reputation and fortune, was careful not to seem overly ambitious for his daughter Anne to marry the Earl of Oxford, who was far above her in social standing. In *Hamlet,* Polonius pretends to downplay his ambition for his commoner daughter Ophelia to marry Prince Hamlet. Both Polonius and Laertes, her brother, remind her that he is far above her social position as a commoner and could probably have his way with her with impunity. This disparity of social class gets unusual emphasis in the play taking up nearly all of act 1 scene 3.

Nothing is known about Oxford's relationship with Anne Cecil during their teenage years in the same household, but it would not be out of the ordinary if they felt attracted to each other, she in a purely romantic way to a sensitive, brilliant earl six years older than she who is driven by teenage male hormones to have a sexual curiosity in a younger girl, especially one who, as a commoner, was vulnerable.

Ophelia's story is in every act in *Hamlet*. In act 1 scene 3, her brother and her father lecture her at length not to believe Hamlet's expressions of love and to resist his attempt to seduce her, which would ruin her reputation and that of her family. In the following act, foreshadowing what is to come, Hamlet in a manic phase and for no apparent reason warns Polonius: "Conception is a blessing, but as your daughter may conceive, friend, look to it." (2.2.184-5)

In act 3, Polonius uses his daughter as bait so that he and the King can spy on Hamlet's conversation with her and learn whether he plans to harm his usurper uncle. She lies to Hamlet about it, and he flies into a manic rage and rejects her. Just as Cecil engaged in spying, if not personally, to further his political scheming, Polonius here does the same.

In act 4, Ophelia in her madness sings lines indicating that she is pregnant and is considering abortion: "Young men will do it if they come to it / By Cock, they are to blame. / Quoth she, 'Before you tumbled me, / You promised me to wed.'" (4.5.60-3) Later, when she is distributing different flowers that have meanings for their recipients, she saves for herself a flower called rue, symbolic for sorrow and repentance but the oil of which was thought to induce abortion. "And here's some for me," she says. (4.5.178, 180) At the end of the act, Gertrude recounts how she has learned that Ophelia drowned in a brook, whether a suicide or by accident in her madness; and at the start of act 5, that issue is debated by the Gravedigger just before her burial.

When Oxford reached his majority at age twenty-one, he and Anne Cecil, fourteen, were engaged to be married in what was probably an arranged betrothal, a common practice at the time. Her father reportedly promised the fatherless and spendthrift Oxford, who faced enormous debts, primarily as a result of his wardship, an enormous dowry, which apparently was never paid. (See Anderson.) Queen Elizabeth raised Cecil to the nobility, making his daughter Anne a noblewoman suitable for marriage to an earl and making Lord Burghley the founder of a noble lineage. By marrying the Earl of Oxford, the fifteen-year-old Anne Cecil became a countess. The Queen attended the elaborate ceremony in Westminster Abbey.

Oxford and his wife were married for three years without producing a child, but shortly after he left for Italy in 1575 Anne, now eighteen, discovered that she was pregnant and asked her doctor for a drug to induce abortion. She apparently feared that Oxford would believe rumors, probably spread by his nemesis the Earl of Leicester, that he was not the father. She did not abort, and her daughter Elizabeth was born before Oxford returned from Italy. He believed the rumors (or, if not, was sorely offended by them) and refused to see his wife for five years, at the end of which time they were reconciled and would have two more daughters and a baby boy, who died in infancy.

The central parallels in the lives of Anne Cecil and Ophelia would not have escaped notice by contemporary readers of *Hamlet* and spectators at performances of the play. Anne was the teenage daughter of the chief minister to the monarch, as is Ophelia. Anne was a young girl living in a household with an older boy, the Earl of Oxford, who was far above her social status. Anne's father, William Cecil, was Oxford's guardian after his father's death, effectively a surrogate father. Anne and Oxford lived almost as sister and brother. Ophelia, daughter of Polonius and a commoner, is living in close proximity to Prince Hamlet in Elsinore, almost as sister and brother. Anne's father controlled whom she would marry, as does Ophelia's father.

Another parallel is the desire to abort a first pregnancy. Anne Cecil sought from her doctor a drug that would cause an abortion. Her doctor informed Queen Elizabeth about it in a letter, and the word may well have spread among the Queen's ladies in waiting and beyond in court circles. In act 4 scene 5, Ophelia in her madness distributes flowers to the King, Queen and Laertes, telling their significance for each. For herself, she keeps some rue, a flower whose oil was thought to cause an abortion.

In her madness Ophelia reveals her innermost feelings and in crafting her character Oxford may well have been working through his tormenting memories of his relations with Anne. He may have rejected her when she was a young teenager and did reject her when she was his countess and a mother. In the play, Ophelia goes mad and drowns while still a young teenager rejected by Hamlet, who nevertheless protests wildly at her burial that he loved her.

Ophelia's story has nothing to do with Hamlet's preoccupation with getting revenge for his father's death. If Ophelia were left out of the play, she would not be missed. She is, however, a major character in the play, and she must be there for a reason, probably to exorcise Oxford's guilty feelings at the end of his life about his treatment of Anne Cecil during their teenage years and early married life. (See Anderson, Green, Whittemore.)

If Burghley is lampooned in Polonius, and Anne Cecil inspired Ophelia, then Thomas Cecil, Burghley's older son, was the model for Laertes, Polonius's son. (See Cecil *Ten Precepts* in the bibliography.) Thomas Cecil had a propensity for the impulsive, irresponsible, rebellious behavior of young men in their late teens and early twenties, behavior that Oxford, eight years younger, may well have appreciated as an adolescent with similar impulses and depicted in the character Laertes.

Thomas Cecil spent a year or two in Paris, ostensibly for his education but mostly in idleness and expensive pastimes. His behavior worried his father, who expressed his concern in letters to him and to Thomas's tutor and companion in Paris. At one point, the father wrote that he had received "watch-word" from one of his spies in Paris that his son spent his time in idleness. (See Charlton.) Laertes is also a student in Paris whose behavior there concerns Polonius.

In act 1 scene 3, Polonius gives Laertes his famous advice, including the line, "Neither a borrower nor a lender be," as Laertes prepares to return to Paris. Implied in his advice is that Polonius had heard that Laertes had been enjoying himself in Paris but had fallen in with the wrong crowd, spending too much on clothes, getting into fights, borrowing money heedlessly. Some commentators have interpreted the lecture that he calls his "precepts" as common-sense advice but others read it as a collection of shallow and cynical platitudes. Oxford may well have intended both readings.

In act 2 scene 1, Polonius directs a servant, Reynaldo, to take money to Laertes in Paris but before meeting up with him to ask around about his behavior. Polonius then gives explicit, lengthy instructions on how to spy on Laertes. He tells Reynaldo to find Laertes' friends in Paris and draw them out by telling them lies about Laertes' past behavior, such as gambling, drinking, fencing, and swearing, and by pretending to have seen him in Paris gambling, quarreling at a tennis match and entering a brothel. For Stratfordians the scene is extraneous to the main action of the play, but it makes sense as Oxford's description of Cecil's use of spies and informers.

Reynaldo's name is very similar to the name of one of Cecil's servants, Reymondo, whom Oxford mentioned in a letter from Paris in 1575 to Cecil. In sly, diplomatic language Oxford told Cecil that his servant did him a number of favors adding that he knows that Reymondo's "friendship" for him was mostly because of his "respect" for Cecil. The servant was no doubt informing Cecil about what Oxford was doing in Paris. (See Detobel.)

The detailed, striking parallels between Oxford's guardian William Cecil and Cecil's daughter and son in real life and Polonius and his daughter and son in the play are strong indications that Oxford wrote *Hamlet*. It is difficult if not impossible to believe that Shakspere of Stratford could have known enough about the Cecil family to have done it, whereas Oxford lived all of his teenage years with the Cecil family. Thus it's to be expected that Oxford's life experience and concerns are reflected throughout the play in matters large and small, and especially at Hamlet's death, representing the coming death of the play's author.

At the end of act 2, Hamlet in soliloquy castigates himself for not avenging Claudius's murder of his father, as the Ghost enjoined him to do, because he's not sure the Ghost was really that of his father. He says he will have a visiting acting company perform a play with a scene that resembles the murder of his father. If the King, who'll be watching the play, visibly flinches, it will betray his guilt. Hamlet concludes his soliloquy by exclaiming, "The play's the thing / Wherein I'll catch the conscience of the king!" (2.2.534-5)

In act 3 scene 2, the acting company performs the translated (and unidentified) Italian play that Hamlet has ordered for King Claudius and his court and that includes lines he has written. In this "play-within-the-play," the murderer Lucianus pours poison in the Duke Gonzago's ear while he's asleep in his garden. Hamlet explains in his running commentary that the murderer will get the love of Gonzago's wife. His dramatic stratagem works. Claudius realizes that Hamlet knows he murdered his father with poison in his ear and "gets the love" of his widow (and married her) and that Hamlet will seek revenge. He flees the scene in terror, and Hamlet has the corroboration he wants for his suspicions about Claudius's regicide. The Ghost indeed was that of Hamlet's father and spoke the truth.

Just as the parallels between the murderer in the play-within-the-play and King Claudius catch the conscience of the King, the parallels here in *Hamlet* between Oxford and Hamlet are hard to miss. Oxford was a playwright, and Hamlet writes lines for the play-within-the-play. Some of the characters in Oxford's plays, often based on older works, like the Gonzago play, could be seen by a knowing audience as representing actual court personages, here the murderer in the play-within-the-play as Claudius in *Hamlet*. His plays were clever, creative entertainments with embedded allegories that told dangerous truths to power, as does Hamlet to the King with his play-within-the-play.

A knowing court audience would also catch the double parallel of poisoners: The murderer of the king by poison in the ear in the play-within-the play represents Claudius in *Hamlet* who by his flight betrays himself as the murderer by poison in the ear of King Hamlet; and Claudius would call to mind the Earl of Leicester with his notorious reputation as a serial poisoner whom Oxford and others in the aristocracy probably suspected of having had his father, the sixteenth Earl of Oxford, assassinated by poison. Also, although the nephew-murderer kisses the sleeping king's crown in the play-within-the-play, Hamlet explains that he kills the king not for his crown but "for his estate," just as Oxford suspected that his father was poisoned not for his title of Earl of Oxford but for his estate (Oxford's inheritance). Although Leicester did not "get the love" of the sixteenth Earl's widow, as the murderer "gets the love" of his victim's widow, he did get the favor, the seeming "love," of his co-conspirator in the plunder of Oxford's estate, Queen Elizabeth, as her life-long favorite courtier and virtual consort king, which served his ambitions much better. To the end of Oxford's life there's no indication that he ever found corroboration for his suspicion that Leicester had his father poisoned and that he ever even attempted to achieve revenge. *Hamlet* was his revenge, tempered by ambiguity at the end.

The seventeenth Earl of Oxford was the only son of an earl who lived the life of a feudal lord, and a nostalgia for feudalism colors *Hamlet.* Oxford was a direct descendant of hereditary aristocracy stretching back five centuries to the time of William the Conqueror. He was born in a Norman castle in the Essex countryside. His father controlled one of the largest feudal estates in England. A feudal lord was expected to have a certain standards of chivalry, responsibility and honor. Significantly, these values even included the embrace sometimes of the ancient feudal requirement for blood revenge.

In *Hamlet*, a nostalgia for feudalism occurs most visibly in the Ghost. In act 1 scene 2 the ghost of Hamlet's admired father is wearing a full suit of feudal armor. Very much in the spirit of feudalism, Hamlet promises to seek revenge for the murder of his father by killing the murderer, Claudius. This desire for retribution, however, will set up a conflict for Hamlet, because the feudal morality of justice through blood revenge was giving way to the new era of the rule of law with justice administered by courts. Hamlet's conflict is between the very human desire, even lust to exact personal revenge for the murder of a close relative versus letting the rule of law determine justice and punishment for the murder, thus avoiding the potential for continuing cycles of revenge killings. In the end, Hamlet does kill Claudius, but his revenge is ambiguous.

A court audience would recognize the conflict for Hamlet that is raised by the Ghost's call for revenge, typical of feudal times, which were fading in England with the rise of the "new men" and their mercantile society and nation state with its laws and courts. Oxford may well have felt the ancient desire to avenge the death of his father by killing Leicester and also felt the artistic compulsion to work through these conflicted emotions by writing *Hamlet*. As Charlton Ogburn wrote, "How singular it was that the Renaissance ideal should have been realized most fully in England in a man [Oxford] who could never cease looking back as [the Stratfordian] A. L Rowse recognized, upon the feudal past." Will Shakspere, the wool merchant, money lender and real estate investor was a lower class "new man," unlikely to have appreciated the significance of feudalism and blood revenge for a story like Hamlet's.

Nor is it likely that Shakspere would have been able to learn about the new astronomy of Copernicus, a Polish mathematician, that was just emerging in scientific circles and that is alluded to in *Hamlet*. In the Copernican model, Earth is no longer the center of the universe, a fundamental belief of science and religion for centuries, based on the work of the Greek Claudius Ptolemy (b. 100 AD). For Copernicus, the Sun is the center of the solar system, and Earth is just one of the planets orbiting the Sun, which, in turn is just one of stars in the universe. Peter D. Usher, emeritus professor of astronomy and astrophysics at Pennsylvania State University, describes an extraordinary number of allusions to astronomy in *Hamlet* and other Shakespeare plays.

One of the most striking allusions occurs when Hamlet suddenly exclaims, "O God, I could be bounded in a nutshell and count myself king of infinite space." (2.2.237-8) The "nutshell" would be the relatively small, fixed shell of stars in Ptolemaic astronomy that was being replaced by the revolutionary and heretical Copernican astronomy, and "infinite space" was from "A Perfit Description" (1576) by Thomas Digges, a mathematician and astronomer, who was one of the earliest admirers of Copernicus's work.

Oxford was well-placed to learn about the emerging Copernican astronomy. His first tutor's library included a copy of Copernicus's work, a rare and expensive book published in Germany. It was written principally for mathematicians. (Hamlet is a student at Wittenberg, Germany, the first university to begin Copernican studies.) The library of William Cecil, Oxford's guardian during his teenage years, also had a copy of Copernicus, and Oxford's course of study in Cecil House included cosmology, the study of Earth and the universe.

Oxford probably knew Digges, not only through their interest in cosmology but also through Cecil, who asked Digges for his opinion of the significance of the supernova of 1572, when Oxford was twenty-two. (See "Astronomy in *Hamlet*" in this edition and Usher in the bibliography.)

Hamlet is often called a revenge play in the tradition of Roman revenge tragedies. In the Elizabethan theater, the first revenge play was the very popular *Spanish Tragedy* (c. 1587), which appeared anonymously and which Oxford probably wrote. Commentators have noted the many similarities to it in *Hamlet*, including a hero who seeks to revenge the murder of a close relative and who feigns madness. Only centuries later was the play ascribed to Thomas Kyd but only indirectly and on very slim evidence. T. S. Eliot wrote that he had no doubt that for some parts of *Hamlet* its author was merely revising passages in *The Spanish Tragedy*. Much more likely, *The Spanish Tragedy* was one of Oxford's forerunners to *Hamlet*, as proposed in "Sources, Influences and Forerunners" in this edition.

The crucial concept of blood revenge is at the center of *Hamlet*, and at the play's climax occurs a dense, extended example of deliberate ambiguity in literature for poetic purpose. In *Hamlet*, the ambiguity about revenge complicates what actually happens in the play, especially at the climax, and sets the audience and reader to thinking hard about the degree of guilt or innocence of the characters.

The ambiguity begins building with Laertes. Several minutes before the start of his fencing match with Laertes, Hamlet apologizes at length to him for killing his father. He says he was not himself and blames his manic madness. Laertes says he is satisfied by Hamlet's apology but only on the condition that some higher authority certify that his reputation is not damaged by his failing to get blood revenge. Then, however, he concludes: "I do receive your offered love like love / And will not wrong it." (5.2.223-4) Laertes sounds sincere but is ambiguous. He knows that he and the King still plan for him to kill Hamlet with the poisoned tip of his foil, which he will do in the duel.

Before they begin fencing, Queen Gertrude drinks to Hamlet's success, but unknowingly she drinks from the cup that King Claudius has poisoned. Sitting next to her, as would king and queen, he could stop her, but he fails to do so. Deliberate ambiguity clouds Claudius's motive, whether he is guilty of her death by deliberate non-action or is innocent because he could not act in time to prevent it. "It is too late," he says in an aside, as if justifying his non-action.

In the duel, Hamlet scores two hits and playfully taunts Laertes to try for his first hit. Incensed, Laertes lunges at him: "Have at you now!" He violates fencing etiquette by omitting the warning "en garde" and stabs him with the poisoned foil, achieving revenge for the death of his father. Then, however it happens, they exchange foils, perhaps in a scuffle, and Hamlet stabs Laertes with the poison-tipped foil, for Horatio exclaims, "They bleed on both sides!"

If Hamlet, who has been contemplating revenge throughout the play, has any thoughts now about finally avenging his father's murder, he says not a word about it. He speaks only of avenging his mother's death. When she dies, Laertes, himself dying, tells Hamlet, "Thy mother's poisoned. . . . The king's to blame." Hearing this, Hamlet impulsively wounds the King with the poisoned foil, and for good measure forces him to drink from the same poisoned cup that killed his mother, crying "Follow my mother!" And the King dies, his death not caused by Hamlet's long-sought revenge for the death of his father according to the feudal precept—a calculated and cold-blooded revenge slaying for the death of a close relative—but in an impulsive rage at the King for what he understands to be the murder of his mother.

Seconds later, knowing that he, too, is dying as a result of Claudius's plotting, Hamlet says, "Wretched queen, adieu." He mourns the death of his mother, again without a word about his father. Hamlet's immediate and final revenge thoughts are solely about his mother's death.

Deliberate ambiguity clouds Claudius's motives, whether he is guilty of her death because he fails to stop her from drinking from the cup he poisoned, or it is accidental because he could not act in time to prevent it. "It is too late," he says in an aside to himself, which could mean he regrets her death or realizes that he welcomes it and can justify it for his own political purposes, reflecting what Leicester would have done.

Deliberate ambiguity for dramatic purposes is a distinctive feature of the Shakespeare plays, (See Whalen "Ambiguity First Folio.") In *Hamlet* it clouds the motives, actions and fates of all the principal characters. In addition to Claudius's ambiguous non-action and Laertes' slippery ambiguity, left unsaid is whether his sister Ophelia died by accidental drowning or by suicide (or both) in despair at Hamlet's rejecting her and slaying her father.

Whether or not Gertrude had guilty knowledge of Claudius's murder of her first husband, King Hamlet, as implied by Hamlet's rage at her. Whether Hamlet's stabbing of Polonius hiding behind the arras is accidental because Hamlet thought he was stabbing the King, or deliberate because he should have recognized Polonius's voice when he shouts for help for Gertrude who fears Hamlet may kill her. And whether Hamlet for the audience and reader succeeds or fails to get his long-desired revenge according to the feudal precept for his father's murder by killing King Claudius, or whether it's an act of impulsive rage at Claudius's guilt in the death of Hamlet's mother, as Laertes has revealed in his dying words.

This greatest of the Shakespeare plays might well have been intended to leave its audience entertained, exhilarated and exhausted, struggling to understand what actually happens in the play and how its deliberate ambiguity might reflect the actual ambiguity in the lives of men and women everywhere, especially those in positions of influence and power.

Finally, it may be legitimate to suggest that Oxford at the end of his life accepted that it was no longer worth agonizing over Leicester's rumored murder of Oxford's father by poison and his own failure to get blood revenge in the traditional feudal manner. In the end, his preoccupation is his mother's betrayal of his father's memory and honor and her too hasty marriage after his death to a man Oxford would have considered far inferior to his father, the sixteenth Earl of Oxford, in political position, social status and accomplishments.

Hamlet's dying words arguably reflect Oxford's final thoughts about his legacy of Shakespeare plays and poems. In his last surviving letter, in 1603, Oxford, sensing that he was near the end of his life, asked Robert Cecil, William Cecil's son and the new monarch's chief minister, to expedite a piece of legal business. He explained that he had exhausted what was the best in him. "I am grown old," he wrote, "and spent the chiefest ["best part" OED obs.] time of mine age." He would die the next year at the age of fifty-four. *Hamlet* would be the last play he worked on. He did not live to see it in print. No Shakespeare plays can be securely dated after 1604, although Stratfordians try to date about a dozen after Oxford died. (See Whalen "A Dozen.")

Oxford had Hamlet regret that he leaves behind "a wounded name, / Things standing thus unknown." (5.2.330-1) Oxford himself left behind a wounded name, a reputation for many admirable traits but also a mercurial, erratic, unpredictable and difficult temperament that most people would find offensive. Oxford's reputation was also wounded because his contemporaries could not understand his disturbing episodes of manic high spirits; nor could they appreciate how the Earl of Leicester and the queen plundered his inheritance, the basis of a nobleman's power and prestige; nor how aristocratic norms of propriety enjoined him from putting his "wounded name" on his plays and poems that appeared as by William Shakespeare.

Hamlet

Dying, Hamlet exhorts Horatio, who knows him best, "to report me and my cause aright / To the unsatisfied" and "to tell my story." This plea by the Earl of Oxford in the voice of Prince Hamlet, however, went unfulfilled for more than three centuries while Stratford's Will Shakspere—a commoner of no documented education, no direct experience of court intrigues and corruption, no travel or military experience, no demonstrated writing ability—was given the credit for writing the works of Shakespeare.

A Note on the Play Text

For this edition of *Hamlet,* Brig. Gen. Jack Shuttleworth (ret.), head of the English department at the U.S. Air Force Academy for two decades, transcribed the play text from a facsimile copy of the second quarto of *Hamlet,* which was published in London in 1604. Most Shakespeare scholars consider this quarto to be the most authentic of the three earliest texts of the play—the 1603 "bad" quarto, the 1604 "good" quarto and even the play text in the 1623 First Folio, the first collection of Shakespeare plays. The facsimile copy, a photomechanical re-print called a collotype, was published by the Huntington Library, San Marino CA, in 1938.

This edition, like most editions of *Hamlet*, includes a few passages from the first quarto and the First Folio, passages that are not in the second quarto, when needed for clarity or for completeness of thought or action. For example, they include from the First Folio lines 224-247 and 310-317 about the visiting players and the childrens acting companies.

As is the case with all Shakespeare plays, *Hamlet* requires much modernizing throughout to produce a text that is more legible for the modern-day reader, but without violating the spirit of the play and the voice of the author. This editorial work includes modernizing Elizabethan orthography, adding punctuation and act/scene divisions, and correcting the occasional and obvious errors by the printer's typesetter, who was working from the author's manuscript, which, as is the case with all Shakespeare plays, has not survived.

The Tragedy of Hamlet

Prince of Denmark

The Principal Characters

Prince Hamlet, son of the late King Hamlet and nephew of Claudius
Claudius, King of Denmark and brother of the late King Hamlet
Gertrude, Queen of Denmark, Hamlet's mother and widow of King Hamlet
The Ghost of Hamlet's father

Polonius, councilor of state and principal adviser to King Claudius
Ophelia, his daughter
Laertes, his son
Reynaldo, his servant

Horatio, Hamlet's close friend and fellow student
Rosencrantz and *Guildenstern*, courtiers and Hamlet's former schoolfellows
Osric, a courtier
Marcellus, *Barnado* and *Francisco*, soldier sentinels
A Gravedigger, and *His Friend*
Fortinbras, Prince of Norway

Actors in the play-within-the-play, a priest, a Norwegian captain, English ambassadors, lords, ladies, officers, soldiers, sailors, messengers, and attendants.

Setting: Castle Elsinore, the capitol of Denmark in the eleventh century (standing for Queen Elizabeth's court in the sixteenth century)

Stage direction (s.d. hereafter)**:** That the setting is nighttime is clear from the text that follows, and it indicates that the play was written for evening performance indoors at Queen Elizabeth's court or at the Blackfriars, a renovated hall in the former monastery, for the upper classes, rather than for performance at a public theater like the Globe that was open to the sky and daylight for daytime performances with much cheaper ticket prices.

1 Who's there?: Barnardo, just coming on guard duty, is the wrong soldier to issue the challenge. It's the guard on duty who challenges someone approaching. This opening line signals that things are not in proper order and are disorderly in Denmark under King Claudius. The reversed challenge and its significance would come naturally to Oxford, who had military experience; Will Shakspere did not.

3 Long live the king: no doubt the password, and somewhat ironic because King Claudius will not live long.

9 sick at heart: probably due to his unease about having seen the Ghost on previous nights or to his dismay at the disorder and corruption in Claudius's court. Or both. Without being explicit, the guards are upset about what's going on in Denmark's court under the new king.

14 rivals: not competitors but having the same purpose, the earliest meaning in the Oxford English Dictionary (OED), here guard duty.

S.d. *Enter Horatio*: Hamlet's best friend, loyal to the end, no doubt named after one of Oxford's best friends, his cousin Horatio Vere. There is no Horatio in any of the literary sources for *Hamlet.*

15 Friends to this ground: probably to this land (OED obsolete) and by extension this country, Denmark, with a veiled implication of not to the current regime.

16 liegemen: a feudal term for vassals who owe allegiance to their overlord; here, to King Claudius "the Dane." The first of many references and allusions to feudalism. (See the Introduction.)

Act 1

Scene 1. A rampart at Castle Elsinore.
Enter Barnardo and Francisco, two sentinels

Barnardo
Who's there?
Francisco
Nay, answer me. Stand and unfold yourself.
Barnardo
Long live the king.
Francisco
Barnardo?
Barnardo
He. 5
Francisco
You come most carefully upon your hour.
Barnardo
'Tis now struck twelve. Get thee to bed, Francisco.
Francisco
For this relief much thanks. 'Tis bitter cold,
And I am sick at heart.
Barnardo
Have you had quiet guard? 10
Francisco
Not a mouse stirring.
Barnardo
Well, good night.
If you do meet Horatio and Marcellus,
The rivals of my watch, bid them make haste.
Enter Horatio and Marcellus
Francisco
I think I hear them. Stand ho! Who is there?
Horatio
Friends to this ground. 15
Marcellus
And liegemen to the Dane.
Francisco
Give you good night.

19 piece of him: part of him (OED obs.), perhaps reflecting his divided mind about reports of the appearance of a ghost of the late king and the disorderly state of Denmark under the new king.

29 approve our eyes: corroborate what we have seen.

38 star . . . pole: referring to the supernova (SN1572A) that appeared in November 1572 in the constellation Cassiopeia. The new star, described by the Danish astronomer Tycho Brahe, raised the question of whether the heavens were permanent, threatening long-held Ptolemaic, cosmological and religious views. Oxford's father-in-law, Lord Burghley, was directed by the queen to determine the truth and implications of the celestial phenomenon. (Oxford was 22; Shakspere 8.) Furthermore, the names Rosenkrantz and Guildenstern, prominent families in Denmark, are among those appearing in a portrait of Tycho known to have been in the possession of Oxford's brother-in-law, Lord Willoughby. The extraordinary number of astronomical references and allusions in *Hamlet* testifies to the author's deep knowledge of the just emerging science of the new, Copernican astronomy, which Will Shakspere could hardly have known. Stratfordian commentators routinely overlook or ignore them. (See Usher and "Astronomy in *Hamlet.*")

41 beating: tolling.

Marcellus
O, farewell, honest soldier. Who hath relieved you?
Francisco
Barnardo hath my place. Give you good night. *Exit Francisco*
Marcellus
Holla, Barnardo!
Barnardo
Say, what, is Horatio there?
Horatio
A piece of him.
Barnardo
Welcome, Horatio, welcome, good Marcellus. 20
Horatio
What, has this thing appeared again tonight?
Barnardo
I have seen nothing.
Marcellus
Horatio says 'tis but our fantasy,
And will not let belief take hold of him
Touching this dreaded sight twice seen of us; 25
Therefore I have entreated him along,
With us to watch the minutes of this night,
That if again this apparition come,
He may approve our eyes and speak to it.
Horatio
Tush, tush, 'twill not appear. 30
Barnardo
Sit down a while,
And let us once again assail your ears,
That are so fortified against our story,
What we have two nights seen.
Horatio
Well, sit we down, 35
And let us hear Barnardo speak of this.
Barnardo
Last night of all,
When yond same star that's westward from the pole
Had made his course to illume that part of heaven
Where now it burns, Marcellus and myself, 40
The bell then beating one —

Enter Ghost

43 In the same figure: appearing as it has before. **the king**: King Hamlet.

44 Thou art a scholar: As a university student, Horatio speaks Latin, which was believed necessary to exorcise a ghost. The soldier Marcellus may be a bit overexcited, and in fact Horatio will speak to it in English, not Latin.

46 harrows me: greatly distresses me.

49 What art . . . usurpest: Horatio questions the Ghost's identity and its right to disturb ("usurpest") the night in the form of the dead King Hamlet. His speech foreshadows that Hamlet will question the identity of the Ghost and that Claudius has usurped the Danish throne.

50 warlike form: wearing feudal armor. Edward de Vere, the seventeenth Earl of Oxford, was the latest in a long line of feudal lords stretching back to the time of William the Conqueror. Putting the ghost of Hamlet's father in feudal armor would have had special significance for the dramatist and for the aristocratic audiences of theater-goers and readers who were living through the fading of the ancestral, feudal times and the emergence of the "new men," commoners who were achieving political power in the court of Queen Elizabeth, who rewarded them with titles of nobility. (See the Introduction.)

51 buried Denmark: the dead King Hamlet.

61 sensible and true avouch: clear testimony.

66 Norway: the King of Norway.

67angry parle: an angry discussion or argument. (OED obs.)

68 He smote the sleaded pollax on the ice.: probably meaning that in anger he struck the frozen ground ("the ice") with his poleaxe ("pollax" OED obs. spelling) made heavy with lead ("sleaded," a printer's error for "leaded.") The phrase has also been taken to mean he struck Poles on sleds on the ice, but that seems bizarre and unlikely.

Marcellus
Peace, break thee off. Look where it comes again!
Barnardo
In the same figure, like the king that's dead.
Marcellus
Thou art a scholar, speak to it, Horatio.
Barnardo
Looks it not like the king? Mark it, Horatio. 45
Horatio
Most like; it harrows me with fear and wonder.
Barnardo
It would be spoke to.
Marcellus
Speak to it, Horatio.
Horatio
What art thou that usurpest this time of night,
Together with that fair and warlike form 50
In which the majesty of buried Denmark
Did sometimes march? By heaven I charge thee speak!
Marcellus
It is offended
Barnardo
See, it stalks away.
Horatio
Stay! Speak, speak, I charge thee speak! *Exit Ghost* 55
Marcellus
'Tis gone, and will not answer.
Barnardo
How now, Horatio? You tremble and look pale.
Is not this something more than fantasy?
What think you on it?
Horatio
Before my God, I might not this believe 60
Without the sensible and true avouch
Of mine own eyes.
Marcellus
Is it not like the king?
Horatio
As thou art to thyself.
Such was the very armor he had on 65
When he the ambitious Norway combated.
So frowned he once when in an angry parle
He smote the sleaded pollax on the ice.

71 martial stalk: marching proudly. (OED obs.)

74 eruption: an outbreak of a disease, here figuratively for the diseased and corrupted Danish "state" under King Claudius. The dominating metaphor in the play will be rottenness, disease and corruption. (See Spurgeon.)

77-84 So nightly toils. . . . inform me?: In this speech Marcellus asks why the Danes are made to work day and night preparing for war. This might well reflect 1584-6 when England was sending an army to the Lowlands and building up its navy. The reference also may suggest when Oxford was beginning to write *Hamlet*; he was active at court and went with the English forces to the Lowlands as a commander.

88 emulate pride: envious ambition. (OED obs.)

92 by law and heraldry: by both written law and the unwritten rules of chivalric precedence (OED obs.); a usage unique in Shakespeare and one that would come readily to a nobleman like Oxford who was very familiar with both the law and chivalry.

86-100 Our last king . . . . fell to Hamlet.: In this long speech, Horatio tells how King Hamlet killed the senior King Fortinbras of Norway in single combat and won back land that King Fortinbras had seized for himself.

101 unimproved: unproven. (OED obs.)

102-3 skirts . . . . resolutes: that is, in the outlying parts ("skirts") of Norway he collected by fraudulent means ("sharked up" OED obs.) a band ("list") of lawless desperadoes ("resolutes" OED obs.).

'Tis strange.

Marcellus

Thus twice before, and jump at this dead hour, 70
With martial stalk hath he gone by our watch.

Horatio

In what particular thought to work I know not,
But in the gross and scope of mine opinion,
This bodes some strange eruption to our state.

Marcellus

Good now, sit down, and tell me, he that knows, 75
Why this same strict and most observant watch
So nightly toils the subject of the land,
And why such daily cast of brazen cannon,
And foreign mart for implements of war,
Why such impress of shipwrights, whose sore task 80
Does not divide the Sunday from the week.
What might be toward, that this sweaty haste
Doth make the night joint-laborer with the day:
Who is it that can inform me?

Horatio

That can I. 85
At least the whisper goes so: Our last king,
Whose image even but now appeared to us,
Was, as you know, by Fortinbras of Norway,
Thereto pricked on by a most emulate pride,
Dared to the combat; in which our valiant Hamlet
(For so this side of our known world esteemed him) 90
Did slay this Fortinbras, who, by a sealed compact
Well ratified by law and heraldry,
Did forfeit with his life all those his lands
Which he stood seized of, to the conqueror;
Against the which a moiety competent 95
Was gaged by our king, which had returned
To the inheritance of Fortinbras,
Had he been vanquisher; as by the same covenant
And carriage of the article designed,
His fell to Hamlet. Now sir, young Fortinbras, 100
Of unimproved mettle hot and full,
Hath in the skirts of Norway here and there
Sharked up a list of lawless resolutes
For food and diet to some enterprise
That hath a stomach in it, which is no other, 105
As it doth well appear unto our state,

107 by strong hand: by main force; word play on "Fortinbras," French for "strong in arm" reflecting Oxford's facility with French, and probably suggesting Fortinbras using "strong-arm" tactics.

112 rummage: commotion, bustle, from an old nautical word for shifting or unloading a ship's cargo. (OED obs.)

123 moist star: the moon, which is associated with tides and the belief that it drew water from the earth.

126 like precurse: similar forerunners. (OED obs.)

130 our climatures: our (temperate) region, per the OED, the first use of the word, probably referring to Denmark's location in the temperate zone.

132 cross it: confront it, perhaps in the form of a cross with his sword's hilt. **Blast me.**: ruin me, destroy me; from blast meaning to blight with an evil wind, per the OED..

136 to thee do ease and grace to me: give relief to you and reflect well on me.

138 happily: perchance. (OED archaic)

140-1 uphoarded . . . earth: that is, in the alternative if you (the Ghost) hoarded stolen ("extorted") treasure and buried it underground (as did the dragon in *Beowulf.* (See "Sources Influences Forerunners" in the appendix.) Horatio reflects the belief that a ghost might deceive humans and not be what he appears to be but someone damned or the devil himself, a possibility that Hamlet will also consider.

But to recover of us, by strong hand
And terms compulsatory, those foresaid lands
So by his father lost; and this, I take it,
Is the main motive of our preparations, 110
The source of this our watch, and the chief head
Of this post-haste and rummage in the land.

Barnardo

I think it be no other but even so.
Well may it sort that this portentous figure
Comes armed through our watch so like the king 115
That was and is the question of these wars.

Horatio

A mote it is to trouble the mind's eye.
In the most high and palmy state of Rome,
A little ere the mightiest Julius fell,
The graves stood tenantless and the sheeted dead 120
Did squeak and gibber in the Roman streets;
As stars with trains of fire, and dews of blood,
Disasters in the sun; and the moist star
Upon whose influence Neptune's empire stands
Was sick almost to doomsday with eclipse. 125
And even the like precurse of feared events,
As harbingers preceding still the fates
And prologue to the omen coming on,
Have heaven and earth together demonstrated
Unto our climatures and countrymen. 130

Enter Ghost

But soft, behold. Lo where it comes again.

It spreads his arms

I'll cross it though it blast me. Stay, illusion!
If thou hast any sound or use of voice,
Speak to me.
If there be any good thing to be done 135
That may to thee do ease, and grace to me,
Speak to me.
If thou art privy to thy country's fate,
Which happily foreknowing may avoid,
O speak!
Or if thou hast uphoarded in thy life 140
Extorted treasure in the womb of earth,
For which, they say, your spirits oft walk in death,
Speak of it, stay and speak!

The cock crows

144 partisan: a long-handled spear with a cutting-edge blade.

149 being so majestical: that is, the Ghost being so majestic.

158 god of day: Sun god, Phoebus Apollo.

160 extravagant: roaming out of its boundaries (OED obs.). **erring**: deviating from its proper course (OED obs.), like a star mistakenly believed to be "erring" from its orbit but which is actually a planet. Another of many references and allusions in the play to astronomy. (See "Astronomy in *Hamlet*" in the appendix.) And with a connotation of "erring" in the sense of having committed errors or sins. **hies:** hurries.

161 confine: place of confinement.

162 This present object made probation.: that is, this ghost gave proof ("probation" OED obs,) of the belief that a ghost could not exist in daylight.

164 ever 'gainst: always before.

168 no planets strike: In astrological belief, planets in an unfavorable position or aspect could strike or destroy men or things.

169 takes: probably, afflicts or bewitches.

Stop it, Marcellus.

Marcellus

Shall I strike it with my partisan?

Horatio

Do, if it will not stand. 145

Barnardo

'Tis here!

Horatio

'Tis here!

Marcellus

'Tis gone!

We do it wrong, being so majestical,

To offer it the show of violence; 150

For it is as the air, invulnerable,

And our vain blows malicious mockery.

Barnardo

It was about to speak when the cock crew.

Horatio

And then it started like a guilty thing

Upon a fearful summons. I have heard 155

The cock, that is the trumpet to the morn,

Doth with his lofty and shrill-sounding throat

Awake the god of day, and at his warning,

Whether in sea or fire, in earth or air,

The extravagant and erring spirit hies 160

To his confine, and of the truth herein

This present object made probation.

Marcellus

It faded on the crowing of the cock.

Some say that ever 'gainst that season comes

Wherein our Savior's birth is celebrated, 165

This bird of dawning singeth all night long,

And then they say no spirit dare stir abroad,

The nights are wholesome, then no planets strike,

No fairy takes, nor witch hath power to charm,

So hallowed, and so gracious, is that time. 170

Horatio

So have I heard and do in part believe it.

But look, the morn in russet mantle clad

Walks over the dew of yon high eastward hill.

Break we our watch up, and by my advice

Let us impart what we have seen tonight 175

S.d. Enter Claudius: Oxford names him "Claudius" only here and in the first speech prefix of the scene perhaps to emphasize that Claudius, although the brother of King Hamlet, is not his natural heir, as is Hamlet. Thereafter, Claudius is "the King."

1-39 our dear brother's death. . . . your duty: With flagrant hypocrisy, Claudius calls the late King Hamlet his "dear brother" whom he grieves for, but whom, it will transpire, he cuckolded and recently killed with poison in order to seize the throne. No one, however, including his audience, knows that he secretly killed him. In this long, cleverly manipulative speech, Claudius, the presumptive king, addresses the court from the throne for the first time. He is quick to use the royal plural and assert, if anyone had any doubts, that he is now in charge. The smooth-talking villain of the play, King Claudius was no doubt inspired by the smooth-talking Earl of Leicester, who had a reputation as a poisoner and whom Oxford probably suspected of having his father poisoned in order to seize control of much of his inheritance. (See the Introduction.)

7 remembrance of ourselves: Claudius guilefully maintains that he must remember that he ("ourselves") is now also king of the Danes.

8-9 sometime sister . . . imperial jointress: To consolidate his taking the throne, Claudius introduces his bride, Gertrude, his "former sister"-in-law, as "the imperial jointress," describing how she had acquired "jointure" property rights to King Hamlet's legacy, the Danish "empire." The adjective "imperial" exaggerates but implies rights as Queen as well. "Jointress" was an arcane legal term for a widow who had acquired certain property rights in special circumstances—evidence for the dramatist's in-depth knowledge of property law, which Shakspere was not likely to have had. (See Regnier.) **warlike state**: referring to the preparations being made for war if the Norwegians attack and implying the need for a man to be in charge.

15-16 Your better wisdoms . . . this affair along.: Finally, to further consolidate his position, Claudius brazenly assumes that his court audience in its collective "wisdoms" agrees "freely" with his taking the throne, even though they know that Hamlet, listening to all this, is the only son and obvious natural heir to it, although as a teenage university student too young to legally exercise its power, just as Oxford, when his father died, was a minor and too young to exercise power over his inheritance. (See the Introduction.)

26 Now for ourself,: Having co-opted the court to accept his claimed right to be king, he gets down to royal business as the new king.

29 impotent and bedrid: confined to sick bed and thus powerless ("impotent").

Unto young Hamlet, for, upon my life,
This spirit, dumb to us, will speak to him.
Do you consent we shall acquaint him with it,
As needful in our loves, fitting our duty?

Marcellus
Let's do it, I pray, and I this morning know 180
Where we shall find him most convenient.

Exeunt

Scene 2. A room of state.
Enter Claudius, King of Denmark; Gertrude the Queen; councilors; Polonius and his son Laertes and daughter Ophelia; Hamlet, and others.

Claudius
Though yet of Hamlet our dear brother's death
The memory be green, and that it us befitted
To bear our hearts in grief, and our whole kingdom
To be contracted in one brow of woe,
Yet so far hath discretion fought with nature 5
That we with wisest sorrow think on him
Together with remembrance of ourselves.
Therefore our sometime sister, now our queen,
The imperial jointress to this warlike state,
Have we, as 'twere with a defeated joy, 10
With an auspicious, and a dropping eye,
With mirth in funeral, and with dirge in marriage,
In equal scale weighing delight and dole,
Taken to wife; nor have we herein barred
Your better wisdoms, which have freely gone 15
With this affair along. For all, our thanks.
Now follows that you know young Fortinbras,
Holding a weak supposal of our worth,
Or thinking by our late dear brother's death
Our state to be disjoint and out of frame, 20
Co-leagued with this dream of his advantage,
He hath not failed to pester us with message
Importing the surrender of those lands
Lost by his father, with all bonds of law,
To our most valiant brother. So much for him. 25
Now for ourself, and for this time of meeting,
Thus much the business is: we have here writ
To Norway, uncle of young Fortinbras—
Who, impotent and bedrid, scarcely hears
Of this his nephew's purpose—to suppress 30

31-33 suppress / His further gait . . . his subject: stop his nephew, young Fortinbras, from taking any further steps ("gait") to raise money ("levies"), recruit men ("lists") in large quantities thereof ("proportions" OED obs.) that must all come from Norway's people, his "subject(s)."

37 dilated: fully detailed. (OED obs.)

39 let your haste commend your duty: Let your speedy accomplishment of your mission prove your loyalty.

43 Laertes: Polonius's son.

46 thou: In oily graciousness, Claudius shifts from the formal "your" to the familiar but a bit condescending "thou" form of address.

58 bow them: submit themselves.

60 slow leave: reluctant permission.

62 Upon . . . consent: that is, upon Laertes "will" (his desire) I and gave my reluctant ("hard") consent to his returning to Paris.

His further gait herein, in that the levies,
The lists, and full proportions are all made
Out of his subject; and we here dispatch
You, good Cornelius, and you, Voltemand,
For bearers of this greeting to old Norway, 35
Giving to you no further personal power
To business with the king, more than the scope
Of these dilated articles allow.
Farewell, and let your haste commend your duty.

Cornelius, Voltemand
In that, and all things, will we show our duty. 40

King Claudius
We doubt it nothing; heartily farewell.
Exeunt Voltemand and Cornelius
And now, Laertes, what's the news with you?
You told us of some suit, what is it, Laertes?
You cannot speak of reason to the Dane 45
And lose your voice. What wouldst thou beg, Laertes,
That shall not be my offer, not thy asking?
The head is not more native to the heart,
The hand more instrumental to the mouth, 50
Than is the throne of Denmark to thy father.
What wouldst thou have, Laertes?

Laertes
My dread lord,
Your leave and favor to return to France,
From whence though willingly I came to Denmark
To show my duty in your coronation, 55
Yet now I must confess, that duty done,
My thoughts and wishes bend again toward France,
And bow them to your gracious leave and pardon.

King
Have you your father's leave? What says Polonius?

Polonius
Hath, my lord, wrung from me my slow leave 60
By laborsome petition, and at last
Upon his will I sealed my hard consent.
I do beseech you give him leave to go.

King
Take thy fair hour, Laertes, time be thine,
And thy best graces spend it at thy will 65
But now, my cousin Hamlet, and my son—

67 A little more than kin and less than kind.: Hamlet interrupts the King, who has boldly called him "my son," to assert that the King, his uncle, cannot claim to be his natural father and that only by marrying his mother did he also become his stepfather, "a little more than kin," kin being the blood relationship of uncle-nephew. For emphasis, Hamlet adds that the King is "less than kind," that is, he is not an offspring or descendent ("kind" OED obs.). In this his first line in the play, Hamlet confronts King Claudius with a quick-witted, riddling response that will be typical of his word play and antic disposition. The King deliberately ignores Hamlet's retort and continues with his question.

69 Not so much, my lord, I am too much in the Sun: Wearing mourning black, Hamlet again contradicts the King probably objecting that he finds himself "too much" in the offensive, bright glare ("the Sun") of the court in colorful, celebratory raiment, everyone having too soon forgot Hamlet's father's death; and also alluding to the fact that Hamlet, as his father's only son/Sun is the natural heir to the throne of Denmark, just as in the new Copernican astronomy the Sun (not the Earth/ Claudius) is the natural and rightful center of the known universe; and also reflecting Oxford's belief that the Earl of Leicester (personified in Claudius) stole his patrimony just as Claudius has stolen Hamlet's inheritance." All in one short line.

70 nighted color: black (OED obs.), and probably also his gloomy countenance ("color").

71 on Denmark: on Claudius, who has made himself King of Denmark.

72 vailed lids: lowered, downcast eyes. (OED obs.).

81 suspiration: deep breathing. (OED rare)

83 havior of the visage: appearance of the face.

89-114 'Tis sweet . . . . toward you: The very length of this hypocritical speech shows a duplicity almost desperate in Claudius's dealings with Hamlet.

94 obsequious: not servile, but with proper funeral rites. (OED obs.)

Hamlet
A little more than kin, and less than kind.
King
How is it that the clouds still hang on you?
Hamlet
Not so, my lord, I am too much in the sun.
Queen
Good Hamlet, cast thy nighted color off, 70
And let thine eye look like a friend on Denmark.
Do not for ever with thy vailed lids
Seek for thy noble father in the dust.
Thou knowest 'tis common, all that lives must die,
Passing through nature to eternity. 75
Hamlet
Ay, madam, it is common.
Queen
If it be,
Why seems it so particular with thee?
Hamlet
Seems, madam? nay, it is, I know not seems.
Tis not alone my inky cloak, good mother,
Nor customary suits of solemn black, 80
Nor windy suspiration of forced breath,
No, nor the fruitful river in the eye,
Nor the dejected havior of the visage,
Together with all forms, moods, shapes of grief,
That can denote me truly. These indeed seem, 85
For they are actions that a man might play;
But I have that within which passes show,
These but the trappings and the suits of woe.
King
'Tis sweet and commendable in your nature, Hamlet,
To give these mourning duties to your father. 90
But you must know your father lost a father,
That father lost, lost his, and the survivor bound
In filial obligation for some term
To do obsequious sorrow. But to persever
In obstinate condolement is a course 95
Of impious stubbornness; 'tis unmanly grief;
It shows a will most incorrect to heaven,
A heart unfortified, or mind impatient,
An understanding simple and unschooled:
For what we know must be, and is as common 100
As any the most vulgar thing to sense,

103 fault: offense.

107 first corpse: the body of Abel, who was traditionally considered the first human to die; a grimly appropriate but probably unconscious allusion by Claudius, who murdered his brother, to Cain's murder of his brother Abel.

115 Wittenberg: the German university and the first where scholars began in the late 16th century to consider the work of the Pole Copernicus; also the city famous for Martin Luther and the birth of Protestantism; and the preferred university for Danish students studying abroad.

116 retrograde: contrary; but its first meaning was astronomical, describing certain planets that appear at times to move backward relative to other planets moving east to west. Its usage here is the first to mean an objection or contrary opinion. (OED obs.) Claudius's objection to Hamlet returning to Wittenberg allies him with Ptolemaic astronomy, which will be discredited. The new Copernican astronomy explains the "retrograde" appearance.

117-118 to remain . . . our eye,: no doubt, however, in order to keep an "eye" on Hamlet, who the King suspects may suspect him of murdering his father and who may be thinking of revenge.

123 obey, you, madam.: After being lectured by the King to stop his mourning, and being entreated by him to stay in England, Hamlet says only that he will do his best to obey his mother, snubbing the king.

127 jocund health: a merry toast or salute.

128 cannon . . . shall tell: the firing of cannon salutes, a Danish custom of the time. Oxford would have learned of it from his brother-in-law, the queen's special envoy to the court of Denmark.

129 rouse: from "carouse," drinking a full bumper of wine; that is, every time the King empties his goblet a cannon salute will be fired. **Bruit again**: make noise (OED archaic from the French) again; here echo.

134 self-slaughter: In this soliloquy, Hamlet falls into a mood of deep, suicidal despair, the polar opposite of his antic disposition, reflecting Oxford's apparent, periodic moods of despair and manic highs. (See the Introduction.)

136-7 unweeded garden: Claudius's regime.

Why should we in our peevish opposition
Take it to heart? Fie, 'tis a fault to heaven,
A fault against the dead, a fault to nature;
To reason most absurd, whose common theme 105
Is death of fathers, and who still hath cried,
From the first corpse till he that died to-day,
This must be so. We pray you throw to earth
This unprevailing woe, and think of us
As of a father; for let the world take note 110
You are the most immediate to our throne,
And with no less nobility of love
Than that which dearest father bears his son,
Do I impart toward you. For your intent
In going back to school in Wittenberg, 115
It is most retrograde to our desire,
And we beseech you bend you to remain
Here in the cheer and comfort of our eye,
Our chiefest courtier, cousin, and our son.

Queen

Let not thy mother lose her prayers, Hamlet, 120
I pray thee stay with us, go not to Wittenberg.

Hamlet

I shall in all my best obey you, madam.

King

Why, 'tis a loving and a fair reply.
Be as ourself in Denmark. Madam, come.
This gentle and unforced accord of Hamlet 125
Sits smiling to my heart, in grace whereof,
No jocund health that Denmark drinks today,
But the great cannon to the clouds shall tell,
And the king's rouse the heaven shall bruit again,
Respeaking earthly thunder. Come, away. 130

Flourish. Exeunt all but Hamlet

Hamlet

O that this too too solid flesh would melt,
Thaw, and resolve itself into a dew.
Or that the Everlasting had not fixed
His canon 'gainst self-slaughter. O God, God,
How weary, stale, flat, and unprofitable 135
Seem to me all the uses of this world.
Fie on it, ah fie! 'Tis an unweeded garden

139 merely: entirely. (OED obs.)

142 Hyperion to a satyr: Hamlet compares his father to the Greek god of light, wisdom and honor, and his uncle King Claudius to a "satyr," a half-man half-goat, drunken, lustful companion of Dionysus.

143 beteem: allow. (OED obs.)

147 within a month: Just as Oxford's mother re-married soon after his father's death to a man of much lower status when Oxford was thirteen and living in the Cecil household, Hamlet's mother re-married "within a month" a man of much lower status and character, in Hamlet's view, when Hamlet was in his teens and away at the university in Wittenberg. She will admit later that their marriage was over-hasty. As Hamlet, Oxford vents his anger at his late mother here and when Hamlet confronts Gertrude in her sitting room in act 3 scene 4. (See the Introduction.)

149 those shoes: The queen's shoes were probably stylish, fragile shoes or slippers of cloth or thin leather that aristocratic ladies wore indoors, shoes that quickly became worn and "old" and that Oxford would have known about, but not likely Shakspere.

151 Niobe: In Greek myth, the personification of inconsolable grief.

155 Hercules: the Greek hero who performed superhuman tasks.

156 unrighteous tears: false, insincere tears. (OED obs.)

159 incestuous: A widow's marriage with her deceased husband's brother was considered incest from Biblical times.

166 what make you: What are you doing here? (OED archaic)

170 truant disposition: an inclination to skip school; probably a tactful evasion of Hamlet's question on a sensitive matter, his father's death and mother's re-marriage.

That grows to seed; things rank and gross in nature
Possess it merely. That it should come to this!
But two months dead, nay, not so much, not two. 140
So excellent a king, that was to this,
Hyperion to a satyr; so loving to my mother
That he might not beteem the winds of heaven
Visit her face too roughly. Heaven and earth,
Must I remember? Why, she should hang on him 145
As if increase of appetite had grown
By what it fed on, and yet, within a month—
Let me not think on it. Frailty, thy name is woman—
A little month, or ere those shoes were old
With which she followed my poor father's body, 150
Like Niobe, all tears—why, she—
O God, a beast that wants discourse of reason
Would have mourned longer—married with my uncle,
My father's brother, but no more like my father
Than I to Hercules. Within a month, 155
Ere yet the salt of most unrighteous tears
Had left the flushing in her galled eyes,
She married. O most wicked speed, to post
With such dexterity to incestuous sheets;
It is not, nor it cannot come to good. 160
But break, my heart, for I must hold my tongue.

Enter Horatio, Marcellus, and Barnardo

Horatio
Hail to your lordship!

Hamlet
I am glad to see you well.
Horatio, or I do forget myself.

Horatio
The same, my lord, and your poor servant ever.

Hamlet
Sir, my good friend, I'll change that name with you. 165
And what make you from Wittenberg, Horatio?—
Marcellus!

Marcellus
My good lord.

Hamlet
I am very glad to see you. *[To Barnardo.]* Good even, sir—
But what, in faith, make you from Wittenberg?

Horatio
A truant disposition, good my lord. 170

174 you are no truant: here, the earliest meaning of truant, an idle vagabond, often in a playful sense. (OED obs.)

176 drink deep: another allusion to the dissolute drinking in King Claudius's court.

181 baked meats: meat pies and pastries.

182 coldly: the leftovers served up cold for the wedding feast; with overtones of callousness ("coldly") in serving leftover funeral dishes at a wedding.

183 met my dearest foe in heaven: that is, seen my worthiest ("dearest" OED obs.) enemy in heaven.

184 Or ever: before. (OED obs.)

193 your admiration: your astonishment. (OED obs.)

194 attent: attentive.

Hamlet
I would not hear your enemy say so,
Nor shall you do my ear that violence
To make it truster of your own report
Against yourself. I know you are no truant.
But what is your affair in Elsinore? 175
We'll teach you to drink deep ere you depart.
Horatio
My lord, I came to see your father's funeral.
Hamlet
I pray thee do not mock me, fellow student,
I think it was to see my mother's wedding.
Horatio
Indeed, my lord, it followed hard upon. 180
Hamlet
Thrift, thrift, Horatio, the funeral baked meats
Did coldly furnish forth the marriage tables.
Would I had met my dearest foe in heaven,
Or ever I had seen that day, Horatio.
My father — methinks I see my father. 185
Horatio
Where, my lord?
Hamlet
In my mind's eye, Horatio.
Horatio
I saw him once; he was a goodly king.
Hamlet
He was a man, take him for all in all,
I shall not look upon his like again.
Horatio
My lord, I think I saw him yesternight. 190
Hamlet
Saw? Who?
Horatio
My lord, the king your father.
Hamlet
The king my father?
Horatio
Season your admiration for a while
With an attent ear, till I may deliver,
Upon the witness of these gentlemen, 195
This marvel to you.

199 dead waste: desolate, uninhabited. (OED the earliest meaning)

201 Armed at point exactly *cap-à-pie*: wearing feudal armor that is correct in every detail ("at point" from the French *à point* meaning just right) from head to foot ("*cap-à-pie*" from Old French). Oxford was fluent in French from his youth. The Ghost's feudal armor may well have been inspired by Titian's 1537 painting of the Duke of Urbino wearing armor, which Oxford could have seen in Italy. This is the same duke who reportedly was murdered in 1538 by a relative who put poison in his ear as he slept in his garden, as happened to King Hamlet. The Stratfordian scholar Geoffrey Bullough was struck by Titian's painting as a likely source for the Ghost's armor. An engraving of it was in a book in Cecil's library, where Oxford also could have seen it. The murder by poison of the Duke of Urbino will inspire the play-within-the-play produced by Hamlet in act 3 scene 2. (See line notes 2.2.468 and 3.2.248.)

205 truncheon: military commander's symbol of office, a marshal's baton. **distilled**: reduced.

206 act: effects, action. (OED obs.)

208 In dreadful secrecy impart: that is, in fearful ("dreadful" OED obs.) secrecy they told me ("impart(ed)" to me).

210-211 delivered . . . of the thing: probably meaning, as they had described "(delivered") what they saw, that is, the Ghost ("the thing") giving both the time of night it appeared and what it looked like.

212 These hands are not more like: Horatio says his two hands are as much alike as was the resemblance of the Ghost to Hamlet's father when alive.

223 writ down in our duty: probably, expected of us, given our loyalty to you.

Hamlet
For God's love let me hear!
Horatio
Two nights together had these gentlemen,
Marcellus and Barnardo, on their watch,
In the dead waste and middle of the night,
Been thus encountered. A figure like your father, 200
Armed at point exactly, *cap-à-pie*,
Appears before them, and with solemn march
Goes slow and stately by them; thrice he walked
By their oppressed and fear-surprised eyes
Within his truncheon's length, whilst they, distilled 205
Almost to jelly with the act of fear,
Stand dumb and speak not to him. This to me
In dreadful secrecy impart they did,
And I with them the third night kept the watch,
Where, as they had delivered, both in time, 210
Form of the thing, each word made true and good,
The apparition comes. I knew your father,
These hands are not more like.
Hamlet
But where was this?
Marcellus
My lord, upon the platform where we watch.
Hamlet
Did you not speak to it?
Horatio
My lord, I did, 215
But answer made it none. Yet once methought
It lifted up its head and did address
Itself to motion like as it would speak;
But even then the morning cock crew loud,
And at the sound it shrunk in haste away 220
And vanished from our sight.
Hamlet
'Tis very strange.
Horatio
As I do live, my honored lord, 'tis true,
And we did think it writ down in our duty
To let you know of it.
Hamlet
Indeed, indeed, sirs. But this troubles me. 225
Hold you the watch tonight?

230 beaver: visor or face guard of a helmet. (OED obs.)

231 What: How. **frowningly:** as befits a warrior.

232 A countenance . . .:sorrow: face or visage, perhaps with a connotation of communicating an attitude or feeling (OED obs.), here "sorrow."

233 red: flushed, as if alive.

240 tell a hundred: count (OED obs.) to a hundred.

243 grizzled: gray.

Marcellus, Barnardo
We do, my lord.
Hamlet
Armed, say you?
Marcellus, Barnardo
Armed, my lord.
Hamlet
From top to toe?
Marcellus, Barnardo
My lord, from head to foot.
Hamlet
Then saw you not his face.
Horatio
O yes, my lord, he wore his beaver up. 230
Hamlet
What looked he, frowningly?
Horatio
A countenance more in sorrow than in anger.
Hamlet
Pale, or red?
Horatio
Nay, very pale.
Hamlet
And fixed his eyes upon you? 235
Horatio
Most constantly.
Hamlet
I would I had been there.
Horatio
It would have much amazed you.

Hamlet
Very like. Stayed it long?
Horatio
While one with moderate haste might tell a hundred. 240
Marcellus, Barnardo
Longer, longer.
Horatio
Not when I saw it.
Hamlet
His beard was grizzled, no?
Horatio
It was, as I have seen it in his life,

245 a sable silvered: dark hair ("sable") turning silver gray.

248 If it assume my noble father's person,: Hamlet confronts the possibility that the Ghost may be a devil that had taken on the appearance of his deceased father to deceive him for wicked purposes. For this reason, Hamlet will not take action against King Claudius precipitously without further evidence. The audience would recognize that he must first verify that the Ghost was not a deceptive devil but was indeed that of his father telling Hamlet that Claudius poisoned him. Hamlet will verify this to his satisfaction with the play-within-the play in act 3 scene 2.

249 hell . . . gape: At the time, it was also believed that speaking to a ghost would condemn one to hell.

252 Let it be tenable in your silence still: Let it continue to be held ("tenable") secret what you have seen and may "still" happen to see tonight.

255 your loves: Hamlet insists here and at line 259 on a relationship of loyal friendship ("loves") that is beyond mere duty and that is reciprocal.

261 doubt some foul play: not "doubt" in the usual sense but suspect, or fear (OED obs.) some wicked deeds. This is the first hint of what Hamlet will discover about how his father died.

262 Foul deeds will rise . . . to men's eyes: A ghost's appearance was thought to be the sign of a crime ("foul deeds"), here especially a hidden one that will, however, eventually be revealed "to men's eyes."

1 My necessaries are embarked.: Everything I need ("necessaries" OED obs.) is on board ship.

3 assistant: standing by. (OED obs.)

5-44 For Hamlet. . . . none else near.: In this long speech, Laertes, like his father Polonius, indulges in long-winded flowery rhetoric that is supposed to impress his listener. Since Polonius was inspired by William Cecil, later Lord Burghley, as is widely accepted, then Laertes is his son, Thomas Cecil, eight years older than Oxford when Oxford was a teenage ward in the Cecil household, and who did leave home and travel to Paris to study; and Ophelia is Cecil's daughter, Anne. She and Oxford both lived in the Cecil household when Oxford was in his teens, and they would marry when he reached the age of twenty-one and she was fifteen. (See the Introduction.)

5 trifling of his favor: his frivolous attention, with a connotation of false or feigning. (OED obs.)

6 toy in blood: probably meaning a transitory sexual fancy.

7 primy: probably, in the prime of life, lustful.

A sable silvered. 245

Hamlet

I will watch tonight; perchance 'twill walk again.

Horatio

I warrant it will.

Hamlet

If it assume my noble father's person,
I'll speak to it though hell itself should gape
And bid me hold my peace. I pray you all, 250
If you have hitherto concealed this sight,
Let it be tenable in your silence still,
And whatsomever else shall hap tonight,
Give it an understanding but no tongue.
I will requite your loves. So fare you well. 255
Upon the platform 'twixt eleven and twelve
I'll visit you.

All

Our duty to your honor.

Hamlet

Your loves, as mine to you; farewell. *Exeunt all but Hamlet*
My father's spirit—in arms! All is not well, 260
I doubt some foul play. Would the night were come!
Till then sit still, my soul. Foul deeds will rise,
Though all the earth overwhelm them, to men's eyes. *Exit*

Scene 3. Enter Laertes and Ophelia, his sister.

Laertes

My necessaries are embarked. Farewell.
And, sister, as the winds give benefit
And convoy is assistant, do not sleep,
But let me hear from you.

Ophelia

Do you doubt that?

Laertes

For Hamlet, and the trifling of his favor, 5
Hold it a fashion and a toy in blood,
A violet in the youth of primy nature,
Forward, not permanent, sweet, not lasting,
The perfume and suppliance of a minute—No more.

Ophelia

No more but so?

Laertes

Think it no more: 10

15 cautel: deceit, trickery. (OED obs.)

17 His greatness: Prince Hamlet's nobility, like Lord Oxford's, whereas Polonius and his family, like the Cecils, were commoners.

23 voice and yielding: proclaimed consent. In his Arden edition (1982) the Stratfordian Harold Jenkins cites Sir Thomas Smith as the source for this description of the political body's action. As it happens, Smith was one of Oxford's tutors. No known connection, however, links Will Shakspere to Smith or to his works, which would be very unlikely.

32 unmastered: uncontrolled.

34-5 rear of your affection . . . danger of desire.: a military image urging Ophelia not to place herself in the front lines of danger, where her "affection" might lead her, but to remain in the "rear," safely protected from physical desire.

38 calumnious strokes: slanderous attacks.

39 canker galls the infants: The canker worm attacks the young plants.

42 contagious blastments: blights that cause young plants to wither

44 to itself rebels: against its own best interests by feeling the stirring of lust.

47 ungracious: wicked, unholy. (OED obs.)

For nature crescent does not grow alone
In thews and bulk, but as this temple waxes,
The inward service of the mind and soul
Grows wide withal. Perhaps he loves you now,
And now no soil nor cautel doth besmirch 15
The virtue of his will; but you must fear,
His greatness weighed, his will is not his own,
For he himself is subject to his birth:
He may not, as unvalued persons do,
Carve for himself, for on his choice depends 20
The safety and health of this whole state,
And therefore must his choice be circumscribed
Unto the voice and yielding of that body
Whereof he is the head. Then if he says he loves you,
It fits your wisdom so far to believe it 25
As he in his particular act and place
May give his saying deed, which is no further
Than the main voice of Denmark goes withal.
Then weigh what loss your honor may sustain
If with too credent ear you list his songs, 30
Or lose your heart, or your chaste treasure open
To his unmastered importunity.
Fear it, Ophelia, fear it, my dear sister,
And keep you in the rear of your affection,
Out of the shot and danger of desire. 35
The chariest maid is prodigal enough
If she unmask her beauty to the moon.
Virtue itself scapes not calumnious strokes.
The canker galls the infants of the spring
Too oft before their buttons be disclosed, 40
And in the morn and liquid dew of youth
Contagious blastments are most imminent.
Be wary then, best safety lies in fear:
Youth to itself rebels, though none else near.

Ophelia

I shall the effect of this good lesson keep 45
As watchman to my heart. But, good my brother
Do not, as some ungracious pastors do,
Show me the steep and thorny way to heaven,
Whiles, like a puffed and reckless libertine,

51 recks not his own rede: ignores his own advice. (OED obs.)

57 There—my blessing: probably meant to accompany a sign of the cross in the air, the presumption of which might raise smiles in the audience.

58-80 these few precepts . . . . false to any man: This now famous speech is seemingly full of good advice but is compiled and embellished from proverbs and commonplace sayings. It looks like Oxford satirizing the propensity of aristocrats, and the commoner William Cecil emulating them, to dispense advice at length to no doubt impatient sons. Given Polonius's pompous garrulity elsewhere in the play, this long, tedious speech also might well bring knowing smiles to an audience of aristocrats at court. (See the Bibliography for Cecil.)

58-9 precepts . . . character: engrave these “precepts” in your “memory.”

65 courage: a bold, swaggering fellow. (OED obs.)

69 censure: opinion, here not necessarily a negative judgment. (OED obs.)

71-4 rich, not gaudy. . . . chief in that: that is, the French of the highest rank and position demonstrate their superiority by the dignified richness of their dress and are leaders in proper dress, "chief in that". When he was twenty-five, Oxford spent a month at the court of Henri III in Paris and would have had seen the courtly dress there.

77 husbandry: economical management of finances. (OED obs.)

81 season: ripen, mature.

Himself the primrose path of dalliance treads 50
And recks not his own rede.

Laertes

O, fear me not.

Enter Polonius

I stay too long—but here my father comes.
A double blessing is a double grace,
Occasion smiles upon a second leave.

Polonius

Yet here, Laertes? Aboard, aboard, for shame! 55
The wind sits in the shoulder of your sail,
And you are stayed for. There—my blessing with thee.
And these few precepts in thy memory,
Look thou, character. Give thy thoughts no tongue,
Nor any unproportioned thought his act. 60
Be thou familiar, but by no means vulgar:
Those friends thou hast, and their adoption tried,
Grapple them unto thy soul with hoops of steel,
But do not dull thy palm with entertainment
Of each new-hatched, unfledged courage. Bewarc 65
Of entrance to a quarrel, but being in,
Bear it that the opposed may beware of thee.
Give every man thy ear, but few thy voice,
Take each man's censure, but reserve thy judgment.
Costly thy habit as thy purse can buy, 70
But not expressed in fancy--rich, not gaudy,
For the apparel oft proclaims the man,
And they in France of the best rank and station
Are of a most select and generous chief in that.
Neither a borrower nor a lender be, 75
For loan oft loses both itself and friend,
And borrowing dulleth the edge of husbandry.
This above all: To thine own self be true,
And it must follow, as the night the day,
Thou canst not then be false to any man. 80
Farewell, my blessing season this in thee.

Laertes

Most humbly do I take my leave, my lord.

Polonius

The time invites you. Go, your servants tend.

Laertes

Farewell, Ophelia, and remember well
What I have said to you. 85

91 Marry: A mild oath from "by the Virgin Mary" that came to have an intensifier meaning, that is, to be sure, certainly, indeed.

95 'tis put on me: told to me, presumably by an informer in his household. William Cecil Lord Burghley, Oxford's guardian and then father-in-law, was well known for his network of informers and spies.

97 do not understand yourself: not know your place nor how to behave properly.

103 Unsifted: untested, inexperienced. (OED obs.)

106-10 Think yourself a baby. . . . tender me a fool: Polonius mockingly turns young Ophelia's innocent use of "tenders" into a commercial transaction; he wants her to believe that Hamlet's tenders of affection are not of value, not real money ("not sterling"). Despite his exasperation with her, he can't resist continuing to indulge in word play on "tender," perhaps to disguise his fear that she'll make "a fool" of him by getting pregnant when she is only a "baby." Oxford was in his late teens and Anne Cecil, Burghley's daughter (and the model for Ophelia), was in her pre-teens and early teens when they were living in the Cecil household. (See the Introduction.)

109-10 (not to crack the wind . . . it thus): a metaphor from horsemanship; that is, not to overwork word play on "tender" as one might make a horse lose its breath ("crack the wind") and become exhausted by being run too fast too long ("wringing" it out). Oxford was expert in horsemanship. There's no evidence for Shakspere owning a horse or riding, which would in any case be most unlikely.

113 Go to, go to.: The Elizabethan way of impatiently saying "Come on, come on."

114 given countenance: given confirmation. (OED obs.)

Ophelia
'Tis in my memory locked,
And you yourself shall keep the key of it.
Laertes
Farewell. *Exit Laertes*
Polonius
What is it, Ophelia, he hath said to you?
Ophelia
So please you, something touching the lord Hamlet. 90
Polonius
Marry, well bethought.
'Tis told me, he hath very oft of late
Given private time to you, and you yourself
Have of your audience been most free and bounteous.
If it be so—as so 'tis put on me, 95
And that in way of caution—I must tell you,
You do not understand yourself so clearly
As it behooves my daughter and your honor.
What is between you? Give me up the truth.
Ophelia
He hath, my lord, of late made many tenders 100
Of his affection to me.
Polonius
Affection, puh. You speak like a green girl,
Unsifted in such perilous circumstance.
Do you believe his tenders, as you call them?
Ophelia
I do not know, my lord, what I should think. 105
Polonius
Marry, I will teach you: Think yourself a baby
That you have taken these tenders for true pay,
Which are not sterling. Tender yourself more dearly,
Or (not to crack the wind of the poor phrase,
Wringing it thus) you'll tender me a fool. 110
Ophelia
My lord, he hath importuned me with love
In honorable fashion.
Polonius
Ay, fashion you may call it. Go to, go to.
Ophelia
And hath given countenance to his speech, my lord,
With almost all the holy vows of heaven. 115

116 springes to catch woodcocks: metaphorically, traps ("springes" OED obs.) to ensnare the gullible, here Ophelia; from the belief that woodcocks were easily caught in traps.

134 slander any moment leisure: that it, disgrace (OED obs.) even a moment of your time.

136 Come your ways: idiomatic at the time for "Let's go."

1 shrewdly: sharply, keenly.

2 eager: sharp, biting. (OED obs.)

s.d.: ***A flourish . . . pieces goes off*****:** A trumpet fanfare, and cannons firing a salute.

Polonius

Ay, springes to catch woodcocks. I do know,
When the blood burns, how prodigal the soul
Lends the tongue vows. These blazes, daughter,
Giving more light than heat, extinct in both
Even in their promise, as it is a-making, 120
You must not take for fire. From this time
Be something scanter of your maiden presence,
Set your entreatments at a higher rate
Than a command to parley. For lord Hamlet,
Believe so much in him, that he is young, 125
And with a larger tether may he walk
Than may be given you. In few, Ophelia,
Do not believe his vows, for they are brokers,
Not of that dye which their investments show,
But mere implorators of unholy suits, 130
Breathing like sanctified and pious bawds,
The better to beguile. This is for all:
I would not, in plain terms, from this time forth
Have you so slander any moment leisure
As to give words or talk with the lord Hamlet. 135
Look to it, I charge you. Come your ways.

Ophelia

I shall obey, my lord. *Exeunt*

Scene 4. On the castle rampart.
Enter Hamlet, Horatio, and Marcellus

Hamlet

The air bites shrewdly, it is very cold.

Horatio

It is a nipping and an eager air.

Hamlet

What hour now?

Horatio

I think it lacks of twelve.

Marcellus

No, it is struck. 5

Horatio

Indeed? I heard it not.
It then draws near the season
Wherein the spirit held his wont to walk.

A flourish of trumpets, and two pieces go off

What does this mean, my lord?

10 his rouse: a round of drinks. (OED archaic)

11 Keeps wassail: has a drinking party, with a connotation of it being disorderly. **swaggering up-spring reels**: That is, the "swaggering" King Claudius dances the gaillard, a dance ("reels") requiring precisely choreographed steps to the music, including much leaping in the air ("up-spring"), a favorite dance of Queen Elizabeth. Or the king drunkenly prances about in wild and riotous manner ("reels" OED obs.). Or both, and deliberately ambiguous to emphasize Claudius' debauchery. Oxford would have been very familiar with the gaillard, an athletic, Renaissance dance favored by wealthy aristocrats and nobility. A painting thought by some to represent Elizabeth and the Earl of Leicester shows him lifting her high in the "volta" step of the gaillard while courtiers look on.

18-19 a custom . . . breach . . . observance: that is, a custom that proves itself to be more honorable ("honored") when it is broken ("breached") than when it is observed.

20-1 heavy-headed . . . taxed: that is, such drunken revelry causes us Danes to be defamed ("traduced") and censured ("taxed" OED obs.) in countries to the east and west.

22 clepe: call or proclaim.

23 addition: reputation. (OED obs.)

25 attribute: honor, credit. (OED obs.)

27 vicious mole: a defect undermining one's character with vice.

31 pales: fencing or palisades.

32 over-leavens: overgrows; as too much yeast will cause bread to overflow its container and be ruined.

33 plausive: approved. (OED rare)

34-5 livery: probably, distinctive mark, as a servant's uniform "(livery") marks his position.

40 dout: extinguish; from the contraction of "do" and "out." (dialectical per the OED)

43-6 Be thou. . . . questionable shape: In this passage, Hamlet expresses his uncertainty whether the Ghost is truly the spirit of his father or is a deceptive devil in disguise.

Hamlet
The king doth wake tonight and takes his rouse, 10
Keeps wassail, and the swaggering up-spring reels;
And as he drains his draughts of Rhenish down,
The kettle-drum and trumpet thus bray out
The triumph of his pledge.

Horatio
Is it a custom? 15

Hamlet
Ay, marry, is it,
But to my mind, though I am native here
And to the manner born, it is a custom
More honored in the breach than the observance.
This heavy-headed revel east and west 20
Makes us traduced and taxed of other nations;
They clepe us drunkards, and with swinish phrase
Soil our addition, and indeed it takes
From our achievements, though performed at height,
The pith and marrow of our attribute. 25
So, oft it chances in particular men,
That for some vicious mole of nature in them,
As in their birth, wherein they are not guilty
(Since nature cannot choose his origin),
By the overgrowth of some complexion 30
Oft breaking down the pales and forts of reason,
Or by some habit, that too much over-leavens
The form of plausive manners—that these men,
Carrying, I say, the stamp of one defect,
Being nature's livery, or fortune's star, 35
His virtues else, be they as pure as grace,
As infinite as man may undergo,
Shall in the general censure take corruption
From that particular fault: The dram of evil
Doth all the noble substance often dout 40
To his own scandal.

Enter Ghost

Horatio
Look, my lord, it comes.

Hamlet
Angels and ministers of grace defend us!
Be thou a spirit of health, or goblin damned,
Bring with thee airs from heaven, or blasts from hell,
Be thy intents wicked or charitable 45

50 thy canonized bones: those of his saintly ("canonized") father. Hamlet makes a saint of his father, as Oxford, twelve years old when his father died, may well at that age have idolized his father figuratively as a saint.

51 cerements: shrouds.

55 complete steel: dressed in full armor.

58 disposition: mind set.

62 impartment: communication.

69 pin's fee: cost of a pin.

73 toward the flood: toward the sea, with a connotation of flood tide, high tide.

75 beetles over: projects dangerously over.

79 toys: sudden urges, tricks of the mind. (OED obs.)

Thou comest in such a questionable shape
That I will speak to thee. I'll call thee Hamlet,
King, father, royal Dane. O, answer me!
Let me not burst in ignorance, but tell
Why thy canonized bones, hearsed in death, 50
Have burst their cerements; why the sepulchre,
Wherein we saw thee quietly interred,
Hath oped his ponderous and marble jaws
To cast thee up again. What may this mean,
That thou, dead corpse, again in complete steel 55
Revisits thus the glimpses of the moon,
Making night hideous, and we fools of nature
So horridly to shake our disposition
With thoughts beyond the reaches of our souls?
Say why is this. Wherefore? What should we do? 60

Horatio *Ghost beckons Hamlet*

It beckons you to go away with it,
As if it some impartment did desire
To you alone.

Marcellus

Look with what courteous action
It waves you to a more removed ground, 65
But do not go with it.

Horatio

No, by no means.

Hamlet

It will not speak, then I will follow it.

Horatio

Do not, my lord.

Hamlet

Why, what should be the fear?
I do not set my life at a pin's fee,
And for my soul, what can it do to that, 70
Being a thing immortal as itself?
It waves me forth again, I'll follow it.

Horatio

What if it tempt you toward the flood, my lord,
Or to the dreadful summit of the cliff
That beetles over his base into the sea, 75
And there assume some other horrible form
Which might deprive your sovereignty of reason,
And draw you into madness? Think of it.
The very place puts toys of desperation,

81 fathoms: here not water depth but the distance down to the water's surface.

86 artery: not a blood vessel, but a ligament. (OED obs.)

87 Nemean lion's nerve: figuratively for the strong point of the lion, its fur. The Nemean lion was a ferocious, mythical lion whose golden fur was impervious to weapons. Hercules strangled it in what would be the first of his twelve heroic labors.

89 lets me!: hinders me! (OED archaic)

92 Have after: Let's follow.

94 Something is rotten . . . Denmark: Prompted by the Ghost's appearance and Hamlet's reaction, Marcellus is struck by what he suspects is corruption ("something rotten") in Denmark under King Claudius. As a court insider, Oxford had first-hand experience of the murderous intrigues, treachery and corruption in the court of Queen Elizabeth, chiefly that of his nemesis the Earl of Leicester. (See the Introduction.)

95 Nay: Probably meaning: "No, do not leave it to heaven; we must follow him."

3 My hour is almost come: Dawn is near, when he must return to purgatory.

Without more motive, into every brain 80
That looks so many fathoms to the sea
And hears it roar beneath.

Hamlet
It waves me still—Go on, I'll follow thee.

Marcellus
You shall not go, my lord.

Hamlet
Hold off your hands.

Horatio
Be ruled, you shall not go.

Hamlet
My fate cries out, 85
And makes each petty artery in this body
As hardy as the Nemean lion's nerve.
Still am I called. Unhand me, gentlemen.
By heaven, I'll make a ghost of him that lets me!
I say away!—Go on, I'll follow thee. *Exeunt Ghost and Hamlet* 90

Horatio
He waxes desperate with imagination.

Marcellus
Let's follow. 'Tis not fit thus to obey him.

Horatio
Have after. To what issue will this come?

Marcellus
Something is rotten in the state of Denmark.

Horatio
Heaven will direct it.

Marcellus
Nay, let's follow him. 95

Exeunt

Scene 5. Enter Ghost and Hamlet

Hamlet
Whither wilt thou lead me? Speak, I'll go no further.

Ghost
Mark me.

Hamlet
I will.

Ghost
My hour is almost come 3
When I to sulphurous and tormenting flames
Must render up myself.

6 unfold: disclose.

11 confined to fast: sentenced to go without food. In Catholic belief, the punishment in purgatory must fit the sin, so the ghost of King Hamlet probably is saying that he must fast presumably as punishment for his gluttony. The concept of purgatory was much debated as England moved away from the Catholic religion of feudalism toward the Anglican religion, which did not include purgatory among its beliefs. Nevertheless, the old notion of an intermediate place where some souls of the dead suffered temporary punishment lingered on.

12 crimes: wrongdoings, sins, not necessarily violations of law.

16 harrow up thy soul: vex and tear up your soul. (OED obs.)

20 porpentine: an early, variant spelling of porcupine.

22 List: listen, hear this. (OED archaic)

21 blazon: revelation; from heraldry for a shield that displays a coat of arms.

24 thy dear father: Hamlet's father, King Hamlet. The Ghost is speaking of himself in the third person singular.

33-4 And duller . . . Lethe wharf: the banks or wharf of Lethe, the river of forgetfulness in the underworld. The Ghost is saying to Hamlet that if he fails to act he will be more apathetic and "duller" than someone affected by "the fat weed." The "fat" weed has not been identified.

Hamlet
Alas, poor ghost.
Ghost
Pity me not, but lend thy serious hearing 5
To what I shall unfold.
Hamlet
Speak, I am bound to hear.
Ghost
So art thou to revenge, when thou shalt hear.
Hamlet
What?
Ghost
I am thy father's spirit,
Doomed for a certain term to walk the night, 10
And for the day confined to fast in fires,
Till the foul crimes done in my days of nature
Are burnt and purged away. But that I am forbid
To tell the secrets of my prison-house,
I could a tale unfold whose lightest word 15
Would harrow up thy soul, freeze thy young blood,
Make thy two eyes like stars start from their spheres,
Thy knotted and combined locks to part,
And each particular hair to stand an end,
Like quills upon the fearful porpentine. 20
But this eternal blazon must not be
To ears of flesh and blood. List, list, O list!
If thou didst ever thy dear father love—
Hamlet
O God!
Ghost
Revenge his foul and most unnatural murder. 25
Hamlet:
Murder!
Ghost
Murder most foul, as in the best it is,
But this most foul, strange, and unnatural.
Hamlet
Haste me to know it, that I with wings as swift
As meditation, or the thoughts of love, 30
May sweep to my revenge.
Ghost
I find thee apt,
And duller shouldst thou be than the fat weed

35 'Tis given out: something officially reported (here by Claudius) but not true.

36-38 whole ear of Denmark . . . abused: that is, everyone in Denmark who heard the false report ("forged process") has been abused.

40 O my prophetic soul: not that Hamlet foresaw his father's death by assassination, but that his instincts about his uncle's true nature as a treacherous assassin are now verified.

42 Ay, that . . . beast,: That is, Claudius ("that beast") committed "incest" by marrying his brother's widow, an act considered incest, and was defiled by committing adultery ("adulterate") with Gertrude, seducing and corrupting her when she was married to King Hamlet. (See Jenkins Long Note, pp 456-7.)

43 witchcraft: fascinating attraction or charm, often devilish, per the OED.

56 sate: satiate, over-satisfy its appetite.

61 secure: safe, unsuspecting.

62 cursed hebona: a poisonous fluid that has not been identified, possibly and vaguely from the henbane plant thought to have some poisonous properties. (OED obs.)

64 leprous distillment: a volatile liquid ("distillment"), causing the skin to become scaly as in leprosy, considered a loathsome disease.

68-9 posset and curd: curdle. Posset was a drink of hot milk curdled with ale or wine. (OED obs.)

71 tetter barked about: a rash ("tetter") on his skin like the bark of a tree.

72 lazar-like: leper-like.

That roots itself in ease on Lethe wharf,
Wouldst thou not stir in this. Now, Hamlet, hear:
'Tis given out that, sleeping in my orchard, 35
A serpent stung me; so the whole ear of Denmark
Is by a forged process of my death
Rankly abused. But know, thou noble youth,
The serpent that did sting thy father's life
Now wears his crown.

Hamlet

O my prophetic soul! 40
My uncle?

Ghost

Ay, that incestuous, that adulterate beast,
With witchcraft of his wits, with traitorous gifts—
O wicked wit and gifts that have the power
So to seduce!—won to his shameful lust 45
The will of my most seeming virtuous queen.
O Hamlet, what a falling-off was there
From me, whose love was of that dignity
That it went hand in hand even with the vow
I made to her in marriage, and to decline 50
Upon a wretch whose natural gifts were poor
To those of mine.
But virtue, as it never will be moved,
Though lewdness court it in a shape of heaven,
So lust, though to a radiant angel linked, 55
Will sate itself in a celestial bed
And prey on garbage.
But soft, methinks I scent the morning air,
Brief let me be. Sleeping within my orchard,
My custom always of the afternoon, 60
Upon my secure hour thy uncle stole,
With juice of cursed hebona in a vial,
And in the porches of my ears did pour
The leprous distillment, whose effect
Holds such an enmity with blood of man 65
That swift as quicksilver it courses through
The natural gates and alleys of the body,
And with a sudden vigor it doth posset
And curd, like eager droppings into milk,
The thin and wholesome blood. So did it mine, 70
And a most instant tetter barked about,
Most lazar-like, with vile and loathsome crust

77 Unhousled, disappointed, unanelled: without the last rites of the Catholic church, that is, not receiving the Eucharist ("unhousled" OED obs.), unprepared for death by confessing his sins ("disappointed"), and not anointed with oil ("unanelled" OED obs.) in the sacrament of Extreme Unction for the dying.

83 luxury: lechery, lustful behavior. (OED obs.)

85 Taint not thy mind: Do not corrupt your mind.

86 Leave her to heaven: Let God be her judge.

93 And shall I couple hell: that is, include the ultimate evil, hell. Hamlet recognizes the moral dilemma of a revenge killing, a feudal dictum requiring revenge for the slaying of a close relative but possibly leading to damnation for murder. He will nevertheless swear to do it (assuming the Ghost indeed proves to be that of his father and not a devil in disguise).

98 table of my memory: metaphorically, the contents of my memory, an allusion to an Elizabethan pocket notebook ("table" OED obs.) waxed so that notes could be inscribed with a stylus and erased to make room for more important new notes, as in this passage. Queen Elizabeth presented Oxford with a diamond-trimmed tablet in 1571 when he won a jousting tournament.

99 fond: foolish. (OED obs.)

105 pernicious woman: wicked woman (OED obs.) with a connotation of ruinous. His mother allowed herself to be seduced by Claudius while still married to the late King Hamlet, per the Ghost. (1.5. 45-6)

106-8 smiling damned villain. . . . smile and be a villain.: Addressing Claudius *in absentia* with a vivid image of a charming villain who hides his treachery by smiling and making a show of friendship reflects the habitual demeanor of the Earl of Leicester, Oxford's nemesis, who apparently had an uncanny talent for hiding his treacherous and deadly plans behind a disarmingly friendly appearance, always escaping official blame and punishment. In 1566 the French ambassador, La Forêt, reported that Leicester confessed to him, "smiling and sighing at the same time, that he does not know what to hope or fear" about whether Queen Elizabeth will marry him. He wanted to be her virtual king consort. In her dual biography, Elizabeth Jenkins quotes La Forêt and also notes that the courtier Christopher Hatton at Leicester's death in 1588 had been "deceived by this smiler with the knife," alluding to the proverb "to smile in one's face and cut one's throat" cited in Hibbard's *Hamlet* at 1.5.109.

107 I set it down: I write it in my notebook. (See note 98 above.)

All my smooth body.
Thus was I, sleeping, by a brother's hand
Of life, of crown, of queen, at once dispatched, 75
Cut off even in the blossoms of my sin,
Unhousled, disappointed, unanelled,
No reckoning made, but sent to my account
With all my imperfections on my head.
O, horrible, O, horrible! Most horrible! 80
If thou hast nature in thee, bear it not,
Let not the royal bed of Denmark be
A couch for luxury and damned incest.
But howsomever thou pursues this act,
Taint not thy mind, nor let thy soul contrive 85
Against thy mother aught. Leave her to heaven,
And to those thorns that in her bosom lodge
To prick and sting her. Fare thee well at once!
The glow-worm shows the matin to be near,
And gins to pale his uneffectual fire. 90
Adieu, adieu, adieu. Remember me. *[Exit]*

Hamlet

O all you host of heaven! O earth! What else?
And shall I couple hell? O fie, hold, hold, my heart,
And you, my sinews, grow not instant old,
But bear me stiffly up. Remember thee. 95
Ay, thou poor ghost, whiles memory holds a seat
In this distracted globe. Remember thee.
Yea, from the table of my memory
I'll wipe away all trivial fond records,
All saws of books, all forms, all pressures past 100
That youth and observation copied there,
And thy commandment all alone shall live
Within the book and volume of my brain,
Unmixed with baser matter. Yes, by heaven!
O most pernicious woman. 105
O villain, villain, smiling damned villain!
My tables—meet it is I set it down
That one may smile, and smile, and be a villain.
At least I am sure it may be so in Denmark.
So, uncle, there you are. Now to my word: 110
It is "Adieu, adieu! remember me."
I have sworn it.

Horatio, Marcellus *[Within]*

My lord, my lord!

115 Illo, ho, ho. . . . come: In a gently mocking response to Marcellus' calling him, Hamlet facetiously converts it to a falconer's call with "Come, bird, come." Metaphors on falconry, the sport of aristocrats, would come naturally to a nobleman like Oxford.

123-4 villain . . . arrant knave: that is, any villain in Denmark must be an unmitigated ("arrant") crafty rogue ("knave"), referring obliquely to Claudius.

126-132 Why, right . . . go pray: Hamlet is slipping into a manic phase.

127 circumstance: ceremony. (OED archaic)

131 poor: probably, insignificant; a bit of false modesty, which Horatio will not accept.

Marcellus
Lord Hamlet! *Enter Horatio and Marcellus*
Horatio
Heavens secure him.
Hamlet
So be it.
Marcellus
Illo, ho, ho, my lord! 115
Hamlet
Hillo, ho, ho, boy! Come, bird, come.
Marcellus
How is it, my noble lord?
Horatio
What news, my lord?
Hamlet
O, wonderful.
Horatio
Good my lord, tell it.
Hamlet
No, you will reveal it.
Horatio
Not I, my lord, by heaven. 120
Marcellus
Nor I, my lord.
Hamlet
How say you then, would heart of man once think it—
But you'll be secret?
Horatio, Marcellus
Ay, by heaven, my lord.
Hamlet
There's never a villain dwelling in all Denmark —
But he's an arrant knave.
Horatio
There needs no ghost, my lord, come from the grave 125
To tell us this.
Hamlet
Why, right, you are in the right,
And so, without more circumstance at all,
I hold it fit that we shake hands and part,
You, as your business and desire shall point you,
For every man hath business and desire, 130
Such as it is, and for my own poor part,
I will go pray.

132 wild and whirling words: Horatio recognizes that Hamlet is in one of his manic phases. (See the introduction.)

135 offense: doubt or disbelief, an early meaning per the OED.

136 by Saint Patrick: The oath is especially appropriate since he was the legendary keeper of purgatory. In medieval Catholic legend, Saint Patrick in the fifth century found what was supposed to be the entrance to purgatory in Lough Derg, County Donegal, Ireland, and established an abbey there, which became a destination for pilgrims.

138 honest: reliable. Hamlet wavers on whether the Ghost is to be suspect or believable.

147 Upon my sword: because the blade and hilt form a cross, thus making the oath sacred.

150 truepenny: an honest fellow (OED archaic), as for a coin of genuine metal; but here it might also be a clever, multilingual pun on the family names of Oxford's father and mother. "True" in Latin is "verum" or "vere," and the Earl of Oxford's family name was Vere. A penny in the 16th century was stamped from a mold called a "trussell" (OED obs.), and Oxford's mother was a descendent of the Trussell family. Hence "Vere+Trussel"= "truepenny," conceivably Oxford inserting his signature into this Shakespeare play.

151 fellow in the cellarge: a feudal term for the cellar level of a castle. Under some stress, Hamlet will continue his jocular, somewhat irreverent, manic references to King Hamlet's ghost ("fellow"), whose voice comes from below.

Horatio
These are but wild and whirling words, my lord.
Hamlet
I am sorry they offend you, heartily,
Yes, faith, heartily.
Horatio
There's no offence, my lord. 135
Hamlet
Yes, by Saint Patrick, but there is, Horatio,
And much offence, too. Touching this vision here,
It is an honest ghost, that let me tell you.
For your desire to know what is between us,
Overmaster it as you may. And now, good friends, 140
As you are friends, scholars, and soldiers,
Give me one poor request.
Horatio
What is it, my lord, we will.
Hamlet
Never make known what you have seen tonight.
Horatio, Marcellus
My lord, we will not. 145
H*amlet*
Nay, but swear it.
Horatio:
In faith, My lord, not I.
Marcellus
Nor I, my lord, in faith.
Hamlet
Upon my sword.
Marcellus
We have sworn, my lord, already.
Hamlet
Indeed upon my sword, indeed.
Ghost
Swear. *Ghost cries under the stage.*
Hamlet
Ha, ha, boy, sayest thou so? Art thou there, truepenny? 150
Come on, you hear this fellow in the cellarage,
Consent to swear.
Horatio
Propose the oath, my lord.
Hamlet
Never to speak of this that you have seen,

156 ***Hic et ubique*?**: Here and everywhere?

162 old mole . . . so fast?: The Ghost, which Hamlet likens to an underground digger, like a mole, seems to move fast from one spot to another.

163 pioner: a military sapper or digger, who dug trenches and tunnels (OED obs.); from Old French "pionier". Another of the many allusions to military operations that would come readily to someone like Oxford who had military experience. **Once more remove**: move again to another spot on stage over the cellar.

169-72 Here, as before . . . . To put an antic disposition on—: In this passage, Hamlet acknowledges that in the past ("as before") he has experienced spells of "antic" behavior and says he plans put on or pretend such behavior sometimes ("perchance hereafter"). Oxford (Hamlet) acknowledges here that he has experienced such spells. An "antic disposition" is a fantastic, bizarre, even grotesque manner of speech or action. An "antic" was a clown, and in Shakespeare plays the clown character simultaneously reveals/conceals truths for the audience and readers to unravel and appreciate.

174 arms encumbered thus: originally, hampered; here probably arms folded across the chest in an attitude of knowing disbelief, which Hamlet demonstrates "thus."

177 "If we list . . .": If we wanted.

179 aught of me: anything of my putting on an antic disposition.

185 friending: probably, friendship.

169-72 Here, as before . . . . To put an antic disposition on—: In this passage, Hamlet acknowledges that in the past ("as before") he has experienced spells of "antic" behavior and says he plans put on or pretend such behavior sometimes ("perchance hereafter"). Oxford (Hamlet) acknowledges here that he has experienced such spells. An "antic disposition" is a fantastic, bizarre, even grotesque manner of speech or action. An "antic" was a clown, and in Shakespeare plays the clown character simultaneously reveals/conceals truths for the audience and readers to unravel and appreciate.

174 arms encumbered thus: originally, hampered; here probably arms folded across the chest in an attitude of knowing disbelief, which Hamlet demonstrates "thus."

177 "If we list . . .": If we wanted.

179 aught of me: anything of my putting on an antic disposition.

185 friending: probably, friendship.

Swear by my sword.

Ghost

Swear. 155

Hamlet

Hic et ubique? Then we'll shift our ground.
Come hither, gentlemen,
And lay your hands again upon my sword.
Swear by my sword
Never to speak of this that you have heard 160

Ghost

Swear by his sword.

*Hamlet***

Well said, old mole, canst work in the earth so fast?
A worthy pioner! Once more remove, good friends.

Horatio

O day and night, but this is wondrous strange!

Hamlet

And therefore as a stranger give it welcome. 165
There are more things in heaven and earth, Horatio,
Than are dreamt of in your philosophy.
But come —
Here, as before, never, so help you mercy,
How strange or odd somever I bear myself— 170
As I perchance hereafter shall think meet
To put an antic disposition on—
That you, at such times seeing me, never shall,
With arms encumbered thus, or this headshake,
Or by pronouncing of some doubtful phrase, 175
As "Well, well, we know," or "We could, and if we would,"
Or "If we list to speak," or "There be, and if they might,"
Or such ambiguous giving out, to note
That you know aught of me—this do swear,
So grace and mercy at your most need help you. 180

Ghost

Swear.

Hamlet

Rest, rest, perturbed spirit. So, gentlemen,
With all my love I do commend me to you,
And what so poor a man as Hamlet is
May do to express his love and friending to you, 185
God willing, shall not lack. Let us go in together,
And still your fingers on your lips, I pray.
The time is out of joint. O cursed spite,
That ever I was born to set it right!
Nay, come, let's go together. *Exeunt* 190

1 him: Polonius's son Laertes, who is in Paris. Polonius is sending Reynaldo, a servant, to spy on him, just as Burghley sent a servant to spy on his dissolute son Thomas in Paris, something Oxford (but not Will Shakspere) would have known given Oxford's close association with Burghley. This scene with Renaldo is quite irrelevant to the plot, but it serves to dramatize court corruption, which would have been of great concern to Oxford.

7 Inquire me . . . Danskers are in Paris: that is, find out for me the Danes (**Danskers**, OED obs.) who are in Paris (and who would know about his son's behavior.) In the detailed instructions to Reynaldo that follow, Polonius unwittingly reveals his propensity, almost an obsession, for spying, lying and corrupt deceptions; here principally how to interrogate Danes in Paris as sources of information about Laertes without raising their suspicions. Burghley was well known for using informers and spies. (See Hume.)

8 keep: lodge. (OED obs.).

10 encompassment and drift: a roundabout and indirect stratagem.

12 Than your particular demands will touch it: than your direct questions would achieve.

13 Take you: Pretend to have.

15 in part: to some extent.

19 put on him: ascribe or attribute to him.

20 forgeries: lies, deceptions (OED obs.), here false accusations.

22 usual slips: ordinary lapses in behavior.

26 Drabbing: whoring; patronizing prostitutes.

Act 2

Scene 1. Enter Polonius and Reynaldo

Polonius
Give him this money and these notes, Reynaldo.
Reynaldo
I will, my lord.
Polonius
You shall do marvelous wisely, good Reynaldo,
Before you visit him, to make inquire
Of his behavior
Reynaldo
My lord, I did intend it. 5
Polonius
Marry, well said, very well said. Look you, sir,
Inquire me first what Danskers are in Paris,
And how, and who, what means, and where they keep,
What company, at what expense; and finding
By this encompassment and drift of question 10
That they do know my son, come you more nearer
Than your particular demands will touch it.
Take you as 'twere some distant knowledge of him,
As thus, "I know his father and his friends,
And in part him." Do you mark this, Reynaldo? 15
Reynaldo
Ay, very well, my lord.
Polonius
"And in part him — but," you may say, "not well.
But if it be he I mean, he's very wild,
Addicted so and so," and there put on him
What forgeries you please: marry, none so rank 20
As may dishonor him, take heed of that,
But, sir, such wanton, wild, and usual slips
As are companions noted and most known
To youth and liberty.
Reynaldo
As gaming, my lord.
Polonius
Ay, or drinking, fencing, swearing, quarrelling, 25
Drabbing— you may go so far.

28 season: temper, shape.

30 open to incontinency: disposed to sexual excess.

31 quaintly: artfully; cunningly. (OED obs.)

34 unreclaimed: untamed, wild; a term from falconry, a sport of the nobility very familiar to Oxford but not to commoners like Shakspere.

38 fetch of wit: a clever contrivance (OED obs.); a stratagem by which something is brought to pass indirectly.

42 the prenominate: the above-named. (OED obs.)

45 He closes . . . consequence: He confides in the following way.

47 addition: style of addressing. (OED obs.)

50 By the mass: a mild oath, originally referring to the Roman Catholic mass. Polonius has lost his train of thought here, perhaps an exaggeration of Burghley's speech ometimes.

Reynaldo
My lord, that would dishonor him.
Polonius
Faith, as you may season it in the charge.
You must not put another scandal on him,
That he is open to incontinency— 30
That's not my meaning. But breathe his faults so quaintly
That they may seem the taints of liberty,
The flash and outbreak of a fiery mind,
A savageness in unreclaimed blood,
Of general assault.
Reynaldo
But, my good lord — 35
Polonius
Wherefore should you do this?
Reynaldo
Ay, my lord, I would know that.
Polonius
Marry, sir, here's my drift,
And I believe it is a fetch of wit:
You laying these slight sullies on my son,
As 'twere a thing a little soiled with the working, 40
Mark you,
Your party in converse, him you would sound,
Having ever seen in the prenominate crimes
The youth you breathe of guilty, be assured
He closes with you in this consequence: 45
"Good sir," or so, or "friend," or "gentleman,"
According to the phrase or the addition
Of man and country.
Reynaldo
Very good, my lord.
Polonius
And then, sir, does he this — he does —
What was I about to say? By the mass, I was about 50
to say something. Where did I leave?
Reynaldo
At "closes in the consequence," at "friend
or so," and "gentleman."
Polonius
At "closes in the consequence," ay, marry.
He closes thus: "I know the gentleman. 55
I saw him yesterday," or " the other day,"
Or then, or then, with such or such, "and as you say,

58 overtook in his rouse: overcome by carousing and drinking.

59 falling out at tennis: quarreling about tennis, a sport of the aristocracy. Oxford confronted Sir Philip Sidney in September 1579 at the royal tennis court in Queen Elizabeth's palace, Whitehall, and they quarreled over who had priority to use the court. The dispute, which included insults, later went all the way to the queen, who noted that the Earl of Oxford outranked Sidney. Standard editions of *Hamlet* make no mention of Polonius's unusual reference to court tennis and the quarrel, which a court audience might be expected to recognize and appreciate, but not something Shakspere would have known about.

61 *Videlicet*: That is to say.

64 windlasses . . . assays of bias: Both terms reflect aristocratic entertainments. A "windlass" (OED obs.) was a circuit made to intercept game in the sport of hunting," hence an indirect, crafty maneuver. "Bias" comes from early forms of lawn bowling and describes how a bowl could be weighted on one side to make it take a curved or oblique course toward its target (OED), hence attempts ("assays") to take an indirect way of reaching one's objective.

68 God buy ye: God be with you; the likely origin of "goodbye."

70 Observe . . . yourself: probably, observe Laertes' tendencies or proclivities ("inclination") of behavior for yourself.

S.d. Enter Ophelia: Polonius's daughter, probably a teenager, who is under the sway of powerful men, as was the teenage Anne Cecil, the daughter of William Cecil Lord Burghley, the inspiration for the character Polonius. Ophelia is thought to be courted by Hamlet; Anne Cecil at age fourteen was betrothed to Oxford, twenty.

77 closet: a private room in a castle for prayer, reading, etc. usually next to a bedroom. (OED archaic)

78 doublet all unbraced. . . down-gived to his ankle: his clothing in disarray. **No hat**: Men customarily wore hats indoors. Ophelia describes Hamlet in a manic phase of behavior, his "madness.' Oxford experienced mood swings from depression to manic highs.

There was he gaming," " there overtook in his rouse,"
"There falling out at tennis"; or, perchance,
"I saw him enter such a house of sale," 60
Videlicet, a brothel, or so forth. See you now,
Your bait of falsehood take this carp of truth,
And thus do we of wisdom and of reach,
With windlasses and with assays of bias,
By indirections find directions out; 65
So by my former lecture and advice
Shall you my son. You have me, have you not?

Reynaldo
My lord, I have.

Polonius
God buy ye, fare ye well.

Reynaldo
Good my lord.

Polonius
Observe his inclination in yourself. 70

Reynaldo
I shall, my lord.

Polonius
And let him ply his music.

Reynaldo
Well, my lord.

Polonius
Farewell. *Exit Reynaldo*

Enter Ophelia

How now, Ophelia, what's the matter?

Ophelia
O my lord, my lord, I have been so affrighted! 75

Polonius
With what, in the name of God?

Ophelia
My lord, as I was sewing in my closet,
Lord Hamlet, with his doublet all unbraced,
No hat upon his head, his stockings fouled,
Ungartered, and down-gyved to his ankle, 80
Pale as his shirt, his knees knocking each other,
And with a look so piteous in purport
As if he had been loosed out of hell
To speak of horrors, he comes before me.

Polonius
Mad for thy love? 85

88 length of all his arm,: holds her at arm's length.

95 his bulk: his body. (OED obs.)

102 ecstasy: frenzy or madness. (OED obs.)

103 fordoes itself: destroys itself. (OED obs.)

112 coted him: overtaken, gotten ahead of him. (OED obs.) From the aristocratic sport of coursing when one hunting dog passes and runs ahead of another in pursuit of the hare.

113 wrack: ruin (by seducing). **Beshrew my jealousy:** probably, blame ("beshrew" OED obs.) my zeal and anxiety to do right ("jealousy" OED obs.).

114-15 proper to our age . . . To cast beyond ourselves: characteristic of people the age of Polonius to search ("cast beyond") for clues beyond what they know; another hunting metaphor, when hounds are spread out to find the lost scent of their prey.

119 More grief . . . utter love: more trouble and grief than the objections and censure ("hate") we might face if we speak of ("utter") this show of "love".

Ophelia
My lord, I do not know,
But truly I do fear it.
Polonius
What said he?
Ophelia
He took me by the wrist, and held me hard,
Then goes he to the length of all his arm,
And with his other hand thus over his brow,
He falls to such perusal of my face 90
As he would draw it. Long stayed he so.
At last, a little shaking of mine arm,
And thrice his head thus waving up and down,
He raised a sigh so piteous and profound
As it did seem to shatter all his bulk 95
And end his being. That done, he lets me go,
And with his head over his shoulder turned,
He seemed to find his way without his eyes,
For out of doors he went without their helps,
And to the last bended their light on me. 100
Polonius
Come, go with me. I will go seek the king.
This is the very ecstasy of love,
Whose violent property fordoes itself,
And leads the will to desperate undertakings
As oft as any passions under heaven 105
That does afflict our natures. I am sorry —
What, have you given him any hard words of late?
Ophelia
No, my good lord, but as you did command
I did repel his letters, and denied
His access to me. 110
Polonius
That hath made him mad.
I am sorry that with better heed and judgment
I had not coted him. I feared he did but trifle
And meant to wrack thee, but beshrew my jealousy.
By heaven, it is as proper to our age
To cast beyond ourselves in our opinions, 115
As it is common for the younger sort
To lack discretion. Come, go we to the king.
This must be known, which, being kept close, might move
More grief to hide, than hate to utter love.
Come. *Exeunt* 120

1 Rosencrantz and Guildenstern: the only Danish names in the play and the names of two families prominent at the Danish court. Oxford would have heard of the two Danes from his brother-in-law, Lord Willoughby, whom Queen Elizabeth had sent to Denmark on diplomatic missions in 1582 and 1585, when Oxford was in his thirties. Lord Willoughby spent five months at the Danish court where he would have met members of the two Danish families. Details about why Oxford used these particular two names are lacking, but the close connection to the Danish court through his brother-in-law seems quite significant. Shakspere had no known such connection. The two names also appear in a 1586 portraits of the Danish astronomer Tycho Brahe owned by Sir Dudley Digges, diplomat-statesman and son of the astronomer Thomas. (See Usher *Hamlet*'s.)

3 to use you: to spy on Hamlet. Getting information on potential adversaries by spying and using informers is a major theme of this play about the political corruption in King Claudius's court, and was a major concern of Oxford in his dealings with Burghley in Queen Elizabeth's court. In three letters to Burghley he protested against Burghley's use of informers. (See Oxford in the Bibliography.)

6 Sith: Since.

13 vouchsafe your rest: promise to remain.

15 To draw him . . . to gather: Claudius directs Hamlet's schoolmates to be informers and find out what he might want to know about Hamlet

18-19 Whether aught . . . our remedy.: that is, whether anything ("aught") afflicting him, when discovered and made known ("opened"), might be helped by the king ("lies within our remedy"). The king would have them believe that he would try to help Hamlet with what "afflicts him," when in reality he wants to know whether and how Hamlet plans to harm him.

22 gentry: courtesy. (OED obs.)

27 dread: that which inspires reverence, awe, fear.

30 full bent: utmost willingness; from archery where "bent" describes the bow when fully drawn.

Scene 2. A room of state.

Flourish.

Enter King and Queen,
Rosencrantz and Guildenstern and others

King
Welcome, dear Rosencrantz and Guildenstern.
Moreover that we much did long to see you,
The need we have to use you did provoke
Our hasty sending. Something have you heard
Of Hamlet's transformation, so I call it, 5
Sith nor the exterior nor the inward man
Resembles that it was. What it should be,
More than his father's death, that thus hath put him
So much from the understanding of himself,
I cannot dream of. I entreat you both 10
That, being of so young days brought up with him,
And sith so neighbored to his youth and havior,
That you vouchsafe your rest here in our court
Some little time, so by your companies
To draw him on to pleasures, and to gather 15
So much as from occasion you may glean,
Whether aught to us unknown afflicts him thus,
That, opened, lies within our remedy.

Queen
Good gentlemen, he hath much talked of you,
And sure I am two men there is not living 20
To whom he more adheres. If it will please you
To show us so much gentry and good will
As to expend your time with us a while
For the supply and profit of our hope,
Your visitation shall receive such thanks 25
As fits a king's remembrance.

Rosencrantz
Both your majesties
Might, by the sovereign power you have of us,
Put your dread pleasures more into command
Than to entreaty.

Guildenstern
But we both obey,
And here give up ourselves, in the full bent, 30
To lay our service freely at your feet,
To be commanded.

36 Go some of you: addressing the other courtiers in attendance.

39 pleasant and helpful to him: joining in the King's subterfuge that he hopes to help Hamlet, while no doubt knowing that they are to try to find out what Hamlet may be up to.

43 father of good news.: probably with a bit of sarcasm, which Polonius catches. As Oxford would know from his life at court, a courtier/aide to a monarch never wants to have to be the bearer of bad news, only good news.

47 Hunts not the trail of policy: doesn't look for and follow the party line, "policy," which can have a negative connotation of crafty stratagems. (OED obs.)

52 fruit to that great feast: dessert, which is his good news, to the "great feast" of news from the ambassadors.

53 do grace: show them our regard (OED archaic), hence a courteous reception.

56 doubt: suspect. (OED archaic)

57 over-hasty marriage: Gertrude may or may not know (it's ambiguous later in the play) that Claudius poisoned his brother King Hamlet, who was her husband and Hamlet's father, in order to seize the throne, and that he then married her quickly to consolidate his *coup d'état*; hence their "over-hasty marriage." Oxford's mother re-married soon after the sudden and unexpected death, as if by poison, of her husband, Oxford's father. Oxford had good reason to suspect that the Earl of Leicester had his father poisoned in order to seize control of much of the underage Oxford's inheritance. (See the Introduction.)

58 sift: examine thoroughly.

59 our brother Norway: our fellow monarch, the king of Norway.

King
Thanks, Rosencrantz and gentle Guildenstern.
Queen
Thanks, Guildenstern and gentle Rosencrantz.
And I beseech you instantly to visit 35
My too much changed son. Go some of you
And bring these gentlemen where Hamlet is.
Guildenstern
Heavens make our presence and our practices
Pleasant and helpful to him.
Queen
Ay, amen!
Exeunt Rosencrantz and Guildenstern
Enter Polonius
Polonius
The ambassadors from Norway, my good lord 40
Are joyfully returned.
King
Thou still hast been the father of good news.
Polonius
Have I, my lord? I assure my good liege
I hold my duty as I hold my soul,
Both to my God and to my gracious king; 45
And I do think, or else this brain of mine
Hunts not the trail of policy so sure
As it hath used to do, that I have found
The very cause of Hamlet's lunacy.
King
O, speak of that, that do I long to hear. 50
Polonius
Give first admittance to the ambassadors;
My news shall be the fruit to that great feast.
King
Thyself do grace to them, and bring them in. *Exit Polonius*
He tells me, my dear Gertrude, he hath found
The head and source of all your son's distemper. 55
Queen
I doubt it is no other but the main,
His father's death and our over-hasty marriage.
Enter Polonius with Voltemand and Cornelius
King
Well, we shall sift him. — Welcome, my good friends!
Say, Voltemand, what from our brother Norway?

61 Upon our first: when we first raised the issue.

63 Polack: the king of Poland.

66 impotence: incapacitation.

67 falsely borne in hand: misconstrued, led astray by false information about his illness and supposed weakness. **arrests:** orders stopping Fortinbras.

71 assay of arms: attempt ("assay" OED obs.) to use armed force.

86 my liege: my lord; a feudal form of address. **expostulate**: to debate, discuss at length. (OED obs.)

Voltemand

Most fair return of greetings and desires. 60
Upon our first, he sent out to suppress
His nephew's levies, which to him appeared
To be a preparation against the Polack;
But better looked into, he truly found
It was against your highness. Whereat grieved, 65
That so his sickness, age, and impotence
Was falsely borne in hand, sends out arrests
On Fortinbras, which he, in brief, obeys,
Receives rebuke from Norway, and in fine,
Makes vow before his uncle never more 70
To give the assay of arms against your majesty.
Whereon old Norway, overcome with joy,
Gives him three thousand crowns in annual fee,
And his commission to employ those soldiers,
So levied, as before, against the Polack, 75
With an entreaty, herein further shown,
That it might please you to give quiet pass
Through your dominions for this enterprise,
On such regards of safety and allowance
As therein are set down.

King

It likes us well, 80
And at our more considered time we'll read,
Answer, and think upon this business.
Meantime, we thank you for your well-took labor.
Go to your rest, at night we'll feast together.
Most welcome home. *Exeunt Voltemand and Cornelius*

Polonius

This business is well ended. 85
My liege, and madam, to expostulate
What majesty should be, what duty is,
Why day is day, night night, and time is time,
Were nothing but to waste night, day, and time;
Therefore, since brevity is the soul of wit, 90
And tediousness the limbs and outward flourishes,
I will be brief. Your noble son is mad:
Mad call I it, for to define true madness,
What is it but to be nothing else but mad?
But let that go.

Queen

More matter with less art. 95

98 figure: figure of speech.

101-3 this effect . . . by cause: Polonius rambles on, trying to make sense of his thoughts.

105 Perpend: listen, consider. (OED archaic)

108 this: this letter.

115 be faithful: report reliably.

116-22 "Doubt . . . I love.": The verse in Hamlet's letter has puzzled Stratfordian commentators, but it makes sense as an extended allusion to recent developments in astronomy. Hamlet is telling Ophelia that she should doubt that the stars—including the planets—are burning ("fire") and that the Sun "moves" around the stationary Earth—both tenets of the newly discredited Ptolemaic system—but that she should doubt, that is, suspect (per the OED), that the widely believed "truth" of Ptolemy's astronomy is false (a "liar"); and that nevertheless she should never doubt his love. The argument of the verse is based on knowledge of Copernicus's recent discrediting of Ptolemaic astronomy, known to mathematician/astronomers who had access to works of Copernicus, and not likely known to Will Shakspere. (See Usher and "Astronomy in *Hamlet.*"

120 ill at these numbers: bad at making verse.

120-1 not art to reckon my groans: to count them (there are so many) or make them metrical (OED obs.). Or both.

122 machine: his body, metaphorically; the first, and quite apt, use of the word in this sense, per the OED.

130 fain: be pleased to.

Polonius
Madam, I swear I use no art at all.
That he's mad, 'tis true, 'tis true 'tis pity,
And pity 'tis 'tis true — a foolish figure,
But farewell it, for I will use no art.
Mad let us grant him then, and now remains 100
That we find out the cause of this effect,
Or rather say, the cause of this defect,
For this effect defective comes by cause:
Thus it remains, and the remainder thus. Perpend. 105
I have a daughter — have whilst she is mine —
Who in her duty and obedience, mark,
Hath given me this. Now gather, and surmise.
[Reads] "To the celestial and my soul's idol, the most beautified
Ophelia" —That's an ill phrase, a vile phrase, ''beautified" is a vile 110
phrase. But you shall hear. Thus: "In her excellent white bosom,
these, et cetera".

Queen
Came this from Hamlet to her?

Polonius
Good madam, stay awhile. I will be faithful. 115
[Reads] "Doubt thou the stars are fire,
"Doubt that the Sun doth move,
"Doubt truth to be a liar,
"But never doubt I love.
"O, dear Ophelia, I am ill at these numbers. I have not art to reckon my 120
"groans, but that I love thee best, O most best, believe it. Adieu. Thine
"evermore, most dear lady, whilst this machine is to him, Hamlet."
This in obedience hath my daughter shown me,
And more above, hath his solicitings,
As they fell out by time, by means, and place, 125
All given to mine ear.

King
But how hath she received his love?

Polonius
What do you think of me?

King
As of a man faithful and honorable.

Polonius
I would fain prove so. But what might you think, 130
When I had seen this hot love on the wing —
As I perceived it (I must tell you that)
Before my daughter told me — what might you,

135 played . . . table-book: probably, simply made notes idly at his desk or in a tablet (and not reported it).

136 winking: closing (OED obs.) and thereby being silent.

137 with idle sight: not taken it seriously.

140 out of thy star: out of reach, above Ophelia's rank. In astrology, one's star determined one's status or fortune.

141 prescripts: instructions, commands.

142 from his resort: from associating with him. (OED obs.)

147 watch: sleeplessness. (OED obs.)

148 lightness: that is, lightheadedness. **declension:** decline.

158-9 Where truth is hid . . . center: that is, even if the truth of the matter were hid "Within the center" of the earth, the place most inaccessible and farthest from the light.

160 four hours: perhaps a printer's error for "for hours."

162 loose my daughter: that is, free her from his order not to see Hamlet in order use her as bait so he and the King can overhear their conversation and learn Hamlet's intentions (in 3.1). Another instance of the spying that goes on at the corrupt court of Elsinore, standing for Queen Elizabeth's court.

163 arras: a large, imported and expensive tapestry of fine quality hung ceiling to floor on the walls of castle chambers initially as insulation against the cold and over time as luxurious decorations, for the nobility and aristocrats. Behind the arras, there could be enough space for an eavesdropper.

Or my dear majesty your queen here, think,
If I had played the desk or table-book, 135
Or given my heart a winking, mute and dumb,
Or looked upon this love with idle sight,
What might you think? No, I went round to work,
And my young mistress thus I did bespeak:
"Lord Hamlet is a prince out of thy star; 140
This must not be." And then I prescripts gave her,
That she should lock herself from his resort,
Admit no messengers, receive no tokens.
Which done, she took the fruits of my advice.
And he, repelled, a short tale to make, 145
Fell into a sadness, then into a fast,
Thence to a watch, thence into a weakness,
Thence to a lightness, and by this declension,
Into the madness wherein now he raves,
And all we mourn for.

King
Do you think 'tis this? 150

Queen
It may be; very like.

Polonius
Hath there been such a time — I would fain know that —
That I have positively said, "'Tis so,"
When it proved otherwise?

King
Not that I know. 155

Polonius: *Pointing to his head and shoulder*
Take this from this, if this be otherwise.
If circumstances lead me, I will find
Where truth is hid, though it were hid indeed
Within the center.

King
How may we try it further?

Polonius
You know sometimes he walks four hours together 160
Here in the lobby.

Queen
So he does, indeed.

Polonius
At such a time I'll loose my daughter to him.
Be you and I behind an arras then,
Mark the encounter: if he love her not,

168 wretch: here, a playful term of pity and commiseration. **reading**: no doubt a book, which traditional scholarship has long suggested is meant to be *Cardanus Comforte* (1573), which had a strong influence on *Hamlet*'s author. What they never say is that it was dedicated to Oxford, who contributed a prefatory letter to the translator and a poem to the reader, and who commissioned publication of the book.

169 board him: figuratively, confront him. **presently**: at once. (OED obs.)

174 fishmonger: a derogatory reference to Lord Burghley, who tried in the 1580s to re-establish Wednesday as a day to eat fish instead of meat (in addition to meatless Friday) as a way to build up the fishing fleet, shipbuilding, and the capacity to build warships, if needed; with a connotation of a seller of flesh, or panderer, the implication being that Polonius is using his daughter as a commodity. In this scene, Hamlet has put on his "antic disposition."

181 For if the sun breed maggots . . . carrion--: something about Ophelia, and possibly disgust with procreation, but Hamlet abruptly interrupts this obscure thought. His talk of breeding, and in his next lines conception and conceiving, and Polonius's mention of pregnancy at line 203 suggest their concern that Hamlet may get Ophelia pregnant. Both are teenagers, Ophelia probably younger and inexperienced. When Oxford and Anne Cecil were growing up in Cecil's household, Oxford was in his teens, she was six years younger and it would not have been unusual for Cecil to worry about a premarital pregnancy. The two would marry at twenty-one and fifteen.

184 Let her not walk in the sun: Don't let her leave sheltered seclusion, go in public and risk becoming pregnant by the Sun (as the Sun supposedly causes maggots to breed) or by a possible future son-in-law, with a pun on son/Sun.

188 extremity: intensity of passion. (OED obs.)

And be not from his reason fallen thereon, 165
Let me be no assistant for a state,
But keep a farm and carters.

King

We will try it.

Enter Hamlet

Queen

But look where sadly the poor wretch comes reading.

Polonius

Away, I do beseech you, both away.
I'll board him presently. *Exeunt King and Queen*
O, give me leave, 170
How does my good lord Hamlet?

Hamlet

Well, God-a-mercy.

Polonius

Do you know me, my lord?

Hamlet

Excellent well, you are a fishmonger.

Polonius

Not I, my lord. 175

Hamlet

Then I would you were so honest a man.

Polonius

Honest, my lord?

Hamlet

Ay, sir, to be honest, as this world goes, is to be one man picked out of ten thousand.

Polonius

That's very true, my lord. 180

Hamlet

For if the sun breed maggots in a dead dog, being a good kissing carrion — Have you a daughter?

Polonius

I have, my lord.

Hamlet

Let her not walk in the sun. Conception is a blessing, but as your daughter may conceive, friend, look to it. 185

Polonius:

[Aside] How say you by that? Still harping on my daughter. Yet he knew me not at first, he said I was a fishmonger. He is far gone. And truly in my youth I suffered much extremity for love — very near this.

191 the matter: the subject. Hamlet deliberately misunderstands "the matter" as meaning a dispute or quarrel. (OED obs.)

198 honesty: decent or fair.

199-200 out of the air: indoors, or out of the drafts. Fresh air was thought to be bad for anyone ill.

203 how pregnant: here, how pointed or loaded with meaning, but harking back to Hamlet's thoughts about conception.

206 suddenly: shortly, immediately.

I'll speak to him again. — What do you read, my lord?

Hamlet

Words, words, words. 190

Polonius

What is the matter, my lord?

Hamlet

Between who?

Polonius

I mean, the matter that you read, my lord.

Hamlet

Slanders, sir; for the satirical rogue says here that old men have grey beards, that their faces are wrinkled, their eyes purging thick amber and 195 plum-tree gum, and that they have a plentiful lack of wit, together with most weak hams; all which, sir, though most powerfully and potently believe, yet I hold it not honesty to have it thus set down; for yourself, sir, shall grow old as I am, if like a crab you could go backward.

Polonius

[Aside] Though this be madness, yet there is method in it. — Will you walk out of the air, my lord? 200

Hamlet

Into my grave.

Polonius

Indeed that's out of the air. *[Aside]* How pregnant sometimes his replies are — a happiness that often madness hits on, which reason and sanity could not so prosperously be delivered of. I will leave him, and 205 suddenly contrive the means of meeting between him and my daughter. — My lord, I will take my leave of you.

Hamlet

You cannot take from me anything that I will not more willingly part withal — except my life, except my life, except my life.

Polonius

Fare you well, my lord.

Hamlet

[Aside] These tedious old fools.

Enter Guildenstern and Rosencrantz

Polonius

You go to seek the lord Hamlet, there he is. 210

Rosencrantz

[To Polonius] God save you, sir! *Exit Polonius*

Guildenstern

My honored lord!

214 My excellent good friends: sarcastically, since he knows that their seeking him is not for friendly reasons.

216 indifferent: ordinary.

217 Fortune's: Fortune is the goddess who could bestow good luck and thus happiness, often depicted naked.

218 button: the ornamental button at the top of a cap.

220 in the middle of her favors: sexual favors.

221 privates: ordinary persons, not officials, sometimes with a connotation of close friends; but here also a probably unintended allusion to Fortune's "privates" or sexual parts of the body.

222 strumpet: describing Fortune as a prostitute who can bestow her (sexual) favors for a price.

224 Then is doomsday near: because only the threat of doomsday could cause the world to become "honest".

236 your ambition: As Claudius directed, Rosencrantz and Guildenstern are pushing Hamlet to reveal whether he is ambitious for the Crown, thus his strange behavior and seeming discontent. Oxford was ambitious for meaningful positions of power in Queen Elizabeth's government. The lines that follow likely reflect his later recognition of the emptiness of such ambitions, even when unrealized.

Rosencrantz
My most dear lord!
Hamlet
My excellent good friends. How dost thou, Guildenstern? Ah, Rosencrantz!
Good lads, how do you both? 215
Rosencrantz
As the indifferent children of the earth.
Guildenstern
Happy, in that we are not over-happy; on Fortune's cap we are not
the very button.
Hamlet
Nor the soles of her shoe?
Rosencrantz
Neither, my lord.
Hamlet
Then you live about her waist, or in the middle of her favors? 220
Guildenstern
Faith, her privates we.
Hamlet
In the secret parts of Fortune? O, most true, she is a strumpet. What news?
Rosencrantz
None, my lord, but the world's grown honest.
Hamlet
Then is doomsday near. But your news is not true. Let me question more
in particular. What have you, my good friends, deserved at the hands 225
of Fortune, that she sends you to prison hither?
Guildenstern
Prison, my lord?
Hamlet
Denmark's a prison.
Rosencrantz
Then is the world one.
Hamlet
A goodly one, in which there are many confines, wards, and dungeons, 230
Denmark being one of the worst.
Rosencrantz
We think not so, my lord.
Hamlet
Why then 'tis none to you; for there is nothing either good or bad, but
thinking makes it so. To me it is a prison. 235
Rosencrantz
Why then your ambition makes it one. 'Tis too narrow for your mind.

237-8 nutshell . . . infinite space . . . bad dreams: In an allusion to astronomy, Hamlet feels that at Elsinore he is confined to a small space, a "nutshell," alluding to the Ptolemaic finite universe of a shell of stars surrounding the Earth, but that he could be or should still be king of "infinite space," alluding to the theory of Thomas Digges, an astronomer and one of the earliest Copernicans, who added in 1576 (when Oxford was 26) his heretical idea of an infinite universe, a concept so difficult for the mind to grasp that it causes "bad dreams." Digges considered his idea so dangerous to orthodox religion that when he published it he "hid" it in an appendix to an edition of his father's almanac. (See "Astronomy in *Hamlet*.")

243-44 Then . . . shadows: Hamlet is perhaps arguing that if ambition is a "shadow's shadow" (as Rosencrantz says) and beggars have "bodies," then "monarchs" are nothing but "beggars' shadows," shadows "outstretched" and looking larger than the beggars' bodies that throw their shadows.

248 beaten way: well-worn path.

250 Beggar that I am.: that is, powerless, emphasizing his lack of position, wealth, power and influence.

255 Anything but to the purpose: Anything but not the reason you are here, probably sarcastically.

256 modesties: deferential feelings. (OED obs.)

259 the consonancy: the harmonious relationship. (OED obs.)

Hamlet
O God, I could be bounded in a nutshell, and count myself a king of infinite space — were it not that I have bad dreams.
Guildenstern
Which dreams indeed are ambition, for the very substance of the ambitious is merely the shadow of a dream. 240
Hamlet
A dream itself is but a shadow.
Rosencrantz
Truly, and I hold ambition of so airy and light a quality that it is but a shadow's shadow.
Hamlet
Then are our beggars bodies, and our monarchs and outstretched heroes the beggars' shadows. Shall we to the court? For, by my fay, I cannot reason.
R*osencrantz* and *Guildenstern*
We'll wait upon you. 245
Hamlet
No such matter. I will not sort you with the rest of my servants; for to speak to you like an honest man, I am most dreadfully attended. But in the beaten way of friendship, what make you at Elsinore?
Rosencrantz
To visit you, my lord, no other occasion.
Hamlet
Beggar that I am, I am even poor in thanks —but I thank you, and sure, 250 dear friends, my thanks are too dear a halfpenny. Were you not sent for? Is it your own inclining? Is it a free visitation? Come, come, deal justly with me. Come, come — nay, speak
G*uildenstern*
What should we say, my lord?
Hamlet
Anything but to the purpose. You were sent for, and there is a kind of 255 confession in your looks, which your modesties have not craft enough to color. I know the good king and queen have sent for you.
Rosencrantz
To what end, my lord?
Hamlet
That you must teach me. But let me conjure you, by the rights of our fellowship, by the consonancy of our youth, by the obligation of our ever-preserved love, and by what more dear a better proposer can 260 charge you withal, be even and direct with me, whether you were sent for or no!
Rosencrantz
[Aside to Guildenstern] What say you?

265 prevent your discovery: forestall the need for you to disclose (OED rare) your secret mission.

266 your secrecy . . . moult no feather: that is, will remain intact, as a bird's plumage remains unchanged before moulting and losing its feathers.

268 so heavily with my disposition: that is, my depression so weighs me down.

269-73 canopy . . . pestilent: Hamlet, a Copernican, alludes to the old theory of Claudius Ptolemy of a "canopy" of stars like a "roof" over the Earth but immediately condemns it—and King Claudius by extension—as "foul and pestilent."

273-78: **What a piece of work is man . . . . Man delights not me**: This passage and the preceding one, while sounding celebratory, probably should be read as bitterly sarcastic and despairing.

278 by your smiling: Rosencrantz and Guildenstern are "smiling" because they take Hamlet to mean sexual "delights" with a man.

282 lenten entertainment: sparse reception. Lent was a period of fasting and penitence, when London theaters were closed.

283 coted: overtook and passed, from hunting with hounds. (See LN 2.1.112.)

285-6 his majesty shall have tribute on me: probably, I will esteem and pay tribute to this player king; but, by implication, not to King Claudius.

288-9 tickled by the sere: quick on the trigger. The sear ("sere") of a gun holds back the hammer until released by the trigger; hence easily tripped or "tickled," here made to laugh by the clown.

291 of the City: the City of London, where the private theaters were located. The childrens acting companies, which grew out of boys choirs, performed plays there and at court. The City was and is at the center of metropolitan London.

295 inhibition: prohibition. Performances were sometimes prohibited because of plague or other reasons. **innovation:** political disturbance (OED obs.), perhaps the change of regime in Denmark.

Hamlet
[Aside.] Nay then, I have an eye of you. — If you love me, hold not off.
Guildenstern
My lord, we were sent for.
Hamlet
I will tell you why, so shall my anticipation prevent your discovery, 265
and your secrecy to the king and queen moult no feather. I have of late
— but wherefore I know not — lost all my mirth, forgone all custom
of exercises; and indeed it goes so heavily with my disposition, that
this goodly frame, the earth, seems to me a sterile promontory; this
most excellent canopy, the air, look you, this brave overhanging 270
firmament, this majestical roof fretted with golden fire, why, it
appeareth nothing to me but a foul and pestilent congregation of
vapors. What a piece of work is a man, how noble in reason, how
infinite in faculties, in form and moving, how express and admirable; 275
in action, how like an angel; in apprehension, how like a god; the
beauty of the world; the paragon of animals; and yet to me what is this
quintessence of dust? Man delights not me — nor women neither,
though by your smiling you seem to say so.
Rosencrantz
My lord, there was no such stuff in my thoughts. 280
Hamlet
Why did ye laugh then, when I said, "Man delights not me"?
Rosencrantz
To think, my lord, if you delight not in man what lenten entertainment the
players shall receive from you. We coted them on the way, and hither are
they coming to offer you service.

Hamlet
He that plays the King shall be welcome — his majesty shall have 285
tribute on me—the the Adventurous Knight shall use his foil and
target, the Lover shall not sigh gratis, the Humorous Man shall end his
part in peace, the Clown shall make those laugh whose lungs are
tickled by the sere, and the Lady shall say her mind freely, or the blank
verse shall halt for it. What players are they? 290
Rosencrantz
Even those you were wont to take such delight in, the tragedians
of the City.
Hamlet
How chances it they travel? Their residence, both in reputation and profit,
was better both ways.
Rosencrantz:
I think their inhibition comes by the means of the late innovation. 295

301 an aerie of children, little eyases,: a nest ("aerie") of children, metaphorically young hawks ("little eyases"), alluding to the childrens acting companies that were active in the City of London and were probably competition for the adult companies. Oxford was the patron of a childrens acting company in the 1580s, when he was writing *Hamlet*.

302 berattle the common theaters: assail or scold with noisy language ("berattle" OED obs.) in the public ("common") theaters.

303-4 many wearing rapiers . . . come thither: that is, many rapier-wearing young aristocrats are deterred from going to plays because they fear the ridicule of the playwrights' pens ("goose quills").

305 escoted: sustained, supported (from Old French, OED obs.).

306 no longer . . . sing?: that is, until their voices change at puberty.

309 succession?: future careers, as adult actors.

311 tarre: goad, urge (from the sport of dog-fighting, OED).

311-12 There was . . . in the question.: probably, that playwrights received no pay for a play's plot ("argument") unless it furthered the competition ("went to cuffs") between the childrens and the adult acting companies.
317 his load: the Earth on his shoulders.

319-20 make mouths at him . . . his picture in little: that is, those who made sneering grimaces ("mouths") at the mention of Claudius before he became king now pay good money ("ducats," silver or gold) for his portrait in miniature ("in little") in a richly decorated and expensive locket; probably not known beyond aristocratic circles. **'Sblood:** short for the oath "God's (Christ's) blood."

***S. d.*:** Players announced their arrival at a castle or town by a trumpet "flourish." They will enter a few minutes later.

Hamlet
Do they hold the same estimation they did when I was in the city? Are they so followed?
Rosencrantz
No indeed are they not.
Hamlet
How comes it? Do they grow rusty?
Rosencrantz
Nay, their endeavor keeps in the wonted pace; but there is, sir, an 300
aerie of children, little eyases, that cry out on the top of question, and are most tyrannically clapped for it. These are now the fashion, and so berattle the common stages— so they call them — that many wearing rapiers are afraid of goose-quills and dare scarce come thither
Hamlet
What, are they children? Who maintains them? How are they 305
escoted? Will they pursue the quality no longer than they can sing? Will they not say afterwards, if they should grow themselves to common players (as it is most like, if their means are no better), their writers do them wrong, to make them exclaim against their own succession?
Rosencrantz
Faith, there has been much to do on both sides, and the nation holds it 310
no sin to tarre them to controversy. There was for a while no money bid for argument, unless the poet and the player went to cuffs in the question.
Hamlet
Is it possible?
Guildenstern
O, there has been much throwing about of brains. 315
Hamlet
Do the boys carry it away?
Rosencrantz
Ay, that they do, my lord — Hercules and his load too.
Hamlet
It is not very strange, for my uncle is king of Denmark, and those that would make mouths at him while my father lived, give twenty, forty, fifty, a hundred ducats apiece for his picture in little. 'Sblood, there is 320
something in this more than natural, if philosophy could find it out.
A flourish off stage
Guildenstern
There are the players.

323 Gentlemen . . . welcome: Only for appearances sake, Hamlet extends a second, more formal welcome to Rosencrantz and Guildenstern.

325 extent: extending. (OED obs.); here, his welcome to the players.

326 fairly outwards: courteously. **entertainment than yours**: my welcome more hospitable than yours.

330 I am but mad north-north-west.: a much debated sentence, probably meaning that he is only a bit out of true sanity, like a compass needle only 15 degrees off true north; but probably also an allusion by Oxford recalling his anger with himself ("mad") at the loss of a £3000 bond he made to invest in Frobisher's third voyage (1578), an expedition to find gold and a "northwest passage" to China, but which failed. (That Antonio in *The Merchant of Venice* owes the same amount in bond to Shylock is not likely a coincidence.) See also Usher *Hamlet's* for quite possible allusions to astronomy in this and the next line note.

331 hawk from a handsaw: another much debated sentence. "Handsaw" may be a printer's error for "heronshaw," a young or small heron (OED archaic) that is prey for hawks, alluding to the aristocratic sport of hawking or falconry. Thus Hamlet knows the difference between hunter and prey, or friends from enemies. See Usher *Hamlet's* for the many interpretations of this sentence and for his own: an allusion to astronomy. (202-3)

337-8: You . . . indeed: Hamlet pretends to be deep in conversation with the two courtiers in order to ignore Polonius.

342 Buzz, buzz.: a scornful reaction to news of something already known.

345-7 The best actors . . . unlimited: no doubt an allusion to Italian *commedia del'arte* performances with their variety of dramatic genres and sometimes clever mash-ups of them. Oxford would have seen performances of *commedia dell'arte* during his five months in northern Italy, but there were none in England for Shakspere to see or hear about. (See Whalen "*Commedia*.") This knowing and rather antic passage and the next seemingly might better be spoken by Hamlet, not the rather dense Polonius.

348 For the law of writ and liberty: There were two types of *commedia* in Italy, *commedia erudita* that were scripted ("writ") and *commedia all'improviso,* the more popular, improvised performances in which the actors took the "liberty" to improvise the action and dialogue of a basic plot. The "law" here refers to the practice of or rules for something. (OED obs.)

Hamlet

Gentlemen, you are welcome to Elsinore. Your hands. Come then: The appurtenance of welcome is fashion and ceremony. Let me comply with you in this garb, lest my extent to the players, which, I tell you, must show fairly outwards, should more appear like entertainment than yours. You are welcome; but my uncle-father and aunt-mother are deceived. 325

Guildenstern

In what, my dear lord?

Hamlet

I am but mad north-north-west. When the wind is southerly I know a hawk from a hand saw. 330

Enter Polonius

Polonius

Well be with you, gentlemen.

Hamlet

Hark you, Guildenstern, and you too — at each ear a hearer — that great baby you see there is not yet out of his swaddling-clouts.

Rosencrantz

Happily he is the second time come to them, for they say an old man is twice a child. 335

Hamlet

I will prophesy, he comes to tell me of the players, mark it — You say right, sir, on Monday morning, 'twas then indeed.

Polonius

My lord, I have news to tell you.

Hamlet

My lord, I have news to tell you. When Roscius was an actor in Rome — 340

Polonius

The actors are come hither, my lord.

Hamlet

Buzz, buzz.

Polonius

Upon my honor —

Hamlet

"Then came each actor on his ass."

Polonius

The best actors in the world, either for tragedy, comedy, history, pastoral, pastoral-comical, historical-pastoral, tragical-historical, tragical-comical-historical-pastoral, scene individable, or poem unlimited; Seneca cannot be too heavy, nor Plautus too light. For the law of writ and the liberty, these are the only men. 345

350 Jephthah: a Biblical warrior who sacrificed his only daughter, a virgin; no doubt an allusion to William Cecil, a commoner, who "sacrificed" his only daughter, fourteen-year-old Anne , by having her marry the seventeenth Earl of Oxford, in order to help induce Queen Elizabeth to elevate him to the nobility as Baron Burghley. (See the Introduction.)

365 chanson: French for song and here the first use of the word in English per the OED, showing Oxford's familiarity with French music.

368 valanced: bearded; from a draped edging of cloth.

371 chopine: an elevated shoe for women that was stylish in Venice when Oxford lived there for several months, but not likely to have been known by Shakspere.

372 cracked within the ring: A coin clipped for its metal content remained legal tender unless the clipping extended into the ring around the monarch's head; it then became a "cracked" crown and no longer legal tender. A boy's singing voice that had "cracked" no longer had the same "ring" thus making him unsuitable for women's roles.

373 like French falconers . . . we see: Let's have a try at the first thing that comes to mind, (sarcastically) like the French witlessly launch their falcons to "fly" at the first prey they see.

378-9 the play . . . caviare to the general: The play, like caviar, was not pleasing to the "general" public of commoners. Caviar was a rare and expensive delicacy imported from Russia for the English nobility and aristocrats who acquired a taste for it, but not something that would be appreciated by those in the general public. Nor something that might be known to a commoner like Shakspere.

380 cried in the top of mine: probably, outweighed, exceeded mine.

382 sallets: salads (OED obs.) with their seasonings.

Hamlet
O Jephthah, judge of Israel, what a treasure hadst thou! 350
Polonius
What a treasure had he, my lord?
Hamlet
Why —
"One fair daughter, and no more, 355
The which he loved passing well."
Polonius
[Aside] Still on my daughter.
Hamlet
Am I not in the right, old Jephthah?
Polonius
If you call me Jephthah, my lord, I have a daughter that I love
passing well. 360
Hamlet
Nay, that follows not.
Polonius
What follows then, my lord?
Hamlet: Why —
"As by lot, God wot," and then, you know, "It came to pass, as most
like it was"—the first row of the pious chanson will show you more, for 365
look where my abridgement comes.

Enter the Players

You are welcome, masters, welcome all. I am glad to see thee well.
Welcome, good friends. O, old friend! Why thy face is valanced since I
saw thee last; comst thou to beard me in Denmark? What, my young
lady
and mistress! By our Lady, your ladyship is nearer to heaven than 370
when I saw you last, by the altitude of a chopine. Pray God your voice
like a piece of uncurrent gold, be not cracked within the ring. Masters,
you are all welcome. We'll even to it like French falconers — fly at
anything we see; we'll have a speech straight. Come give us a taste of
your quality, come, a passionate speech. 375
First Player
What speech, my good lord?
Hamlet
I heard thee speak me a speech once, but it was never acted, or if it was,
not above once; for the play, I remember, pleased not the million, 'twas
caviare to the general, but it was — as I received it, and others, whose
judgments in such matters cried in the top of mine — an excellent play, 380
well digested in the scenes, set down with as much modesty as cunning.
I remember one said there were no sallets in the lines to make the matter

384 affection: not fondness but affectation. (OED obs.)

387 Priam's slaughter: In Virgil's *Aeneid*, Aeneas relates to Dido the story of the fall of Troy, including the death of King Priam.

388 let me see: The speech that Hamlet will recall and recite has special significance for him, relating as it does the revenge of a son, Pyrrhus, for the death of his father, Achilles, as well as the reaction of Priam's wife, Queen Hecuba, to his death. The speech is written in an elaborate style already outdated and considered far inferior to Shakespearean verse.

389 *rugged*: hairy, shaggy (OED obs.). ***Hyrcanian beast***: a tiger, from Hyrcania on the Caspian Sea, famous in antiquity for tigers.

393 *ominous horse*: the Greeks' wooden Trojan horse, which contributed to their defeat of the Trojans. "Ominous" could mean auspicious, fortunate (OED obs.) as well as ill-omened, foreboding.

402 *carbuncles*: mythical gemstones, fiery red and thought to generate light.

418 *as a painted tyrant*: as a tyrant in a painting, thus immobilized.

421 *against*: before, in preparation for. (OED obs.)

422 *rack*: clouds in the upper air. (OED obs.)

savory, nor no matter in the phrase that might indict the author of affection, but called it an honest method, as wholesome as sweet, and by very much more handsome than fine. One speech in it I chiefly loved, 385
'twas Aeneas' tale to Dido, and thereabout of it especially when he speaks of Priam's slaughter. If it live in your memory, begin at this line — let me see, let me see:

"The rugged Pyrrhus, like the Hyrcanian beast —
'Tis not so, it begins with Pyrrhus: 390
"The rugged Pyrrhus, he whose sable arms,
Black as his purpose, did the night resemble
When he lay couched in the ominous horse,
Hath now this dread and black complexion smeared
With heraldry more dismal: head to foot 395
Now is he total gules, horridly tricked
With blood of fathers, mothers, daughters, sons;
Baked and impasted with the parching streets,
That lend a tyrannous and a damned light
To their lord's murder. Roasted in wrath and fire, 400
And thus over-sized with coagulate gore,
With eyes like carbuncles, the hellish Pyrrhus
Old grandsire Priam seeks."

So proceed you.

Polonius

'Fore God, my lord, well spoken, with good accent and good discretion. 405

First Player

"Anon he finds him
Striking too short at Greeks. His antique sword,
Rebellious to his arm, lies where it falls,
Repugnant to command. Unequal matched
Pyrrhus at Priam drives, in rage strikes wide, 410
But with the whiff and wind of his fell sword
The unnerved father falls. Then senseless Ilium,
Seeming to feel this blow, with flaming top
Stoops to his base, and with a hideous crash
Takes prisoner Pyrrhus' ear; for lo his sword, 415
Which was declining on the milky head
Of reverent Priam, seemed in the air to stick.
So as a painted tyrant Pyrrhus stood
And, like a neutral to his will and matter,
Did nothing. 420
But as we often see, against some storm
A silence in the heavens, the rack stand still,
The bold winds speechless, and the orb below

428 ***proof eterne*****:** to be impenetrable forever. (OED)

433 ***spokes and fellies . . . wheel*****:** the spokes and the curved pieces of wood ("fellies") on the outer circumference of the wheel.

434 ***nave*****:** hub of the wheel.

437 barber's . . . beard: It will be trimmed, cut short. **He's:** that is, Polonius. **a jig:** a farcical or comical dance.

439 ***mobled*****:** muffled. (OED obs.) Hamlet will question what it means, perhaps to draw a foolish comment by Polonius.

442 ***bisson rheum*****:** blinding tears. (OED obs.) **clout**: rag. (OED obs.)

444 ***over-teemed*****:** worn out from child-bearing (OED obs.); legendarily, Hecuba bore nineteen children.

447 ***Fortune's state*****:** Fortune's rule, control.

453 ***milch*****:** milky (from tears). ***burning eyes of heaven*****:** stars.

454 ***passion*****:** here, probably overwhelming grief.

As hush as death, anon the dreadful thunder
Doth rend the region; so after Pyrrhus' pause, 425
A roused vengeance sets him new at work,
And never did the Cyclops' hammers fall
On Mars's armor forged for proof eterne
With less remorse than Pyrrhus' bleeding sword
Now falls on Priam. 430
Out, out, thou strumpet Fortune! All you gods,
In general synod take away her power!
Break all the spokes and fellies from her wheel,
And bowl the round nave down the hill of heaven
As low as to the fiends!" 435

Polonius
This is too long.

Hamlet
It shall to the barber's with your beard. Prithee say on, he's for a jig or a tale of bawdry, or he sleeps. Say on, come to Hecuba.

First Player
"But who, ah woe, had seen the mobled queen" —

Hamlet
"The mobled queen"?

Polonius
That's good, "mobled queen" is good. 440

First Player
"Run barefoot up and down, threatening the flames
With bisson rheum, a clout upon that head
Where late the diadem stood, and for a robe,
About her lank and all over-teemed loins,
A blanket, in the alarm of fear caught up — 445
Who this had seen, with tongue in venom steeped,
'Gainst Fortune's state would treason have pronounced.
But if the gods themselves did see her then,
When she saw Pyrrhus make malicious sport
In mincing with his sword her husband's limbs, 450
The instant burst of clamor that she made,
Unless things mortal move them not at all,
Would have made milch the burning eyes of heaven,
And passion in the gods."

Polonius
Look where he has not turned his color and has tears in his eyes. Prithee, no more. 455

458 bestowed: lodged.

459 abstract and brief chronicles of the time: Hamlet's description of the role of actors and their plays and the topicality ("of the time") of their plays supports the understanding of Oxford's Shakespeare plays as often alluding to and commenting on contemporary political events, geopolitical issues, court gossip and affairs, and on royal and noble personages in Elizabethan times.

462 after their desert: according to their merit.

463 God's bodkin: short for the oath "God's dear body."

468 The Murder of Gonzago: The play will be performed for King Claudius and the Danish court as the play-within-the-play in act 3 scene 2. A play with that title or subject has not been found; it is Oxford's invention, inspired by the assassination in 1538 of an Italian duke, which resembled the way he suspected his own father, the sixteenth Earl of Oxford died. (See line notes 1.2.201 and 3.2.248.) Hamlet later will impulsively rename it "The Mousetrap."

470 for need: if needed.

479 what a rogue and peasant slave am I: Like an idle vagabond ("rogue"), he has taken no action and feels contemptible, "slave" being a term of contempt. (OED archaic)

483 her: the soul's. **wanned:** grew pale, wan.

485-6 his whole function . . . conceit?: probably, the player's gestures, expressions, actions ("whole function") matching ("suiting") the imaginary character ("conceit") he is portraying on stage.

Hamlet

'Tis well, I'll have thee speak out the rest of this soon. Good my lord, will you see the players well bestowed? Do you hear, let them be well used, for they are the abstract and brief chronicles of the time. After your death you were better have a bad epitaph than their ill report 460 while you live.

Polonius

My lord, I will use them according to their desert.

Hamlet

God's bodkin, man, much better! Use every man after his desert, and who shall scape whipping? Use them after your own honor and dignity — the less they deserve, the more merit is in your bounty. Take them in. 465

Polonius

Come, sirs.

Hamlet

Follow him, friends, we'll hear a play tomorrow.

[Aside to First Player] Dost thou hear me, old friend? Can you play "The Murder of Gonzago"?

First Player

Ay, my lord.

Hamlet

We'll have it tomorrow night. You could, for need study a speech of some 470 dozen or sixteen lines, which I would set down and insert in it, could you not?

First Player

Ay, my lord.

Hamlet

Very well. Follow that lord, and look you mock him not. My good friends, I'll leave you till night. You are welcome to Elsinore. 475

Exeunt Polonius and Players

Rosencrantz

Good my lord.

Hamlet

Ay so, God buy to you.

Exeunt Rosencrantz and Guildenstern

Now I am alone.
O, what a rogue and peasant slave am I.
Is it not monstrous that this player here, 480
But in a fiction, in a dream of passion,
Could force his soul so to his own conceit
That from her working all the visage wanned,
Tears in his eyes, distraction in his aspect,
A broken voice, and his whole function suiting 485
With forms to his conceit? And all for nothing.

492 horrid: hair-raising. (OED obs.)

497 muddy-mettled: probably, dull-spirited. **peak:** mope about. (OED obs.)

498 unpregnant: not influenced by, not stirred by. (OED obs.)

499-501 Can say nothing . . . defeat was made.: In this passage and the speech that follows, Oxford (like Hamlet) can be seen as castigating himself for failing to take action against the Earl of Leicester (King Claudius) to avenge the suspected murder of his father, the sixteenth Earl of Oxford (King Hamlet), whose estate or "property" (the kingdom of Denmark) was stolen ("a damned defeat") from the underage Oxford.

506 'swounds: short for the oath "God's (Christ's) wounds.

507 pigeon-livered and lack gall: gentle, mild; lacking boldness ("gall"). Pigeons were believed to be gentle because their livers secreted no gall, thought to cause anger and resentment.

509 fatted all the region kites: fattened all the birds of prey ("kites") in the sky. ("region" OED)

510 With this slave's offal: with King Claudius's entrails ("offal" OED obs.) contemptuously, from "slave," a term of contempt. (OED archaic)

511 kindless: unnatural; without natural feelings. (OED obs.)

512 most brave: most admirable, but with bitter sarcasm.

516 drab: prostitute.

517 stallion.: a male prostitute. (OED obs.)

518 About, my brains!: Get going! Be "about" it!

520 cunning of the scene: skill of the presentation.

521 presently: at once. (OED obs.)

527 tent: probe, as a wound. (OED obs.) **blench:** flinch, turn away. (OED obs.)

528-9 The spirit . . . May be a devil,: Hamlet repeats his concern that the ghost of his father ("the spirit") may have been a "devil" in disguise that lied about King Claudius murdering his father. He may seem to delay getting revenge, when in fact he wants some corroborating evidence for it.

For Hecuba!
What's Hecuba to him, or he to her
That he should weep for her? What would he do
Had he the motive and the cue for passion 490
That I have? He would drown the stage with tears,
And cleave the general ear with horrid speech,
Make mad the guilty, and appall the free,
Confound the ignorant, and amaze indeed
The very faculties of eyes and ears. 495
Yet I,
A dull and muddy-mettled rascal, peak
Like John-a-dreams, unpregnant of my cause,
Can say nothing; no, not for a king
Upon whose property and most dear life 500
A damned defeat was made. Am I a coward?
Who calls me villain, breaks my pate across,
Plucks off my beard and blows it in my face,
Tweaks me by the nose, gives me the lie in the throat
As deep as to the lungs? Who does me this? 505
Hah, 'swounds, I should take it; for it cannot be
But I am pigeon-livered, and lack gall
To make oppression bitter, or ere this
I should have fatted all the region kites
With this slave's offal. Bloody, bawdy villain! 510
Remorseless, treacherous, lecherous, kindless villain!
Why, what an ass am I! This is most brave,
That I, the son of a dear father murdered,
Prompted to my revenge by heaven and hell,
Must like a whore unpack my heart with words, 515
And fall a-cursing like a very drab,
A stallion. Fie upon it, foh!
About, my brains! Hum — I have heard
That guilty creatures sitting at a play
Have by the very cunning of the scene 520
Been struck so to the soul, that presently
They have proclaimed their malefactions:
For murder, though it have no tongue, will speak
With most miraculous organ. I'll have these players
Play something like the murder of my father 525
Before mine uncle. I'll observe his looks,
I'll tent him to the quick. If he do blench,
I know my course. The spirit that I have seen
May be a devil, and the devil hath power

531 Out of . . . melancholy,: using my uncertainty and depression.

532 he is very potent with such spirits: That is, the devil has great power exploiting the vapors ("spirits") which cause melancholy.

533 Abuses me: deceives, misleads me.

533-4 grounds / More relative: evidence more relevant, more convincing. Hamlet needs more evidence than just the Ghost's testimony.

To assume a pleasing shape, yea, and perhaps, 530
Out of my weakness and my melancholy,
As he is very potent with such spirits,
Abuses me to damn me. I'll have grounds
More relative than this. The play's the thing
Wherein I'll catch the conscience of the king! 535
Exit

3.1

1 no drift of conference: no idea or hints from your conversation (with Hamlet).

3 Grating so: making so discordant.

4 dangerous lunacy: Claudius floats the idea that Hamlet may be dangerously insane.

7 forward: willing.

13 his disposition: his (antic) attitude, mood, behavior. (OED obs.)

14 Niggard of question: reluctant and unwilling to ask anything or engage in conversation. But this is not true. Rosencrantz apparently does not want the King to think that Hamlet, by his questions, showed that he knows that Rosencrantz and Guildenstern had been set to spy on him.

15 assay: tempt, coax. (OED obs.)

17 overraught: overtook. (OED obs.)

26 edge: stimulus, incitement. (OED obs.)

Act 3

Scene 1. The audience chamber
Enter King, Queen, Polonius, Ophelia, Rosencrantz, Guildenstern

King
And can you by no drift of conference
Get from him why he puts on this confusion,
Grating so harshly all his days of quiet
With turbulent and dangerous lunacy?
Rosencrantz
He does confess he feels himself distracted, 5
But from what cause he will by no means speak.
Guildenstern
Nor do we find him forward to be sounded,
But with a crafty madness keeps aloof
When we would bring him on to some confession
Of his true state. 10
Queen
Did he receive you well?
Rosencrantz
Most like a gentleman.
Guildenstern
But with much forcing of his disposition.
Rosencrantz
Niggard of question, but of our demands
Most free in his reply.
Queen
Did you assay him to any pastime? 15
Rosencrantz
Madam, it so fell out that certain players
We overraught on the way; of these we told him,
And there did seem in him a kind of joy
To hear of it. They are here about the court,
And as I think, they have already order 20
This night to play before him.
Polonius
'Tis most true,
And he beseeched me to entreat your majesties
To hear and see the matter.
King
With all my heart, and it doth much content me
To hear him so inclined. 25
Good gentlemen, give him a further edge,

28 us two: Claudius and Polonius (ignoring Ophelia's presence).

31 Affront: meet face-to-face. (OED obs.)

32 (lawful espials): observers, spies (OED obs.), and trying to make their spying sound legitimate ("lawful").

33 bestow ourselves: place ourselves.

38-42 Ophelia, I do wish . . . . To both your honors.: Queen Gertrude subtly indicates that she would support them if Lord Hamlet and Ophelia, a commoner, were to marry, which would in her view be to the "honors" of both of them. Queen Elizabeth supported the marriage of Lord Oxford to Anne Cecil, even though she was born a commoner.

41 wonted: ordinary, customary.

44 Read on this book,: a prayer book, given what he says next.

51 beautied with plastering art: beautified with thick ("plastering") cosmetics, often used to cover the disfiguring marks of small pox.

53 my deed: his assassination of King Hamlet.

55 Withdraw my lord: Polonius and the king quickly (and rather ignominiously) hide behind an arras.

And drive his purpose into these delights.
Rosencrantz
We shall, my lord. *Exeunt Rosencrantz and Guildenstern*
King
Sweet Gertrude, leave us two,
For we have closely sent for Hamlet hither,
That he, as 'twere by accident, may here 30
Affront Ophelia.
Her father and myself (lawful espials)
Will so bestow ourselves that, seeing unseen,
We may of their encounter frankly judge,
And gather by him, as he is behaved, 35
If it be the affliction of his love or no
That thus he suffers for.
Queen
I shall obey you.
And for your part, Ophelia, I do wish
That your good beauties be the happy cause
Of Hamlet's wildness. So shall I hope your virtues 40
Will bring him to his wonted way again,
To both your honors.
Ophelia
Madam, I wish it may. *Exit Queen*
Polonius
Ophelia, walk you here. *[To the king]* Gracious, so please you,
We will bestow ourselves. *[To Ophelia]* Read on this book,
That show of such an exercise may color 45
Your loneliness. We are oft to blame in this —
'Tis too much proved — that with devotion's visage
And pious action we do sugar over
The devil himself.
King
[Aside] O, 'tis too true.
How smart a lash that speech doth give my conscience. 50
The harlot's cheek, beautied with plastering art,
Is not more ugly to the thing that helps it
Than is my deed to my most painted word.
O heavy burthen.
Polonius
I hear him coming. Withdraw, my lord. 55

56-88 To be . . . action: In this most famous speech, Hamlet swings back and forth between thoughts of living a noble life of action, despite its troubles, heartaches and sufferings, and thoughts of their ending in death, an outcome "devoutly to be wished," even by suicide with a "bare bodkin." Several leading characters in Shakespeare tragedies die by suicide, including Antony and Cleopatra, Romeo and Juliet, Othello, Brutus and Cassius, Lady Macbeth and probably Macbeth. There is circumstantial evidence that Oxford committed suicide at age fifty-four shortly after finishing his final version of *Hamlet*. The manner and cause of his death were not recorded and no will has been found, but shortly before he died in 1604 he took pains to put his affairs in order presumably so that if his death was determined to be suicide his property would not go the government, as was the rule for suicides, but to his wife. (See Detobel.)

60-1 To die, to sleep--No more;: probably, to die is nothing more than to sleep.

67 shuffled off this mortal coil: shed this bustle and turmoil of life. ("coil" OED archaic.)

68 respect: consideration. (OED obs.)

74 patient . . . takes: that the person of "merit" patiently accepts from the "unworthy."

75 quietus: release from an office or duty (OED obs.); here, release from life.

76 bare bodkin: an unsheathed dagger. **fardels:** burdens of sin, sorrow. (OED archaic)

79 bourn: boundary. (OED obs.)

85 sicklied over: made sickly, hence weakened.

86 enterprises of great pitch: of great height or scope of resolution (OED obs.), hence ambitions.

88 Soft you now: "Be still," to himself, as he sees Ophelia approaching.

89 Nymph: in mythology, a beautiful, nubile maiden of rivers and forests who loves to sing. **orisons**: prayers. (OED archaic)

92 well.: doing well.

Enter Hamlet

Hamlet

To be, or not to be, that is the question
Whether 'tis nobler in the mind to suffer
The slings and arrows of outrageous fortune,
Or to take arms against a sea of troubles,
And by opposing, end them. To die, to sleep — 60
No more; and by a sleep to say we end
The heart-ache and the thousand natural shocks
That flesh is heir to; 'tis a consummation
Devoutly to be wished—to die, to sleep —
To sleep, perchance to dream — ay, there's the rub, 65
For in that sleep of death what dreams may come,
When we have shuffled off this mortal coil,
Must give us pause; there's the respect
That makes calamity of so long life.
For who would bear the whips and scorns of time, 70
The oppressor's wrong, the proud man's contumely,
The pangs of despised love, the law's delay,
The insolence of office, and the spurns
That patient merit of the unworthy takes,
When he himself might his quietus make 75
With a bare bodkin. Who would fardels bear,
To grunt and sweat under a weary life,
But that the dread of something after death,
The undiscovered country from whose bourn
No traveler returns, puzzles the will, 80
And makes us rather bear those ills we have
Than fly to others that we know not of.
Thus conscience does make cowards of us all,
And thus the native hue of resolution
Is sicklied over with the pale cast of thought, 85
And enterprises of great pitch and moment
With this regard their currents turn awry
And lose the name of action. — Soft you now,
The fair Ophelia. Nymph, in thy orisons
Be all my sins remembered. 90

Ophelia

Good my lord,
How does your honor for this many a day?

Hamlet

I humbly thank you; well.

93 remembrances: gifts, notes or letters, held as mementoes.

94 longed long to redeliver: presumably because he has been ignoring her or not been kind to her.

99 perfume: the sweetness, now lost by Hamlet's denial.

101 wax poor: become or grow poor.

102 There, my lord.: presumably, Ophelia thrusts his letters at him.

103 honest?: chaste, virtuous? (OED archaic when describing a woman.)

105 fair?: good looking, beautiful? almost always describing a woman.

108 should admit no discourse: should allow no one to become (overly) familiar ("discourse" OED obs.)

109 commerce: dealings, relations.

112 his: its (honesty's).

115-6 for virtue . . . relish of it: that is, for virtue cannot be engrafted ("inoculated," from horticulture) on our (presumably sinful, wicked) customary character and behavior ("old stock") without our continuing to savor and enjoy ("relish") our "old" ways of behaving.

116 I loved you not.: Hamlet is probably admitting that it was not mature, true love but only the sexual impulses of an adolescent boy toward a much younger girl. When Oxford was a teenager in the household of William Cecil, Anne Cecil was six years younger. They would marry when she was fifteen.

118 nunnery: where women take a vow of chastity.

119 indifferent honest: not particularly virtuous.

Ophelia
My lord, I have remembrances of yours
That I have longed long to redeliver.
I pray you now receive them. 95
Hamlet
No, not I,
I never gave you aught.
Ophelia
My honored lord, you know right well you did,
And with them words of so sweet breath composed
As made these things more rich. Their perfume lost,
Take these again, for to the noble mind 100
Rich gifts wax poor when givers prove unkind.
There, my lord.
Hamlet
Ha, ha! are you honest?
Ophelia
My lord?
Hamlet
Are you fair? 105
Ophelia
What means your lordship?
Hamlet
That if you be honest and fair, your honesty should admit no discourse to your beauty.
Ophelia
Could beauty, my lord, have better commerce than with honesty?
Hamlet
Ay, truly, for the power of beauty will sooner transform honesty from 110 what it is to a bawd than the force of honesty can translate beauty into his likeness. This was sometime a paradox, but now the time gives it proof. I did love you once
Ophelia
Indeed, my lord, you made me believe so.
Hamlet
You should not have believed me, for virtue cannot so inoculate our old 115 stock but we shall relish of it. I loved you not.
Ophelia
I was the more deceived.
Hamlet
Get thee to a nunnery. Why, wouldst thou be a breeder of sinners? I am myself indifferent honest, but yet I could accuse me of such things that it were better my mother had not borne me. I am very proud, 120

121 offenses at my beck: misdeeds and sins at my "beck" and call, that is, readily called to mind.

136 paintings: cosmetic make-up.

138 make wantonness your ignorance: You (then) try to excuse your affected, would-be seductive behavior ("wantonness") as just ignorance.

145 glass: mirror. **mould of form:** pattern of good form or model behavior.

146 observed of all observers: the center of attention.

150 Like sweet bells jangled out of time: like music whose rhythm or tempo, the length and number of beats in a measure ("time," a term in musicology) is irregular and mixed up ("jangled"); her description of Hamlet in a manic phase.

151 blown youth: youth in full bloom.

152 ecstasy: a frenzy of passion; with a connotation of tumultuous outbursts. (OED obs.).

revengeful, ambitious, with more offenses at my beck than I have
thoughts to put them in, imagination to give them shape, or time to act
them in. What should such fellows as I do crawling between earth and
heaven? We are arrant knaves, believe none of us. Go thy ways to a
nunnery. Where's your father? 125

Ophelia

At home, my lord.

Hamlet

Let the doors be shut upon him, that he may play the fool nowhere but in his
own house. Farewell.

Ophelia

O, help him, you sweet heavens!

Hamlet

If thou dost marry, I'll give thee this plague for thy dowry: be thou as 130
chaste as ice, as pure as snow, thou shalt not escape calumny. Get thee
to a nunnery, farewell. Or if thou wilt needs marry, marry a fool, for
wise men know well enough what monsters you make of them. To a
nunnery, go, and quickly too. Farewell.

Ophelia

Heavenly powers, restore him! 135

Hamlet

I have heard of your paintings, well enough. God hath given you one
face, and you make yourselves another. You jig and amble, and you
lisp, you nickname God's creatures, and make your wantonness your
ignorance. Go to, I'll no more on it, it hath made me mad. I say we
will have no more marriage. Those that are married already (all but 140
one) shall live, the rest shall keep as they are. To a nunnery, go.

Exit Hamlet

Ophelia

O, what a noble mind is here overthrown!
The courtier's, soldier's, scholar's, eye, tongue, sword,
The expectation and rose of the fair state,
The glass of fashion and the mould of form, 145
The observed of all observers, quite, quite down.
And I, of ladies most deject and wretched,
That sucked the honey of his musicked vows,
Now see that noble and most sovereign reason
Like sweet bells jangled out of time and harsh; 150
That unmatched form and feature of blown youth
Blasted with ecstasy. O, woe is me
To have seen what I have seen, see what I see. *Exit*

The King and Polonius emerge from behind the arras

156 something in his soul: no doubt Hamlet's suspicion that Claudius killed his father.

157 sits on brood: like a brooding hen sitting on eggs.

158 doubt the hatch and the disclose: fear ("doubt" OED obs.) the outcome ("hatch") and public disclosure of the "something in his soul."

162 For the demand of our neglected tribute: to insist on payment to Denmark of overdue "neglected" tribute. For centuries, Denmark from time to time extorted tribute called Danegeld from England as protection money by threatening marauding raids and pillaging of coastal towns. Something Oxford and his court audiences would have known about, but probably not Shakspere.

165 something-settled matter: referring to the "something in his soul" (at 156).

167 From fashion of himself: so unlike his normal self.

175 grief: grievances. (OED obs.) **be round with him**: be frank and severe (OED obs.) in her dealings with Hamlet about his behavior.

177 If she find him not,: If she does not find out what troubles him.

1-34 Speak the speech . . . . make you ready: In this long passage Hamlet instructs the players not in the voice of a fellow actor, an equal, but in that of a director and author, as was Oxford, a patron of acting companies and a dramatist who would be offended by incompetent actors who fail to suit the action to the word and who bellow and strut upon the stage no matter the play text.

2 I had as lief: I would rather. (OED archaic)

7 a robustious periwig-pated fellow: a boisterous, noisy actor wearing a wig.

8 groundlings: Oxford's disparaging word for the unrefined, uncritical spectators on the bare ground of the pit of the public theaters (per the OED), mostly uneducated, even illiterate commoners who would be unable to appreciate his sophisticated plays.

King

Love? His affections do not that way tend,
Nor what he spake, though it lacked form a little, 155
Was not like madness. There's something in his soul
Over which his melancholy sits on brood,
And I do doubt the hatch and the disclose
Will be some danger; which for to prevent,
I have in quick determination 160
Thus set it down he shall with speed to England
For the demand of our neglected tribute.
Haply the seas, and countries different,
With variable objects, shall expel
This something-settled matter in his heart, 165
Whereon his brain's still beating puts him thus
From fashion of himself. What think you on it?

Polonius

It shall do well; but yet do I believe
The origin and commencement of his grief
Sprung from neglected love. How now, Ophelia? 170
You need not tell us what Lord Hamlet said,
We heard it all. My lord, do as you please,
But if you hold it fit, after the play
Let his queen-mother all alone entreat him
To show his grief. Let her be round with him, 175
And I'll be placed (so please you) in the ear
Of all their conference. If she find him not,
To England send him, or confine him where
Your wisdom best shall think.

King

It shall be so.
Madness in great ones must not unwatched go. 180

Exeunt

Scene 2.

Enter Hamlet and three of the Players

Hamlet

Speak the speech, I pray you, as I pronounced it to you, trippingly on the tongue; but if you mouth it, as many of our players do, I had as lief the town-crier spoke my lines. Nor do not saw the air too much with your hand, thus, but use all gently; for in the very torrent, tempest, and, as I may say, whirlwind of your passion, you must acquire and beget a temperance 5 that may give it smoothness. O, it offends me to the soul to hear a robustious periwig-pated fellow tear a passion to tatters, to very rags, to

9 inexplicable dumb shows and noise: that is, the miming, shouting and sound effects without any meaning ("inexplicable"). It seems quite unlikely that Shakspere, a commoner, would have written this denigration of his audience of fellow commoners. More likely, it's Oxford's opinion of the audiences in the public theaters, such as the Rose and the Globe.

11 Termagant: the traditional companion of the Mohammed character in the English mystery plays, depicted as noisy, violent and overbearing (OED). **out-Herods Herod:** exceeds even the ranting rages of the traditional tyrant of medieval plays and the mystery plays.

18-19 the very age . . . form and pressure.: probably, the true state of contemporary life ("the very age"), conveyed in topicalities, as if impressed ("form and pressure") accurately in wax.

24 Christians: here, ordinary people.

26 Nature's journeymen: workers learning a trade under master craftsmen such as Nature herself.

28 indifferently: reasonably well. (OED obs.)

31-33 barren spectators . . . considered: spectators dull and unable to conceive ("barren") what the author has written for the clowns and the point of their lines. In his Shakespeare plays Oxford often has the clowns addressing "some necessary question" that eludes the other characters and expressing the truth of the matter.

36 presently: right now.

split the ears of the groundlings, who for the most part are capable of nothing but inexplicable dumb shows and noise. I would have such fellow whipped for overdoing Termagant; it out-Herods Herod. 10
Pray you avoid it.

First Player

I warrant your honor.

Hamlet

Be not too tame neither, but let your own discretion be your tutor. Suit the action to the word, the word to the action, with this special observance, that you overstep not the modesty of nature for anything 15
so overdone is from the purpose of playing, whose end, both at the first and now, was and is, to hold, as 'twere, the mirror up to Nature to show Virtue her feature, Scorn her own image, and the very age and body of the time his form and pressure. Now this overdone, or come tardy off, though it makes the unskillful laugh, cannot but make the 20
judicious grieve, the censure of which one must in your allowance overweigh a whole theater of others. O, there be players that I have seen play — and heard others praise, and that highly — not to speak it profanely, that, neither having the accent of Christians nor the gait of Christian, pagan, nor man, have so strutted and bellowed that I have 25
thought some of Nature's journeymen had made men, and not made them well, they imitated humanity so abominably.

First Player

I hope we have reformed that indifferently with us, sir.

Hamlet

O, reform it altogether. And let those that play your clowns speak no more than is set down for them, for there be of them that will 30
themselves laugh to set on some quantity of barren spectators to laugh too, though in the mean time some necessary question of the play be then to be considered. That's villainous, and shows a most pitiful ambition in the fool that uses it. Go make you ready. *Exeunt Players*

Enter Polonius, Rosencrantz and Guildenstern

How now, my lord? Will the king hear this piece of work? 35

Polonius

And the queen too, and that presently.

Hamlet

Bid the players make haste. *Exit Polonius*
Will you two help to hasten them?

Rosencrantz

Ay, my lord. *Exeunt the two*

Hamlet

What ho, Horatio! 40

41 sweet: an affectionate term of address; also conveying respect. (OED archaic)

43 conversation: dealings, not just talk. (OED obs.) **Coped:** encountered, met. (OED obs.)

49 let the candied tongue lick absurd pomp: let the sweet-talking, flattering tongue speak to (figuratively "lick") the ludicrous, vain ostentation ("pomp" OED obs.), no doubt referring derisively to the obsequious behavior in a monarch's court, behavior that Oxford would have seen at Queen Elizabeth's court and been disgusted by it.

50 pregnant hinges of the knee: readily disposed ("pregnant" OED obs.) to genuflect.

51 thrift: success, prosperity. (OED obs.)

55 As one . . . nothing: because he transcends suffering, a stoic virtue.

58 blood: figuratively for emotions, passions.

60 stop: note, as on a wind instrument.

63 Something too much of this.: probably parenthetically, I'm going on altogether ("something") too long about this; then abruptly changing the subject.

68 comment of thy soul: note attentively. (OED obs.)

69 occulted: hidden. (OED obs.)

70 itself unkennel: force itself out of hiding and reveal itself; as a fox is forced out from its lair into the open in fox hunting, a sport of aristocrats.

71 damned ghost: Hamlet yet again recognizes that the Ghost might not have been that of his father but a "damned ghost," a devil disguised as his father.

73 Vulcan's stithy: his anvil, here figuratively for his smithy. Vulcan was the Roman god of blacksmiths, and his smithy was thought to be dirtier and blacker than anything on Earth.

76 In censure of his seeming: in judgment of his actions and appearance.

77 If he steal aught : conceals (OED obs.) anything.

78 pay the theft.: Doubting that the king will be able to conceal his reaction and escape detection, Horatio says that if he is wrong he will make recompense for the king's withholding of valuable information, likely an allusion to the crime of theft of services.

Horatio
Here, sweet lord, at your service.
Hamlet
Horatio, thou art even as just a man
As ever my conversation coped withal.
Horatio
O my dear lord —
Hamlet
Nay, do not think I flatter, 45
For what advancement may I hope from thee
That no revenue hast but thy good spirits
To feed and clothe thee? Why should the poor be flattered?
No, let the candied tongue lick absurd pomp,
And crook the pregnant hinges of the knee 50
Where thrift may follow fawning. Dost thou hear?
Since my dear soul was mistress of her choice
And could of men distinguish, her election
She hath sealed thee for herself, for thou hast been
As one in suffering all that suffers nothing, 55
A man that Fortune's buffets and rewards
Hast taken with equal thanks; and blest are those
Whose blood and judgment are so well co-meddled,
That they are not a pipe for Fortune's finger
To sound what stop she please. Give me that man 60
That is not passion's slave, and I will wear him
In my heart's core, ay, in my heart of heart,
As I do thee. Something too much of this.
There is a play tonight before the king,
One scene of it comes near the circumstance 65
Which I have told thee of my father's death.
I prithee, when thou seest that act afoot,
Even with the very comment of thy soul
Observe my uncle. If his occulted guilt
Do not itself unkennel in one speech, 70
It is a damned ghost that we have seen,
And my imaginations are as foul
As Vulcan's stithy. Give him heedful note,
For I mine eyes will rivet to his face,
And after we will both our judgments join 75
In censure of his seeming.
Horatio
Well, my lord.
If he steal aught the whilst this play is playing,
And scape detecting, I will pay the theft.

79 idle: not only unoccupied and not appearing to conspire with Horatio but also seeming foolish and incoherent ("idle" OED obs.), by putting on his antic disposition.

83 the chameleon's dish: The chameleon was believed to live on air. **promise-crammed:** filled with promises of air, perhaps alluding to the king's promise that Hamlet would be his heir.

84 capons: castrated roosters that are fattened for the table.

87 nor mine now: because they have been uttered and are in the air.

89 university: In the sixteenth century university students often performed plays. Oxford would have seen and perhaps participated in plays during his time at Cambridge and at Gray's Inn law school. No record links Shakspere to university study or to the study of law.

92 calf: a dolt, sometimes meek and inoffensive; also a term of endearment, per the OED.

97 here's metal more attractive: something more alluring, alluding to magnetism and perhaps a topical allusion to Robert Norman's *The Newe Attractive* (1581) describing his experiments with magnetism, the first systematic study of the phenomenon, which was not widely known, almost certainly not by commoners like Shakspere.

99 lie in your lap: an ambiguous line with sexual overtones (OED), which Ophelia rejects.

Enter Trumpets and Kettle-drums, King, Queen, Polonius, Ophelia, Rosencrantz, Guildenstern [and others with guards carrying torches]

Hamlet

They are coming to the play. I must be idle;
[To Horatio] Get you a place. 80

King

How fares our cousin Hamlet?

Hamlet

Excellent, in faith.
Of the chameleon's dish I eat the air, promise-crammed;
You cannot feed capons so.

King

I have nothing with this answer, Hamlet. 85
These words are not mine.

Hamlet

No, nor mine now. *[To Polonius].*My lord,
You played once in the university, you say?

Polonius

That did I, my lord, and was accounted a good actor.

Hamlet

What did you enact? 90

Polonius

I did enact Julius Caesar. I was killed in the Capitol;
Brutus killed me.

Hamlet

It was a brute part of him to kill so capital a calf there.
Be the players ready?

Rosencrantz

Ay, my lord, they stay upon your patience. 95

Queen

Come hither, my dear Hamlet, sit by me.

Hamlet

No, good mother, here's metal more attractive.

Polonius

[Aside to the king] O ho, do you mark that?

Hamlet

Lady, shall I lie in your lap?

Ophelia

No, my lord. 100

Hamlet

I mean, my head upon your lap?

Ophelia

Ay, my lord.

101 country matters: sexual intercourse with rural wenches; with an obscene pun on the first syllable of "country."

107 nothing: continuing the sexual puns, no-thing meaning without a penis, and the numeral "0" for nothing, suggesting the vagina.

111 jig-maker: a clown who performed a farcical song and danced a jig at the end of a play's performance. In this satirical passage, Hamlet has put on his manic disposition and recalls how his mother has forgotten the recent death of her husband, as did Oxford's mother, in his view.

115 suit of sables: expensive mourning clothes made of dark brown or black furs of the sable.

117-18 by Our Lady: by the Virgin Mary, a mild oath,

118 build churches: where a "great man" (line 117) could be memorialized.

119-20 "For O, for O, the hobbyhorse is forgot.": the refrain of a ballad, which for some long lost reason refers to someone or something forgotten. The hobbyhorse in the traditional Morris dances of the May games was a costume depicting the front part of a horse that was fastened at the waist.

S.d.: Dumb- show follows: The actors silently foreshadow the plot of the play-within-the-play, miming the action of the plot without dialogue. Commentators on *Hamlet* debate why King Claudius does not seem to grasp the meaning of it for him, which Hamlet has intended for the play-within-the-play to do in order to catch the conscience of the king. The best explanation is probably that the King, Queen and Polonius are talking to each other (perhaps about Hamlet's wild words) and ignoring the silent dumb-show while awaiting the real show to begin—royal behavior that might well have occurred in Queen Elizabeth's court and that Oxford would have seen. (See Wilson *What Happens*.)

123 *declines*: leans.

125 *his crown*: the sleeping king's crown.

127 *makes passionate action*: emotionally expresses love and sorrow.

128 *mutes*: silent actors.

Hamlet
Do you think I meant country matters?
Ophelia
I think nothing my lord.
Hamlet
That's a fair thought to lie between maids' legs. 105
Ophelia
What is, my lord?
Hamlet
Nothing.
Ophelia
You are merry, my lord.
Hamlet
Who, I?
Ophelia
Ay, my lord. 110
Hamlet
O God, your only jig-maker. What should a man do but be merry, for look you how cheerfully my mother looks, and my father died within two hours.
Ophelia
Nay, 'tis twice two months, my lord.
Hamlet
So long? Nay then let the devil wear black, for I'll have a suit of 115
sables. O heavens, die two months ago, and not forgotten yet? Then there's hope a great man's memory may outlive his life half a year, but, by Our Lady, he must build churches then, or else shall he suffer not thinking on, with the hobbyhorse, whose epitaph is, "For O, for O, the hobby-horse is forgot." 120

The trumpets sound. Dumb-show follows

Enter a King and a Queen very lovingly, the Queen embracing him and he her. She kneels and makes show of protestation unto him. He takes her up and declines his head upon her neck. He lies him down upon a bank of flowers. She, seeing him asleep, leaves him. Anon come in another man, takes off his crown, 125
kisses it, pours poison in the sleeper's ears, and leaves him. The Queen returns, finds the King dead, makes passionate action. The poisoner with some three or four mutes come in again, seem to condole with her. The dead body is carried away. The poisoner woos the Queen with gifts; she seems harsh and 130
unwilling awhile, but in the end accepts love.

Exeunt

132 miching malicho: a surreptitious ("miching" OED obs.) misdeed ("malicho.) The word "malicho" is probably from the Spanish "malhecho," wrongdoing or misdeed, per the OED; here troublemaking through disobedience. The OED editors found no evidence of its use in English except in *Hamlet*. The Spanish "malhecho" is not a word that Will Shakspere would have known, but Oxford was an accomplished linguist in several languages.

135 keep counsel: keep a secret. (OED obs.)

138 any show . . . show him: implying that what she might show him would be something intimate or sexual.

140 naught: immoral, indecent. (OED obs.)

144 posy: a short motto or verse, often engraved inside a finger ring.

147 *Phoebus' cart*: Apollo's chariot, the Sun. The players' language in the play-within-the-play, which differs markedly from that of the play proper, imitates (parodies?) an ornate, grandiose, and outdated style of writing.

148 *Neptune's . . . ground,*: the sea and Earth. Neptune was the god of the sea; ***Tellus***, goddess of the Earth.

151 *Hymen*: the Greek and Roman god of marriage.

152 *commutual*: reciprocal.

157 *I distrust you*: I'm apprehensive, fearful for you. (OED obs.)

Ophelia
What means this, my lord?
Hamlet
Marry, this is miching malicho, it means mischief.
Ophelia
Belike this show imports the argument of the play.
Enter Prologue
Hamlet
We shall know by this fellow. The players cannot keep counsel, 135
they'll tell all.
Ophelia
Will he tell us what this show meant?
Hamlet
Ay, or any show that you will show him. Be not you ashamed to show,
he'll not shame to tell you what it means.
Ophelia
You are naught, you are naught. I'll mark the play. 140
Prologue
For us, and for our tragedy,
Here stooping to your clemency,
We beg your hearing patiently. *Exit*
Hamlet
Is this a prologue, or the posy of a ring?
Ophelia
'Tis brief, my lord. 145
Hamlet
As woman's love.
Enter [Player] King and Queen.
Player King
Full thirty times hath Phoebus' cart gone round
Neptune's salt wash and Tellus' orbed ground,
And thirty dozen moons with borrowed sheen
About the world have times twelve thirties been, 150
Since love our hearts and Hymen did our hands
Unite commutual in most sacred bands.
Player Queen
So many journeys may the sun and moon
Make us again count over ere love be done!
But woe is me, you are so sick of late, 155
So far from cheer and from your former state,
That I distrust you. Yet though I distrust,
Discomfort you, my lord, it nothing must,
For women fear too much, even as they love,

160 *hold quantity,*: are in proportion.

161 *In neither aught, or in extremity*: either both are totally absent or both are fully present.

167 *operant powers*: probably, vital faculties. ***leave to do*:** cease to function.

172 *In second husband . . . accursed!*: If I should marry again, let my second husband be a curse on me. Gertrude's marriage to a second husband, Claudius, put a curse on her. And in the next line, Hamlet will react with bitterness, probably reflecting Oxford's bitter memory of his mother's marriage to a second husband, a man far below her status as the Countess of Oxford.

174 wormwood! an herbal purgative imported from the Middle East and noted for its bitter taste. It was typically taken to destroy and expel worms from the intestines, perhaps alluding to Hamlet's plan to have this play-within-the-play cause Queen Gertrude to purge herself of her incestuous sin (worms in her gut) of marrying her late husband's brother, in addition to causing a purgation of King Claudius's "worms," exposing his guilt of murdering his brother. A bitter medicine for both of them.

175 *instances . . . move*: motives that lead to a second marriage.

185-6 *Most necessary . . . debt*: It's inevitably human ("*Most necessary*") to forget what we promise ourselves.

190 *enactures*: fulfillments, expressions. (OED obs)

192 *on slender accident*: at the slightest chance.

193 *aye*: always. (OED obs.)

For women's fear and love hold quantity, 160
In neither aught, or in extremity.
Now what my love is, proof hath made you know,
And as my love is sized, my fear is so.
Where love is great, the littlest doubts are fear;
Where little fears grow great, great love grows there. 165

Player King
Faith, I must leave thee, love, and shortly too;
My operant powers their functions leave to do,
And thou shalt live in this fair world behind,
Honored, beloved, and haply, one as kind
For husband shalt thou —

Player Queen
O, confound the rest! 170
Such love must needs be treason in my breast.
In second husband let me be accursed!
None wed the second but who killed the first.

Hamlet
[Aside] That's wormwood!

Player Queen
The instances that second marriage move 175
Are base respects of thrift, but none of love.
A second time I kill my husband dead,
When second husband kisses me in bed.

Player King
I do believe you think what now you speak,
But what we do determine, oft we break. 180
Purpose is but the slave to memory,
Of violent birth, but poor validity,
Which now, the fruit unripe, sticks on the tree,
But fall unshaken when they mellow be.
Most necessary 'tis that we forget 185
To pay ourselves what to ourselves is debt.
What to ourselves in passion we propose,
The passion ending, doth the purpose lose.
The violence of either grief or joy
Their own enactures with themselves destroy. 190
Where joy most revels, grief doth most lament;
Grief joys, joy grieves, on slender accident.
This world is not for aye, nor 'tis not strange
That even our loves should with our fortunes change
For 'tis a question left us yet to prove, 195
Whether love lead fortune, or else fortune love.

197-8 *The great man . . . enemies*: If a great man falls, watch his chosen favorites abandon him to make friends with his enemies.

201 *try*: put to a test.

202 *seasons him*: matures him, hardens him.

206 *ends*: consequences.

212 *anchor's cheer*: An anchorite was a religious hermit who lived in a cell attached to a Roman Catholic church in the Middle Ages. "Cheer" was food and provisions, per the OED; thus his or her way of living.

213 *blanks*: turns pale, blanches.

215 *here and hence*: in this life and after.

217 break it: break her vow never to remarry.

226 they do but jest: tell an idle tale (OED obs.) **Poison**: something unfit for its purpose, per the OED; here, sardonically a play unfit for a court entertainment. Four lines later Hamlet will call it "knavish," that is, roguish, rascally, mischievous. (OED obs.)

228 "The Mousetrap": Hamlet impulsively makes up a new name for the play he had called "The Murder of Gonzago," which he asked the visiting players to perform. **How tropically!:** that is, how metaphorically (from "trope"); perhaps with a pun on "topically," that is, pertinent to what's happening in real life, or "trapically," word play on the mousetrap in the title. Or all three.

The great man down, you mark his favorite flies,
The poor advanced makes friends of enemies.
And hitherto doth love on fortune tend,
For who not needs shall never lack a friend, 200
And who in want a hollow friend doth try,
Directly seasons him his enemy.
But orderly to end where I begun,
Our wills and fates do so contrary run
That our devices still are overthrown, 205
Our thoughts are ours, their ends none of our own
So think thou wilt no second husband wed,
But die thy thoughts when thy first lord is dead.

Player Queen
Nor earth to me give food, nor heaven light,
Sport and repose lock from me day and night, 210
To desperation turn my trust and hope,
An anchor's cheer in prison be my scope.
Each opposite that blanks the face of joy
Meet what I would have well and it destroy.
Both here and hence pursue me lasting strife, 215
If once I be a widow, ever I be a wife.

Hamlet
If she should break it now.

Player King
'Tis deeply sworn. Sweet, leave me here a while,
My spirits grow dull, and fain I would beguile
The tedious day with sleep.

Player Queen
And never come mischance between us twain. *Exit*

Hamlet
Madam, how like you this play?

Queen
The lady doth protest too much, methinks.

Hamlet
O, but she'll keep her word.

King
Have you heard the argument? Is there no offence in it? 225

Hamlet
No, no, they do but jest, poison in jest — no offence in the world.

King
What do you call the play?

Hamlet
"The Mousetrap." Marry, how tropically! This play is the image of a murder

231 free souls: innocent souls, free of sin, here sarcastically.

231-2 Let the galled jade wince. . .unwrung: Let the saddle-sore horse ("galled jade") wince from the pain. **withers**: the highest part of a horse's back, between the shoulder blades. **Unwrung**: not pinched or twisted, hence not affected. A multi-metaphor from horsemanship, which would come naturally to Oxford, who was expert in it.

233 nephew to the king.: Although it was King Hamlet's brother, Claudius, who assassinated him, Hamlet identifies the assassin Lucianus as the Player King's nephew, and Hamlet of course is King Claudius's nephew; no doubt a veiled threat to further unnerve him.

237 keen: sharp-tongued; bitterly witty is the meaning Ophelia no doubt intends, but. Hamlet in his antic disposition will take it to mean sexually ready.

238 groaning to take off mine edge: take the edge off my sexual desire in the "groaning" of making love.

239 better, and worse: wittier, but also more offensive.

240 So you mis-take: probably, you may take your husbands for better or for "worse" but are mistaken because they turn out worse.

248 for his estate.: not for his crown but for his property and wealth ("estate"), just as the Earl of Leicester contrived to profit financially by the unexpected death of Oxford's father but not to seize the earldom. **His name's Gonzago**: A source for the murder of King Hamlet by his brother and also for the murder of the Player King "Gonzago" by his "nephew" was the murder of the Duke of Urbino in Italy in 1538. Urbino, a powerful nobleman of high rank, reportedly died after a relative poured poison in his ear while he was sleeping in his garden. When Oxford was in Italy, he would have heard about the murder of a fellow nobleman. (See LNs 1.2.201, 2.2.468.)

249 extant . . . choice Italian: But no such play has been found.

252 Frighted with false fire?: referring to the flickering flames of marsh gas called "false fire," thought to frighten and mislead travelers at night.

254 Away!: King Claudius realizes that Hamlet suspects that the king killed his father with poison. He flees the scene and the court follows.

done in Vienna; Gonzago is the duke's name, his wife, Baptista. You shall
see anon. 'Tis a knavish piece of work, but what of that? 230
Your majesty and we that have free souls, it touches us not. Let the
galled jade wince, our withers are unwrung.

Enter Lucianus

This is one Lucianus, nephew to the king.

Ophelia

You are as good as a chorus, my lord.

Hamlet

I could interpret between you and your love, 235
If I could see the puppets dallying.

Ophelia

You are keen, my lord, you are keen.

Hamlet

It would cost you a groaning to take off mine edge.

Ophelia

Still better, and worse.

Hamlet

So you mis-take your husbands. Begin, murderer, leave thy damnable 240
faces and begin. Come, the croaking raven doth bellow for revenge.

Lucianus

Thoughts black, hands apt, drugs fit, and time agreeing,
Confederate season, else no creature seeing,
Thou mixture rank, of midnight weeds collected,
With Hecate's ban thrice blasted, thrice infected, 245
Thy natural magic and dire property
On wholesome life usurps immediately. *Pours a potion in his ear*

Hamlet

He poisons him in the garden for his estate. His name's Gonzago, the
story is extant, and written in very choice Italian. You shall see anon
how the murderer gets the love of Gonzago's wife. 250

Ophelia

The king rises.

Hamlet

What? Frighted with false fire?

Queen

How fares my lord?

Polonius

Give over the play.

King

Give me some light! Away! 255

257-60 Why . . . away: probably lines from a lost ballad.

261 forest of feathers: typically a decoration of an actor's hat. From here to the end of the scene, Hamlet appears to be genuinely manic.

261-2 my fortunes turn Turk with me: if my good fortune and wealth desert me, as might happen to a Christian turning to Islam and becoming a Turkish Moslem; probably also an inside joke for a Elizabethan court audience. Queen Elizabeth, who may have called Oxford her "Turk," colluded with Leicester to misappropriate much of Oxford's fortune.

262 roses . . . razed shoes: rosettes covering the laces of shoes vented with slashes ("razed"), both referring to shoes of aristocrats.

263 cry: contemptuously for an acting company. A "cry" in the aristocratic sport of hunting was the pack of dogs, called a "cry" from their yelping.

266 Damon: Addressing Horatio, Hamlet alludes to the celebrated male friendship of Damon and Pythias in Greek legend.

268 Of Jove himself: King Hamlet.

269 paiock: an obscure, much debated word that is Oxford's creation and may combine "peacock", figuratively a vainglorious, showy person (OED), with "patchcock", a contemptible person (OED obs), here both describing King Claudius. (The expected rhyme might be "ass.") See the OED definitions and Jenkins' Longer Note.

277 comedy: probably ironically, for a play that is a tragedy but happily has served its purpose for him.

278 belike: to all appearances (per the OED). **perdy:** a mild oath from Old French "par dieu," by God; hence assuredly.

Polonius
Lights, lights, lights!

Exeunt all but Hamlet and Horatio

Hamlet
"Why, let the strucken deer go weep,
The hart ungalled play,
For some must watch while some must sleep,
Thus runs the world away." 260
Would not this, sir, and a forest of feathers--if the rest of my fortunes turn Turk with me--with two Provincial roses on my razed shoes, get me a fellowship in a cry of players?

Horatio
Half a share.

Hamlet
A whole one, I. 265
"For thou dost know, O Damon dear,
This realm dismantled was
Of Jove himself, and now reigns here
A very, very" – paiock!

Horatio
You might have rhymed. 270

Hamlet
O good Horatio, I'll take the ghost's word for a thousand pound.
Didst perceive?

Horatio
Very well, my lord.

Hamlet
Upon the talk of the poisoning?

Horatio
I did very well note him. 275

Hamlet
Ah, ha! Come, some music! Come, the recorders.
For if the king like not the comedy,
Why then belike he likes it not, perdy.
Come, some music.

Enter Rosencrantz and Guildenstern

Guildenstern
Good my lord, vouchsafe a word with you. 280

Hamlet
Sir, a whole history.

Guildenstern
The king, sir —

284 retirement: withdrawal. **marvelous distempered**: very upset; but Hamlet, continuing to bait Guildenstern, will pretend to take the word to mean inebriated "with drink" ("distempered" OED obs.)

286 choler: anger, but Hamlet will choose to understand it as dysfunction of his liver that has too much bile.

287 more richer: far more beneficial.

288 his purgation: probably a triple meaning: purging his liver of excess bile, purging his soul of its sin of murder and purging him from his royal position in Denmark.

290 some frame: shape; some coherent form. **start not**: not jump suddenly, escaping to another subject; probably from hunting, when the hounds "start" their quarry from its lair.

296 not of the right breed: not the right kind, but also not according to courtly breeding in manners.

297 wholesome: sensible.

306 admiration: surprised astonishment. (OED archaic)

308 admiration?: here probably in the sense of admiring.

Hamlet
Ay, sir, what of him?
Guildenstern
Is in his retirement marvelous distempered.
Hamlet
With drink, sir? 285
Guildenstern
No, my lord, with choler.
Hamlet
Your wisdom should show itself more richer to signify this to the doctor, for, for me to put him to his purgation would perhaps plunge him into more choler.
Guildenstern
Good my lord, put your discourse into some frame, and start not so 290 wildly from my affair.
Hamlet
I am tame, sir. Pronounce.
Guildenstern
The queen, your mother, in most great affliction of spirit, hath sent me to you.
Hamlet
You are welcome. 295
Guildenstern
Nay, good my lord, this courtesy is not of the right breed. If it shall please you to make me a wholesome answer, I will do your mother's commandment; if not, your pardon and my return shall be the end of my business.

Hamlet
Sir, I cannot. 300
Rosencrantz
What, my lord?
Hamlet
Make you a wholesome answer — my wit's diseased. But, sir, such answer as I can make, you shall command, or rather, as you say, my mother. Therefore no more, but to the matter my mother, you say —
Rosencrantz
Then thus she says your behavior hath struck her into amazement and 305 admiration.
Hamlet
O wonderful son, that can so astonish a mother! But is there no sequel at the heels of this mother's admiration? Impart.

310 closet: private chamber, usually adjoining or near a bedroom.

311 trade: business, but with overtones of contempt.

314 these pickers and stealers: his hands, from the catechism in *The Book of Common Prayer*: "To keep my hands from picking and stealing."

317 I lack advancement: to be king, as the rightful, natural heir to the throne by birth; Hamlet is suddenly forthright.

318 How can that be: Rosencrantz does not understand or more likely feigns not to understand what Hamlet has said.

321 proverb . . . musty: too stale and not even worth finishing. The proverb was "While the grass grows, the horse starves." Perhaps alluding to Claudius flourishing while Hamlet hungers for advancement.

321 withdraw: probably asking Guildenstern to step aside with him.

322 why do you . . . recover the wind of me: trap me by deceit; from hunting, to get downwind ("recover the wind" OED obs.) of me as would a hunter to trick his quarry into scenting him and running the other way into the trap the hunter has set.

323 toil: a net enclosure or snare to trap wild animal. (OED obs.)

324 if my duty . . . unmannerly: If I have offended by my boldness, my concern for you is the cause.

325 pipe: a wind instrument, such as a recorder

Rosencrantz

She desires to speak with you in her closet ere you go to bed. 310

Hamlet

We shall obey, were she ten times our mother. Have you any further trade with us?

Rosencrantz

My lord, you once did love me.

Hamlet

And do still, by these pickers and stealers.

Rosencrantz

Good my lord, what is your cause of distemper? You do surely bar the 315
door upon your own liberty if you deny your griefs to your friend.

Hamlet

Sir, I lack advancement.

Rosencrantz

How can that be, when you have the voice of the king himself for your succession in Denmark?

Enter the Players with recorders

Hamlet

Ay, sir, but "While the grass grows" — The proverb is something 320
musty. O, the recorders! Let me see one. To withdraw with you, why do you go about to recover the wind of me, as if you would drive me into a toil?

Guildenstern

O my lord, if my duty be too bold, my love is too unmannerly.

Hamlet

I do not well understand that. Will you play upon this pipe? 325

Guildenstern

My lord, I cannot.

Hamlet

I pray you.

Guildenstern

Believe me, I cannot.

Hamlet

I pray you.

Guildenstern

Believe me, I cannot. 330

Hamlet

I do beseech you.

Guildenstern

I know no touch of it, my lord.

333 as easy as lying.: implying that Guildenstern is a liar. **ventages:** the finger holes of a wind instrument, such as a recorder.

340 sound me: play on me to examine me with indirect questions to "sound me" out; with a goal of understanding me. (OED obs.)

341 compass: the full range of musical tones an instrument can produce.

342 organ: recorder, with a pun on vocal chords, an organ of speech.

344 fret me: irritate me, with a pun on the frets, the ridges on stringed instruments to mark fingering. These music metaphors came easily to Oxford from his training in music, which was part of an aristocrat's education but not that of a commoner, like Shakspere.

346 presently: immediately.

348 By the mass: a mild oath alluding to the Catholic Church service, the Mass.

350 backed like a weasel: shaped like a weasel, with its rounded back.

354 fool me to the top of my bent: that is, fool with me, accepting my antic fooling even if I take it to my limit (my "bent" from archery, the limit to which a bow can be bent. (OED archaic).

Hamlet
It is as easy as lying. Govern these ventages with your fingers and thumbs, give it breath with your mouth, and it will discourse most eloquent music. Look you, these are the stops 335
Guildenstern
But these cannot I command to any utterance of harmony. I have not the skill.
Hamlet
Why, look you now, how unworthy a thing you make of me. You would play upon me, you would seem to know my stops, you would pluck out the heart of my mystery, you would sound me from my 340
lowest note to the top of my compass; and there is much music, excellent voice, in this little organ, yet cannot you make it speak. 'Sblood, do you think I am easier to be played on than a pipe? Call me what instrument you will, though you fret me, yet you cannot play upon me.

Enter Polonius

God bless you, sir. 345
Polonius
My lord, the queen would speak with you, and presently.
Hamlet
Do you see yonder cloud that's almost in shape of a camel?
Polonius
By the mass and 'tis like a camel indeed.
Hamlet
Methinks it is like a weasel.
Polonius
It is backed like a weasel. 350

Hamlet
Or like a whale.
Polonius
Very like a whale.
Hamlet
Then I will come to my mother by and by.
[Aside] They fool me to the top of my bent.--
I will come by and by. 355
Polonius
I will say so. *Exit Polonius*
Hamlet
"By and by" is easily said. Leave me, friends.
Exeunt all but Hamlet
'Tis now the very witching time of night,

362 Soft,: (to himself) quiet, be calm. (OED rare)

363 nature: natural feeling (of a son's love for his mother).

364 Nero: the Roman emperor who had his mother executed for the alleged murder by poison of his stepbrother. Nero had been adopted by his great-uncle the emperor Claudius, who named him his heir after he married Nero's mother Agrippina. Nero was notorious for the corruption and cruelty during his rule.

365 cruel: here, severe, strict (OED obs.), not to inflict suffering.

368 somever she be shent: however much ("somever" OED obs.) she be reproved ("shent" OED archaic).

368-9 my words . . . seals never: probably an allusion to the Great Seal of England, which authenticated and ratified legal decrees that required taking some action, per the OED. With his legal training, Oxford would have been familiar with the term.

1 nor stands it safe with us: nor is the state (the royal "us") safe; and for the audience, which knows of Hamlet's intentions, "nor is it safe for me."

5 terms of our estate: his position as king.

8 holy . . . fear: the king's judicious caution.

11 peculiar life: one's own particular life.

13 noyance: harm, distress.

15 cess of majesty: death (OED obs.) of the king.

16 gulf: here, a profound depth or whirlpool that swallows or devours everything in it (chiefly poetic per the OED). Rosencrantz, like Guildenstern before him, launches into an obsequious, but foolish, attempt to please the king with an elaborate metaphor about the consequences of his death, which the king must have found offensive but ignores. Probably a parody of courtiers' flattering that Oxford would have seen in Queen Elizabeth's court and found ridiculous; in this play drawing chuckles from a court audience.

17 it is a massy wheel . . . summit: a massive wheel (of Fortune) with the monarchy at the top ("summit"); unsaid is that when the wheel turns, as it inevitably does, his monarchy will be at the bottom.

23 general groan: by the people of his kingdom.

When churchyards yawn and hell itself breathes out
Contagion to this world. Now could I drink hot blood, 360
And do such bitter business as the day
Would quake to look on. Soft, now to my mother.
O heart, lose not thy nature. Let not ever
The soul of Nero enter this firm bosom,
Let me be cruel, not unnatural; 365
I will speak daggers to her, but use none.
My tongue and soul in this be hypocrites—
How in my words somever she be shent,
To give them seals never my soul consent! *Exit Hamlet*

Scene 3.

Enter King, Rosencrantz, and Guildenstern

King
I like him not, nor stands it safe with us
To let his madness range. Therefore prepare you.
I your commission will forthwith dispatch,
And he to England shall along with you.
The terms of our estate may not endure 5
Hazard so near us as doth hourly grow
Out of his brows.

Guildenstern
We will ourselves provide.
Most holy and religious fear it is
To keep those many many bodies safe
That live and feed upon your Majesty. 10

Rosencrantz
The single and peculiar life is bound
With all the strength and armor of the mind
To keep itself from noyance, but much more
That spirit upon whose weal depends and rests
The lives of many. The cess of majesty 15
Dies not alone, but like a gulf doth draw
What's near it with it. Or it is a massy wheel
Fixed on the summit of the highest mount,
To whose huge spokes ten thousand lesser things
Are mortised and adjoined, which when it falls, 20
Each small annexment, petty consequence,
Attends the boistrous ruin. Never alone
Did the king sigh, but with a general groan.

24 viage: voyage. (OED obs.)

28 Behind . . . convey myself: In this corrupt court, spying is routine. Polonius will conceal himself ("convey," with a connotation of secrecy (OED obs.) behind the wall-hanging, an "arras," to spy on Hamlet and Gertrude as he and the king did earlier to spy on Hamlet and Ophelia.

29 tax him: call him to account, chastise him.

37 primal eldest curse: on Cain for murdering his brother Abel.

47 confront the visage of offence: to confront the sin ("offence") directly in the face ("visage").

48 twofold force: to prevent sin or be forgiven for it.

57 In the corrupted currents of this world: that is, in the generally accepted ("currents") corrupt ways of the world.

58 Offence's gilded hand . . . justice: The offender's hand bearing gold (as well as guilt) may push justice aside with a bribe.

King
Arm you, I pray you, to this speedy viage,
For we will fetters put about this fear, 25
Which now goes too free-footed.
Rosencrantz
We will haste us. *Exeunt Rosencrantz and Guildenstern*
Enter Polonius
Polonius
My lord, he's going to his mother's closet.
Behind the arras I'll convey myself
To hear the process. I'll warrant she'll tax him home,
And as you said, and wisely was it said, 30
'Tis meet that some more audience than a mother,
Since nature makes them partial, should overhear
The speech, of vantage. Fare you well, my liege,
I'll call upon you ere you go to bed,
And tell you what I know. 35
King
Thanks, dear my lord. *Exit Polonius*
O, my offence is rank, it smells to heaven,
It hath the primal eldest curse upon it,
A brother's murder. Pray can I not,
Though inclination be as sharp as will.
My stronger guilt defeats my strong intent, 40
And, like a man to double business bound,
I stand in pause where I shall first begin,
And both neglect. What if this cursed hand
Were thicker than itself with brother's blood,
Is there not rain enough in the sweet heavens 45
To wash it white as snow? Whereto serves mercy
But to confront the visage of offence?
And what's in prayer but this twofold force,
To be forestalled ere we come to fall,
Or pardoned being down? Then I'll look up. 50
My fault is past; but, O, what form of prayer
Can serve my turn? "Forgive me my foul murder"?
That cannot be, since I am still possessed
Of those effects for which I did the murder:
My crown, mine own ambition, and my queen. 55
May one be pardoned and retain the offence?
In the corrupted currents of this world
Offence's gilded hand may shove by justice,
And oft 'tis seen the wicked prize itself

61 There is no shuffling: that is, in heaven "above" ("There") there is no "shuffling" putting aside something in an underhanded way. (OED obs.)

68 limed: caught; from the practice of trapping birds with birdlime, a sticky substance spread on twigs.

63 teeth and forehead: probably, teeth bared in defiance and a forehead wrinkled in hostility.

72 All may be well. : This line may be taken as the king, pausing for further thought, tries to comfort himself that despite his moral anguish everything may turn out all right for him.

73 I do it pat: take the opportunity to strike (him) as I planned (per the OED).

75 scanned: carefully considered, as Hamlet goes on to explain.

79 hire and salary: hiring an assassin for pay.

80 full of bread: not fasting and thus not spiritually ready.

81 broad blown: in full bloom. **flush:** full of life.

86 seasoned: prepared, ready.

87 Up, sword: return to your scabbard.

88 hent: plan, design (OED obs.), hence opportunity.

90 incestuous: In Church doctrine the marriage of a widow and the brother of her deceased husband was considered incest for both.

95 stays: awaits.

96 This physic: this medicine or purgative of prayer.

Buys out the law; but 'tis not so above. 60
There is no shuffling, there the action lies
In his true nature, and we ourselves compelled,
Even to the teeth and forehead of our faults,
To give in evidence. What then? What rests?
Try what repentance can. What can it not? 65
Yet what can it, when one cannot repent?
O wretched state! O bosom black as death!
O limed soul, that struggling to be free
Art more engaged. Help, angels! Make assay,
Bow, stubborn knees, and heart, with strings of steel, 70
Be soft as sinews of the new-born babe!
All may be well.

Enter Hamlet

Hamlet
[Aside] Now might I do it pat, now he is a-praying;
And now I'll do it. *Draws his sword*
And so he goes to heaven,
And so am I revenged. That would be scanned: 75
A villain kills my father, and for that
I, his sole son, do this same villain send
To heaven.
Why, this is hire and salary, not revenge.
He took my father grossly, full of bread, 80
With all his crimes broad blown, as flush as May,
And how his audit stands who knows save heaven?
But in our circumstance and course of thought
'Tis heavy with him. And am I then revenged,
To take him in the purging of his soul, 85
When he is fit and seasoned for his passage?
No!
Up, sword, and know thou a more horrid hent
When he is drunk asleep, or in his rage,
Or in the incestuous pleasure of his bed, 90
At game a-swearing, or about some act
That has no relish of salvation in it —
Then trip him that his heels may kick at heaven,
And that his soul may be as damned and black
As hell, whereto it goes. My mother stays, 95
This physic but prolongs thy sickly days. *Exit Hamlet*

King
My words fly up, my thoughts remain below
Words without thoughts never to heaven go. *Exit the king*

3.4

1 straight: straightaway, immediately. **Lay home to him:** chastise him thoroughly.

2 pranks too broad: disgraceful actions (his antic behavior).

4 I'll silence me even here: I'll hide silently (behind the arras).

5 be round with him.: straightforward, blunt.

10 thy father: Claudius, his stepfather.

11 my father: King Hamlet.

12 with an idle tongue: speaking nonsense. (OED obs.)

16 forgot me?: forgotten who I am?

17 by the rood: by the holy cross on which Christ died. (OED archaic)

20 I'll set . . . speak: I'll get someone who can deal with you. (Gertrude is about to leave.)

22 glass: mirror.

Scene 4. The Queen's room
Enter Queen Gertrude and Polonius

Polonius
He will come straight. Look you lay home to him.
Tell him his pranks have been too broad to bear with,
And that your Grace hath screened and stood between
Much heat and him. I'll silence me even here;
Pray you be round with him. 5

Queen
I'll warrant you, fear me not.
Withdraw, I hear him coming. *Polonius hides behind the arras*

Enter Hamlet

Hamlet
Now, mother, what's the matter?

Queen
Hamlet, thou hast thy father much offended. 10

Hamlet
Mother, you have my father much offended.

Queen
Come, come, you answer with an idle tongue.

Hamlet
Go, go, you question with a wicked tongue.

Queen
Why, how now, Hamlet?

Hamlet
What's the matter now? 15

Queen
Have you forgot me?

Hamlet
No, by the rood, not so
You are the queen, your husband's brother's wife,
And would it were not so, you are my mother.

Queen
Nay then, I'll set those to you that can speak. 20

Hamlet
Come, come, and sit you down, you shall not budge;
You go not till I set you up a glass
Where you may see the inmost part of you.

Queen
What wilt thou do? Thou wilt not murder me?
Help, ho! 25

Polonius
What ho, help!

27 Dead for a ducat, dead!: probably an elated, antic cry that the victim whom he suspects is King Claudius, will be dead quickly and easily and at almost no cost, that is, for only a "ducat," sometimes implying small change, and much less than the cost of a royal assassination by a hired killer.

33 Nay, I know not.: Quickly, Hamlet tries to claim, falsely, that he did not know he was stabbing someone, which would absolve him of murder. His statement reflects his attempt to invoke the new, emerging legal doctrine of common law that gave priority to "intent" when judging the slaying of someone. For centuries, it had been the status of the victim that determined the killer's guilt or innocence, not his "intent." (See Regnier.)

33 As kill . . . brother: Hamlet reveals here his suspicion that his mother was somehow complicit, if only after the fact, with Claudius in his assassination of King Hamlet and its consequences.

34 As kill a king!: Her seemingly shocked reaction, perhaps disingenuous, may (or may not) dispel Hamlet's suspicion of her involvement in King Hamlet's death.

37 thy better: your social superior, the King. **Take thy fortune**: Accept this accidental misfortune. (OED obs.)

38 to be too busy: to be a meddling busybody.

42 damned custom: habitual sin. **brassed it:** hardened, made shameless. (per the OED)

45 Such an act: her adultery with Claudius and marriage with him.

49 blister: the mark of a branding iron supposedly applied to a prostitute's forehead as punishment.

51 body of contraction: the text ("body") of a contract, esp. the marriage contract. (OED obs.)

53 rhapsody: a confused mass. (OED obs.)

54 solidity and compound mass: the solid earth compounded of the four elements.

55 heated: flushed. **as against the doom:** as if anticipating judgment day ("doom").

Hamlet
How now? A rat? Dead for a ducat, dead!
Thrusts his sword through the arras
Polonius.
O, I am slain.
Queen
O me, what hast thou done?
Hamlet
Nay, I know not, is it the king? 30
Queen
O, what a rash and bloody deed is this!
Hamlet
A bloody deed--almost as bad, good mother,
As kill a king, and marry with his brother.
Queen
As kill a king!
Hamlet
Ay, lady, it was my word. 35
[To Polonius] Thou wretched, rash, intruding fool, farewell.
I took thee for thy better. Take thy fortune;
Thou find'st to be too busy is some danger.
[To Gertrude] Leave wringing of your hands. Peace, sit you down,
And let me wring your heart, for so I shall, 40
If it be made of penetrable stuff,
If damned custom have not brassed it so
That it be proof and bulwark against sense.
Queen
What have I done, that thou darest wag thy tongue
In noise so rude against me?
Hamlet
Such an act 45
That blurs the grace and blush of modesty,
Calls virtue hypocrite, takes off the rose
From the fair forehead of an innocent love
And sets a blister there, makes marriage vows
As false as dicers' oaths. O, such a deed 50
As from the body of contraction plucks
The very soul; and sweet religion makes
A rhapsody of words. Heaven's face does glow
Over this solidity and compound mass
With heated visage, as against the doom, 55
Is thought-sick at the act.

58 index: preface, as at the start of a book (OED obs.), here presaging something bad.

59 counterfeit: picture. (OED obs. without meaning fraudulent).

61 front: forehead. (OED poetic)

63 A station: a posture of standing tall. (OED obs.)

69 like a mildewed ear: like an ear of rotten corn.

70 Blasting: blighting, infecting and ruining (per the OED); here perhaps hinting at Claudius' murder of King Hamlet by putting poison in his ear.

72 moor: rank, low-lying, marshy ground; perhaps with word play on "blackamoor."

78 apoplexed: paralyzed.

82 hoodman-blind: blindman's bluff, suggesting that Gertrude was figuratively blindfolded when she agreed to marry Claudius.

86 mope: be unconscious. (OED obs.)

87 Rebellious hell: probably the hell of uncontrolled sexual desire, rebelling against reason.

88 mutine: revolt against. (OED obs) Here, fight against.

92 Since frost . . . burn: perhaps, since intense cold figuratively can also "burn" the flesh.

Queen
Ay me, what act
That roars so loud and thunders in the index?
Hamlet
Look here upon this picture, and on this,
The counterfeit presentment of two brothers.
See what a grace was seated on this brow 60
Hyperion's curls, the front of Jove himself,
An eye like Mars, to threaten and command,
A station like the herald Mercury
New lighted on a heaven-kissing hill;
A combination and a form indeed, 65
Where every god did seem to set his seal
To give the world assurance of a man.
This was your husband. Look you now what follows
Here is your husband, like a mildewed ear,
Blasting his wholesome brother. Have you eyes? 70
Could you on this fair mountain leave to feed,
And batten on this moor? Ha, have you eyes?
You cannot call it love, for at your age
The heyday in the blood is tame, it's humble,
And waits upon the judgment, and what judgment 75
Would step from this to this? Sense sure you have,

Else could you not have motion, but sure that sense
Is apoplexed, for madness would not err,
Nor sense to ecstasy was never so thralled
But it reserved some quantity of choice 80
To serve in such a difference. What devil was it
That thus hath cozened you at hoodman-blind?
Eyes without feeling, feeling without sight,
Ears without hands or eyes, smelling sans all;
Or but a sickly part of one true sense 85
Could not so mope. O shame, where is thy blush?
Rebellious hell,
If thou can'st mutine in a matron's bones,
To flaming youth let virtue be as wax
And melt in her own fire. Proclaim no shame 90
When the compulsive ardor gives the charge,
Since frost itself as actively doth burn,
And reason panders will.

96 grained spots: Facial "spots" were considered the outward signs of inward sins.

97 not leave their tinct: not give up their color or stain ("tinct").

99 enseamed: greasy. (OED obs.)

101 sty.: animal pen, but also a brothel.

107 vice of kings: the worst of kings; and alluding to the villainous clown Vice of the morality plays.

108 A cutpurse . . . the rule: robber of the Danish kingdom.

109 diadem: crown, symbolizing royal authority and dignity.

113-14 Save me . . . guards!: Apparently remembering his uncertainty about whether the Ghost is that of his father or a devil, Hamlet entreats angels ("guards") to protect him.

115 he's mad: The Ghost being invisible and inaudible for Gertrude, she exclaims that Hamlet must be hallucinating.

117 lapsed in time and passion: having allowed over time the eagerness for revenge to fade ("lapsed").

123 Conceit: imagining things. (per the OED)

Queen
O Hamlet, speak no more!
Thou turnest my eyes into my very soul, 95
And there I see such black and grained spots
As will not leave their tinct.
Hamlet
Nay, but to live
In the rank sweat of an enseamed bed,
Stewed in corruption, honeying and making love 100
Over the nasty sty.
Queen
O, speak to me no more!
These words like daggers enter in my ears.
No more, sweet Hamlet!
Hamlet
A murderer and a villain! 105
A slave that is not twentieth part the tithe
Of your precedent lord, a vice of kings,
A cutpurse of the empire and the rule,
That from a shelf the precious diadem stole,
And put it in his pocket. 110
Queen
No more!

Enter Ghost in his night-gown

Hamlet
A king of shreds and patches —
Save me, and hover over me with your wings,
You heavenly guards! What would your gracious figure?
Queen
Alas, he's mad. 115
Hamlet
Do you not come your tardy son to chide,
That, lapsed in time and passion, lets go by
The important acting of your dread command?
O, say.
Ghost
Do not forget. This visitation
Is but to whet thy almost blunted purpose. 120
But look, amazement on thy mother sits,
O, step between her and her fighting soul.
Conceit in weakest bodies strongest works,
Speak to her, Hamlet.

127 vacancy: empty space.

131 excrements: inanimate growths of the body, such as the nails and hair. (OED obs.)

137 stones . . . make them capable: even make stones understand and able to respond. (OED obs.)

138 convert: turn someone from his purpose. (OED obs.)

139 My stern effects: my determined and steadfast ("stern") purpose ("effects" OED obs.) to kill King Claudius.

140 Will want true color . . . perchance for blood.: probably, will lack the correct characteristics of a cold-blooded revenge slaying in the feudal manner, even "perchance" with colorless tears (the "true color"), not an angry, impulsive, red-blooded slaying.

147 habit: clothing, appearance. (OED obs.)

149 coinage: fabrication.

150 creation ecstasy . . . cunning in.: that is, this frenzy of passion (his apparent "ecstasy" or "madness") is very "cunning in" creating this kind of hallucination; ironic since Hamlet is "cunning" when he puts on his antic disposition.

156 re-word: in this context, repeat.

157 gambol from: leap spiritedly away from.

Hamlet
How is it with you, lady? 125
Queen
Alas, how is it with you,
That you do bend your eye on vacancy,
And with the incorporal air do hold discourse?
Forth at your eyes your spirits wildly peep,
And as the sleeping soldiers in the alarm, 130
Your bedded hair, like life in excrements,
Start up and stand an end. O gentle son,
Upon the heat and flame of thy distemper
Sprinkle cool patience. Whereon do you look?
Hamlet
On him, on him! Look you how pale he glares, 135
His form and cause conjoined, preaching to stones
Would make them capable. *[to the Ghost]* Do not look upon me,
Lest with this piteous action you convert
My stern effects, then what I have to do
Will want true color, tears perchance for blood. 140
Queen
To whom do you speak this?
Hamlet
Do you see nothing there?
Queen
Nothing at all, yet all that is, I see.
Hamlet
Nor did you nothing hear?
Queen
No, nothing but ourselves. 145
Hamlet
Why, look you there, look how it steals away.
My father, in his habit as he lived.
Look where he goes, even now, out at the portal. *Exit Ghost*
Queen
This is the very coinage of your brain,
This bodiless creation ecstasy 150
Is very cunning in.
Hamlet
Ecstasy? My pulse as yours doth temperately keep time,
And makes as healthful music. It is not madness
That I have uttered. Bring me to the test, 155
And I the matter will re-word, which madness
Would gambol from. Mother, for love of grace,

158 unction: ointment that soothes but not does not heal.

160 skin and film: cover over as with skin or a thin film.

166 pursy: short-winded because so fat**.**

168 curb: bend and bow. (OED obs.)

174 custom . . . doth eat: habit devours good "sense."

175 habits devil: devilish habits.

184 to be blest: to be confessed and forgiven.

185 this same lord: Polonius.

188 scourge and minister: instrument of punishment.

189 bestow him: dispose (OED archaic) of Polonius's body.

195 Not this . . . I bid you do.: that is, don't do this that I'm about to tell you to do.

Lay not that flattering unction to your soul,
That not your trespass but my madness speaks;
It will but skin and film the ulcerous place, 160
Whiles rank corruption, mining all within,
Infects unseen. Confess yourself to heaven,
Repent what's past, avoid what is to come;
And do not spread the compost on the weeds
To make them ranker. Forgive me this my virtue, 165
For in the fatness of these pursy times
Virtue itself of vice must pardon beg,
Yea, curb and woo for leave to do him good.

Queen

O Hamlet, thou hast cleft my heart in twain.

Hamlet

O, throw away the worser part of it, 170
And live the purer with the other half.
Good night, but go not to my uncle's bed.
Assume a virtue, if you have it not.
That monster custom, who all sense doth eat,
Of habits devil, is angel yet in this, 175
That to the use of actions fair and good
He likewise gives a frock or livery
That aptly is put on. Refrain tonight,
And that shall lend a kind of easiness
To the next abstinence, the next more easy; 180
For use almost can change the stamp of nature,
And either admit the devil or throw him out
With wondrous potency. Once more good night,
And when you are desirous to be blest,
I'll blessing beg of you. For this same lord, 185
I do repent; but heaven hath pleased it so
To punish me with this, and this with me,
That I must be their scourge and minister.
I will bestow him, and will answer well
The death I gave him. So again good night. 190
I must be cruel only to be kind.
This bad begins and worse remains behind.
One word more, good lady.

Queen

What shall I do?

Hamlet

Not this, by no means, that I bid you do. 195

196-210 Let the bloat king . . . . break your own neck down.: In this speech Hamlet is bitterly and elaborately sarcastic, appearing to tell her to reveal to Claudius that he is feigning madness ("mad in craft"), while in fact advising her to do the opposite and not reveal it, adding that to reveal it would hurt her ("break your own neck").

198 reechy: filthy. (OED obs.)

200 ravel . . . out: disclose, unravel, disentangle and make clear, per the OED.

204 paddock: a toad. (OED obs.) **gib**: a tomcat. (OED obs), alluding to King Claudius, as does "bat," a mouse-like (or rat-like) creature that shuns daylight.

205 Who would do so?: sarcastically, with the implied answer, "anyone would."

207-210 Unpeg . . . . neck down: metaphorically, reveal what he has just told her ("Let the birds fly"). The rest of the metaphor about the ape (Gertrude!) hoping also to fly but breaking its neck may seem vulgar and contrary to Hamlet's intentions, but it probably reflects his sudden realization, and blurting it out, that if she does reveal what he told her, she will be hurt ("break your own neck").

212 no life to breathe: Understanding the real meaning behind her son's wild sarcasm, Gertrude says she will not "breathe" a "word(s)" of what he has told her.

220 marshal me to knavery: lead me to some dishonest trickery.

221-2 the enginer hoist with his own petard: the soldier-engineer ("enginer" OED obs.) who builds an explosive device ("petard" OED rare) and is blown up ("hoist") by his own device; from the French "petard," an explosive device used to penetrate walls and fortifications. The image suggests Oxford's familiarity with both the military and the French language. No evidence suggests such familiarity by Will Shakspere.

225 Two crafts directly meet: deceit and counter-deceit collide.

223 their mines: their explosive devices.

226 This man shall set me packing: that is, Polonius in dying sends me off to stash his corpse somewhere.

Let the bloat king tempt you again to bed,
Pinch wanton on your cheek, call you his mouse,
And let him, for a pair of reechy kisses,
Or paddling in your neck with his damned fingers,
Make you to ravel all this matter out, 200
That I essentially am not in madness,
But mad in craft. 'Twere good you let him know,
For who that's but a queen, fair, sober, wise,
Would from a paddock, from a bat, a gib,
Such dear concernings hide? Who would do so? 205
No, in despite of sense and secrecy,
Unpeg the basket on the house's top,
Let the birds fly, and like the famous ape,
To try conclusions in the basket creep,
And break your own neck down. 210

Queen

Be thou assured, if words be made of breath,
And breath of life, I have no life to breathe
What thou hast said to me.

Hamlet

I must to England, you know that?

Queen

Alack, I had forgot. 215
'Tis so concluded on.

Hamlet

There's letters sealed, and my two schoolfellows,
Whom I will trust as I will adders fanged,
They bear the mandate, they must sweep my way
And marshal me to knavery. Let it work, 220
For 'tis the sport to have the enginer
Hoist with his own petard, and it shall go hard
But I will delve one yard below their mines,
And blow them at the moon. O, 'tis most sweet
When in one line two crafts directly meet. 225
This man shall set me packing;
I'll lug the guts into the neighbor room.
Mother, good night indeed. This counsellor
Is now most still, most secret, and most grave,
Who was in life a foolish prating knave. 230
Come, sir, to draw toward an end with you.
Good night, mother.

Exit Hamlet dragging Polonius

4 Bestow: Leave. (OED archaic)

7-12 Mad as the sea and wind . . . . good old man: As she promised Hamlet but thereby being drawn further into the corruption of King Claudius's court, Gertrude lies to the King, describing Hamlet when he killed Polonius as "mad" and in an uncontrollable "lawless fit"(and thus innocent of any crime). The nautical simile of Hamlet being as "mad" as an unusually rough sea when the wind blows hard in one direction and a strong tide is running in the opposite direction would come naturally to someone who had been to sea, as had Oxford but not Shakspere.

11 brainish: headstrong. (OED obs.)

12 heavy: serious, profoundly significant.

13 us: me, the royal "we."

17 providence: foresight and planning.

18 kept . . . out of haunt: kept out of circulation. (OED obs.)

22 divulging: being revealed.

25 ore: precious metal, usually gold, from the French "or."

Act 4

Scene 1. The Queen's room
Enter the King, Rosencrantz and Guildenstern

King
There's matter in these sighs, these profound heaves —
You must translate, 'tis fit we understand them.
Where is your son?
Queen
Bestow this place on us a little while. *Exeunt Rosencrantz and Guildenstern*
Ah, mine own lord, what have I seen tonight. 5
King
What, Gertrude? How does Hamlet?
Queen
Mad as the sea and wind when both contend
Which is the mightier. In his lawless fit,
Behind the arras hearing something stir,
Whips out his rapier, cries, "A rat, a rat!" 10
And in this brainish apprehension kills
The unseen good old man.
King
O heavy deed.
It had been so with us had we been there.
His liberty is full of threats to all,
To you yourself, to us, to everyone. 15
Alas, how shall this bloody deed be answered?
It will be laid to us, whose providence
Should have kept short, restrained, and out of haunt
This mad young man; but so much was our love,
We would not understand what was most fit, 20
But like the owner of a foul disease,
To keep it from divulging, let it feed
Even on the pith of life. Where is he gone?
Queen
To draw apart the body he hath killed,
Over whom his very madness, like some ore 25
Among a mineral of metals base,
Shows itself pure. He weeps for what is done.
King
O Gertrude, come away.
The sun no sooner shall the mountains touch,
But we will ship him hence, and this vile deed 30
We must with all our majesty and skill

32 countenance: appear to condone.

33 some further aid: men to help you.

38 call up: summon.

40 [so, haply, Slander]: Editors have added these words, or something similar, to fill an obvious gap in the printed text and supply a suitable speaker for "whose whisper" in the next line. "Rumor" might be the better whisperer since it could imply accusations and false elaborations.

42 As level . . . blank: the "cannon's" line of fire at point-blank range; that is directly.

43 miss our name: that is, not mention King Claudius' name.

44 woundless: invulnerable.

1 Safely stowed: Sarcastically, Polonius's body is put away somewhere, with a connotation of hidden.

6 compounded it: mixed it.

11 your counsel: your secret (OED obs.) that they are spying on him. **Mine own**: his secret that he is sometimes feigning madness.

Both countenance and excuse. Ho, Guildenstern!

Enter Rosencrantz and Guildenstern

Friends both, go join you with some further aid.
Hamlet in madness hath Polonius slain,
And from his mother's closet hath he dragged him. 35
Go seek him out, speak fair, and bring the body
Into the chapel. I pray you haste in this.

Exeunt Rosencrantz and Guildenstern

Come, Gertrude, we'll call up our wisest friends
And let them know both what we mean to do
And what's untimely done. [So, haply, Slander,] 40
Whose whisper over the world's diameter,
As level as the cannon to his blank,
Transports his poisoned shot, may miss our name,
And hit the woundless air. O, come away!
My soul is full of discord and dismay. 45

Exeunt

Scene 2. Another room in the castle

Enter Hamlet

Hamlet

Safely stowed.

Gentlemen

[Offstage] Hamlet! Lord Hamlet!

Hamlet

But soft, what noise? Who calls on Hamlet?
O, here they come.

Enter Rosencrantz and Guildenstern and others

Rosencrantz

What have you done, my lord, with the dead body? 5

Hamlet

Compounded it with dust, whereto 'tis kin.

Rosencrantz

Tell us where 'tis, that we may take it thence,
And bear it to the chapel.

Hamlet

Do not believe it.

Rosencrantz

Believe what? 10

Hamlet

That I can keep your counsel and not mine own. Besides, to be demanded

12 sponge: Hamlet calls Rosencantz a "sponge," an obsequious courtier who soaks up royal favors and rewards that the king knows he can later squeeze out of him, as Hamlet will explain. An image of royal corruption that would come naturally to Oxford but not to Shakspere. **replication**: rejoinder (from law).

20 knavish speech . . . ear: that is, my mischievous ("knavish" OED obs.) speech doesn't reach the understanding of one too stupid to listen and understand, one who has a "foolish ear."

22-3 The body . . . a thing: Riddling, Hamlet may be saying that although Polonius's body is "with" King Claudius somewhere in the royal castle, thus the monarchy of Denmark, the true "king," is not with Polonius's body (since Claudius is an illegitimate usurper of the throne), concluding that Claudius is nothing but a "thing" without legitimate royal status, which shocks Guildenstern. A subtle complex image about royal succession and legitimacy that, again, would come naturally to Oxford but not to Shakspere.

4 distracted: confused by conflicting interests.

6 scourge is weighed: figuratively, his punishment ("scourge") is considered ("weighed").

7 To bear all smooth and even,: to manage this affair with apparent calm and not raise suspicions of an ulterior motive.

9 Deliberate pause: a short, temporary interruption in the course of events, nothing of urgent importance.

10 appliance: actions (per the OED); in this medical metaphor "treatment."

12 befallen?: happened? (OED archaic)

of a sponge, what replication should be made by the son of a king?

Rosencrantz

Take you me for a sponge, my lord?

Hamlet

Ay, sir, that soaks up the king's countenance, his rewards, his
authorities. But such officers do the king best service in the end; he 15
keeps them, like an ape, in the corner of his jaw, first mouthed, to be
last swallowed. When he needs what you have gleaned, it is but
squeezing you, and, sponge, you shall be dry again.

Rosencrantz

I understand you not, my lord.

Hamlet

I am glad of it, a knavish speech sleeps in a foolish ear. 20

Rosencrantz

My lord, you must tell us where the body is, and go with us to the king.

Hamlet

The body is with the king, but the king is not with the body. The king
is a thing —

Guildenstern

A thing, my lord?

Hamlet

Of nothing, bring me to him. 25

Exeunt

Scene 3. Castle hall

Enter King and two or three Attendants

King

I have sent to seek him, and to find the body.
[Aside] How dangerous is it that this man goes loose.
Yet must not we put the strong law on him.
He's loved of the distracted multitude,
Who like not in their judgment, but their eyes, 5
And where 'tis so, the offender's scourge is weighed,
But never the offence. To bear all smooth and even,
This sudden sending him away must seem
Deliberate pause. Diseases desperate grown
By desperate appliance are relieved, 10
Or not at all.

Enter Rosencrantz.

How now, what hath befallen?

Rosencrantz

Where the dead body is bestowed, my lord,
We cannot get from him.

20-21 convocation of politic worms . . . . diet: Hamlet manages to pun on four words in two sentences—worms, emperor, diet and convocation. He says "worms" are feeding on Polonius's corpse their "diet," which puns on the Diet of Worms (a town in Germany), and for which the Holy Roman Emperor issued the "convocation." The 1521 Diet (an official conference or congress, per the OED) was an assembly of church officials called to hear the monk Martin Luther defend his Ninety-Five Theses for church reforms, which he had promulgated in five books the year before and which the Diet condemned as heresy. The punning probably also alludes to Lord Burghley, Oxford's father-in-law, who is caricatured by Oxford in the Polonius character. Burghley was born in December 1520 during the convocation of the Diet ("politic worms"), which began a month later, in January 1521. A patriotic Protestant, Burghley is sometimes thought to have liked having his birth associated with the convocation of the Diet of Worms, the birth of Protestantism.

23 variable service . . . : probably, two choices ("variable") of food, whether kings or beggars, both served at "one table" of "maggots."

29 go a progress: literally, travel; but here a zany image evoking a formal tour of a monarch and court, called "a progress," through "the guts of a beggar," an image that an audience of courtiers would immediately recognize and appreciate. A "progress" was a royal tour to the provinces and castles by the English monarch accompanied by a retinue of courtiers and court officials and large entourage of servants. Two examples: Oxford's father entertained Elizabeth at Hedingham Castle during her 1561 progress through Essex County when Oxford was eleven, and Oxford accompanied her on her progress to Warwick Castle in 1572 and organized the spectacular entertainment, a mock battle with cannons and fireworks.

King
But where is he?
Rosencrantz
Without, my lord, guarded, to know your pleasure.
King
Bring him before us. 15
Rosencrantz
Ho, bring in the lord.
Hamlet and Guildenstern enter.
King
Now, Hamlet, where's Polonius?
Hamlet
At supper.
King
At supper? Where?
Hamlet
Not where he eats, but where he is eaten. A certain convocation of 20
politic worms are even at him. Your worm is your only emperor for
diet. We fat all creatures else to fat us, and we fat ourselves for
maggots. Your fat king and your lean beggar is but variable service,
two dishes, but to one table. That's the end.
King
Alas, alas. 25
Hamlet
A man may fish with the worm that hath eat of a king, and eat of the fish
that hath fed of that worm.
King
What dost thou mean by this?
Hamlet
Nothing but to show you how a king may go a progress through
the guts of a beggar. 30
King
Where is Polonius?
Hamlet
In heaven. Send thither to see. If your messenger find him not there,
seek him in the other place yourself. But if indeed you find him not
within this month, you shall nose him as you go up the stairs into the
lobby.
King
Go seek him there.
Hamlet
He will stay till you come. *Exeunt attendants* 35

36 for thine especial safety: This is a lie. The king has arranged to have Hamlet killed when he arrives in England.

40 at help: favorable.

41 everything is bent: everything has been directed and prepared for this purpose. ("bent" OED obs.)

46 our purposes: a double meaning for Hamlet and the audience; ostensibly for Hamlet's "safety" (line 36) but with dramatic irony really for the safety of Claudius, who suspects Hamlet may try to harm him.

46 cherub: Cherubs were thought to be keen-sighted and knowledgeable; Hamlet hints that he knows Claudius's purpose.

49 Thy loving father: Claudius tries to elicit a farewell directed specifically to himself as his step-father, which Hamlet rejects.

53 at foot: closely at his heels. **Tempt him**: test his adherence to a requirement (here, for "speed"), the earliest meaning of "tempt" per the OED.

56 leans on: depends on or pertains to. (OED obs.)

57 And, England: alone now, King Claudius addresses the king of England *in absentia*. **if my love . . . aught**: if you hold my friendship ("love') as worth anything ("aught').

59 cicatrice: a scar left by healed wound. .

60-1 After the Danish sword . . . pays homage to us: referring again (as at 3.2.162) to Danegeld, tribute payments that Denmark occasionally demanded from England over the centuries, and recently reinstated, for protection from raids (by the "Danish sword") on English coastal towns by Danish marauders for booty. Insiders in a court audience would recognize the reference to Denmark's extortion for payments from England's treasury. **thy free awe**: the English monarch's respectful fear ("awe").

61-2 not coldly set . . . of Hamlet: must not coolly ignore the order in my "letters" (which Rosencrantz and Guildenstern carry) for Hamlet's immediate ("present") death.

66 hectic: fever (per the OED).

67 However my haps: whatever my good fortune ("haps" OED obs. with a connotation of possible bad luck or a bad outcome).

King
Hamlet, this deed, for thine especial safety —
Which we do tender as we dearly grieve
For that which thou hast done — must send thee hence
With fiery quickness; therefore prepare thyself,
The bark is ready, and the wind at help, 40
The associates tend, and everything is bent
For England.
Hamlet
For England.
King
Ay, Hamlet.
Hamlet
Good. 45
King
So is it, if thou knew'st our purposes.
Hamlet
I see a cherub that sees them. But come, for England!
Farewell, dear mother.
King
Thy loving father, Hamlet.
Hamlet
My mother. Father and mother is man and wife, man and wife is one flesh 50
so, my mother —
Come, for England! *Exit Hamlet*
King
Follow him at foot, tempt him with speed aboard.
Delay it not, I'll have him hence tonight.
Away, for everything is sealed and done 55
That else leans on the affair. Pray you make haste. *Exeunt all but the* king
And, England, if my love thou hold'st at aught —
As my great power thereof may give thee sense,
Since yet thy cicatrice looks raw and red
After the Danish sword, and thy free awe 60
Pays homage to us — thou mayst not coldly set
Our sovereign process, which imports at full,
By letters congruing to that effect,
The present death of Hamlet. Do it, England, 65
For like the hectic in my blood he rages,
And thou must cure me. Till I know 'tis done,
However my haps, my joys were never begun.
Exit

3 conveyance: passage. (OED obs.)

5 would aught with us: would anything from us.

6 express our duty in his eye: pay our respects in person.

S.d. *Exeunt . . . and others*: Time and space are extremely condensed here.

14 old Norway: the former king of Norway, now an invalid.

15 main: center, heart.

18-19 a little patch of ground . . . but the name.: a strange and vivid passage, probably an allusion to Copernicus, the great astronomer who died in 1543 in obscurity and was buried in an unmarked grave in Poland, and whose "name" and scholarly accomplishments gave the "patch of ground" its value ("profit"). The allusion would explain an otherwise puzzling passage unrelated to the plot. (See Usher *Hamlet*'s.)

20 farm it: lease it. (OED obs.)

22 A ranker rate . . . sold in fee: a higher ("ranker" OED obs.) rate of return even if sold outright ("in fee," a legal term).

23 the Polack never will defend it.: conceivably alluding to the fact that Copernicus, a Pole, died the year his book was published and thus never had to "defend it."

Scene 4. A field some distance from Elsinore
Enter Fortinbras with his army

Fortinbras
Go, captain, from me greet the Danish king.
Tell him that by his license Fortinbras
Craves the conveyance of a promised march
Over his kingdom. You know the rendezvous.
If that his majesty would aught with us, 5
We shall express our duty in his eye,
And let him know so.

Captain
I will do it, my lord.

Fortinbras
Go softly on. *Exeunt all but the Captain*

Enter Hamlet, Rosencrantz, Guildenstern and others

Hamlet
Good sir, whose powers are these?

Captain
They are of Norway, sir. 10

Hamlet
How purposed, sir, I pray you?

Captain
Against some part of Poland.

Hamlet
Who commands them, sir?

Captain
The nephew to old Norway, Fortinbras.

Hamlet
Goes it against the main of Poland, sir, 15
Or for some frontier?

Captain
Truly to speak, and with no addition,
We go to gain a little patch of ground
That hath in it no profit but the name.
To pay five ducats, five, I would not farm it; 20
Nor will it yield to Norway or the Pole
A ranker rate, should it be sold in fee.

Hamlet
Why then the Polack never will defend it.

Captain
Yes, it is already garrisoned.

26 Will not debate . . . straw.: probably, would be meaningless in the contention over this insignificant parcel of land (“this straw”).

27 imposthume: abscess (OED rare) with a connotation of moral corruption, perhaps suggesting that Fortinbras, also a corrupt ruler, is dissembling his true intention, to attack Denmark.

28 without: outward, in contrast to “inward.”

32 all occasions: everything that happens, like this chance meeting with Fortinbras’ captain.

33 dull revenge: inactive, sluggish revenge.

34 market of his time: use of (OED obs.) his time.

39 To fust: to become mouldy. (OED obs.)

42 quartered: divided into four parts (as for examination).

48 tender: youthful, inexperienced (Fortinbras).

50 makes mouths: makes faces of scorn.

53 an egg-shell: which is hollow and useless, probably alluding to the “little patch of ground” in Poland.

54 Is not . . . argument: Not to act without good reason.

55-6 find quarrel . . . stake: go into action even over an insignificant matter (“a straw”) when one’s honor is at stake.

57 a father killed: Polonius, whose daughter will appear in the next scene. **stained**: dishonored.

58 Excitements: motives, incitements to action. (OED obs.) **my blood**: figuratively for my emotions, passion.

61 trick: a deceptive trifle.

Hamlet
Two thousand souls and twenty thousand ducats 25
Will not debate the question of this straw.
This is the imposthume of much wealth and peace,
That inward breaks, and shows no cause without
Why the man dies. I humbly thank you, sir.
Captain
God buy you, sir. 30
Exit the Captain
Rosencrantz
Will it please you go, my lord?
Hamlet
I'll be with you straight — go a little before. *Exeunt all but Hamlet*
How all occasions do inform against me,
And spur my dull revenge. What is a man,
If his chief good and market of his time
Be but to sleep and feed? A beast, no more. 35
Sure He that made us with such large discourse,
Looking before and after, gave us not
That capability and godlike reason
To fust in us unused. Now whether it be
Bestial oblivion, or some craven scruple 40
Of thinking too precisely on the event—
A thought which quartered hath but one part wisdom
And ever three parts coward—I do not know
Why yet I live to say, "This thing's to do,"
Sith I have cause, and will, and strength, and means 45
To do it. Examples gross as earth exhort me
Witness this army of such mass and charge,
Led by a delicate and tender prince,
Whose spirit with divine ambition puffed
Makes mouths at the invisible event, 50
Exposing what is mortal and unsure
To all that fortune, death, and danger dare,
Even for an egg-shell. Rightly to be great
Is not to stir without great argument,
But greatly to find quarrel in a straw 55
When honor's at the stake. How stand I then,
That have a father killed, a mother stained,
Excitements of my reason and my blood,
And let all sleep, while to my shame I see
The imminent death of twenty thousand men, 60
That for a fantasy and trick of fame

62-3 a plot . . . try the cause: the little patch of ground where sheer "numbers" of fighters cannot determine the truth of the matter (from the law, "to try a cause").

65 continent: space. (OED obs.)

2 distract: deranged, out of her mind. (OED archaic)

5 tricks: frauds, deceptions. (OED obs.)

6 enviously: maliciously, spitefully. (OED obs.)

7 is nothing: means nothing.

9 collection: inferences. (OED obs.) **yawn:** gape, in astonishment. (OED obs.)

18 toy: trifle. **great amiss:** disaster.

19 jealousy: zeal or vehemence. (OED obs.)

Go to their graves like beds, fight for a plot
Whereon the numbers cannot try the cause,
Which is not tomb enough and continent
To hide the slain? O, from this time forth, 65
My thoughts be bloody, or be nothing worth! *Exit*

Scene 5. A castle room
Enter Horatio, Queen Gertrude, and a Gentleman

Queen
I will not speak with her.
Gentleman
She is importunate, indeed distract.
Her mood will needs be pitied.
Queen
What would she have?
Gentleman
She speaks much of her father, says she hears
There's tricks in the world, and hems, and beats her heart, 5
Spurns enviously at straws, speaks things in doubt
That carry but half sense. Her speech is nothing,
Yet the unshaped use of it doth move
The hearers to collection; they yawn at it,
And botch the words up fit to their own thoughts, 10
Which as her winks and nods and gestures yield them,
Indeed would make one think there might be thought,
Though nothing sure, yet much unhappily.
Horatio
'Twere good she were spoken with, for she may strew
Dangerous conjectures in ill-breeding minds. 15
Queen
Let her come in.
[Aside] To my sick soul, as sin's true nature is,
Each toy seems prologue to some great amiss,
So full of artless jealousy is guilt,
It spills itself in fearing to be spilt.
20

Enter Ophelia

Ophelia
Where is the beauteous majesty of Denmark?
Queen
How now, Ophelia?

23 your true love: In her distracted state Ophelia alternates between alluding in her songs as here to Hamlet, her "true love," who has apparently rejected her (and as in her song at lines 58-66), and alluding to her deceased father, as in her song "He is dead" that follows this one.

25-6 cockle hat . . . shoon: A hat with "cockle" shells as a decoration and a walking stick ("staff") denoted a pilgrim returning from the shrine of Saint James of Compostella in Spain and came to symbolize a lover making a pilgrimage. **Shoon**: shoes. (OED obs.)

28 He is dead: Her father Polonius.

38 Larded: strewn; decorated (OED obs.); originally from the pieces of fat ("lard") added to a meat dish, which came to mean "decorated."

39 not: The intrusive "not" disrupts the meter of the line and alters the sense of it, perhaps suggesting that Ophelia is reminding them that she knows that Hamlet killed her father.

42 God dild you: God yield (a reward) to you.

45 Conceit: fantasies.

53 dupped: opened up (OED archaic, from "do up").

Ophelia
[Sings]"How should I your true love know
From another one?
By his cockle hat and staff, 25
And his sandal shoon."
Queen
Alas, sweet lady, what imports this song?
Ophelia
Say you? Nay, pray you mark.
[Sings] "He is dead and gone, lady,
He is dead and gone, 30
At his head a grass-green turf,
At his heels a stone."
O ho!
Queen
Nay, but, Ophelia —
Ophelia
Pray you mark. 35
[Sings] "White his shroud as the mountain snow" —
Enter King.
Queen
Alas, look here, my lord.
Ophelia
[Sings] "Larded all with sweet flowers,
Which bewept to the ground did not go
With true-love showers." 40
King
How do you, pretty lady?
Ophelia
Well, God dild you! They say the owl was a baker's daughter. Lord, we know what we are, but know not what we may be. God be at your table.
King
Conceit upon her father. 45
Ophelia
Pray, let's have no words of this, but when they ask you what it means, say you this.
[Sings] "Tomorrow is Saint Valentine's day,
All in the morning betime,
And I a maid at your window, 50
To be your Valentine.
Then up he rose and donned his clothes,
And dupped the chamber-door,
Let in the maid, that out a maid

58 By Gis: By Jesus (a mild oath).

61 By Cock: By God (OED archaic), and in this context probably with a double meaning of "penis."

62 tumbled me: handled me roughly (per the OED), with a connotation of in bed for sex.

66 An: If. (OED obs.)

74 All from her father's death: King Claudius avoids recognizing that if there's any truth in her madness Ophelia is also saying in her songs that Hamlet promised to marry her in order to get her into bed for sexual intercourse. If Hamlet represents the teenage Oxford and Ophelia Anne Cecil, who was six years younger, this song suggests that he had sex with her.

76 single spies: as lone scouts.

79 muddied: confused.

81 greenly: unskillfully, not having any experience (OED archaic) in these matters.

82 in hugger-mugger: secretly, clandestinely. (OED obs.)

84 we are pictures: that is, for Ophelia we are just uncomprehending images of ourselves without life and thus unable take in the meaning of her singing.

87 Feeds . . . clouds,: probably, obsesses about ("feeds on") his father's horrible death ("this wonder" OED obs.), and keeps himself "in clouds" away from anyone who wants to talk to him about it.

88 buzzers: whisperers; rumor-mongers.

Never departed more." 55

King

Pretty Ophelia.

Ophelia

Indeed without an oath I'll make an end on it.

[Sings] "By Gis, and by Saint Charity,
Alack, and fie for shame!
Young men will do it if they come to it, 60
By Cock, they are to blame."
Quoth she, 'Before you tumbled me,
You promised me to wed.'"
He answers,
'So would I have done, by yonder sun, 65
An thou hadst not come to my bed.' "

King

How long hath she been thus?

Ophelia

I hope all will be well. We must be patient, but I cannot choose but weep to think they would lay him in the cold ground. My brother shall know of it, and so I thank you for your good counsel. Come. My 70 coach! Good night, ladies, good night. Sweet ladies, good night, good night.

Exit Ophelia

King

Follow her close, give her good watch, I pray you.
O, this is the poison of deep grief, it springs
All from her father's death — and now behold –
O Gertrude, Gertrude, 75
When sorrows come, they come not single spies,
But in battalions first, her father slain;
Next, your son gone, and he most violent author
Of his own just remove; the people muddied,
Thick and unwholesome in their thoughts and whispers 80
For good Polonius' death; and we have done but greenly
In hugger-mugger to inter him; poor Ophelia
Divided from herself and her fair judgment,
Without the which we are pictures, or mere beasts;
Last, and as much containing as all these, 85
Her brother is in secret come from France,
Feeds on this wonder, keeps himself in clouds,
And wants not buzzers to infect his ear
With pestilent speeches of his father's death,

90-92 Wherein necessity . . . In ear and ear.: King Claudius assumes that Laertes believes that he was involved in Polonius's death. Hence, he argues here that the rumor-mongers, who need ("necessity") something to talk about, even if without anything of substance ("of matter beggared") will stop at nothing ("nothing stick") to make accusations against him ("our person to arraign") and tell these to everyone ("In ear and ear"). The Earl of Leicester was the subject of many rumors that he was involved in the death of adversaries or targets of opportunity, and like Claudius would have been concerned about the rumors.

93-4 Like to a murdering-piece . . . gives me superfluous death: like an artillery piece that fires many cannon balls at once ("murdering piece" OED obs.) that hit me in many deadly ways that are uncalled for ("superfluous").

95 Switzers: Swiss mercenary guards.

102-4 world . . . word,: an allusion to the feudal world of order with its hierarchies, rules and customs, which the rabble forget as if the world were about to begin, an idea important to Oxford whose ancestors were feudal nobility.

105 "Laertes shall be king!": Laertes, who has heard about his father's death and thinks the King Claudius must have been responsible, has apparently incited citizens into a "rabble" in his support.

108-9 How . . . dogs! The metaphor is from hunting with hounds, the sport of aristocrats, when the yelping pack (a "cry") follows the scent backwards ("counter") from the direction taken by its prey.

115 Keep the door: Guard the door.

118 proclaims me bastard: Laertes' outburst in this passage, which seems to be an overreaction to Gertrude's "Calmly," may well reflect Oxford's troubling memory that in an inheritance dispute he was alleged to be a bastard. He was in his early teens and living with other young aristocrats in William Cecil's household, when his half-sister and her husband alleged that Oxford's father was a bigamist when Oxford was born and that Oxford was not the legitimate heir to his father's title and estate; but nothing ever came of it. Queen Elizabeth (probably teasing him) once called him a bastard. Bastardy and the distressing consequences of it for a nobleman's career and reputation figure prominently in two of Oxford's Shakespeare plays: the bastard Edmund in *King Lear* and Philip the Bastard in *King John*.

Wherein necessity, of matter beggared, 90
Will nothing stick our person to arraign
In ear and ear. O my dear Gertrude, this,
Like to a murdering-piece, in many places
Gives me superfluous death. *A shouting off-stage*
Attend!
Where is my Switzers? Let them guard the door. 95
Enter a Messenger
What is the matter?

Messenger
Save yourself, my lord!
The ocean, overpeering of his list,
Eats not the flats with more impitious haste
Than young Laertes, in a riotous head, 100
Overbears your officers. The rabble call him lord,
And as the world were now but to begin,
Antiquity forgot, custom not known,
The ratifiers and props of every word,
They cry, "Choose we, Laertes shall be king!" 105
Caps, hands, and tongues applaud it to the clouds,
"Laertes shall be king! Laertes king!" *A shouting off-stage*

Queen
How cheerfully on the false trail they cry.
O, this is counter, you false Danish dogs!
Enter Laertes with others

King
The doors are broke. 110

Laertes
Where is this king? Sirs, stand you all without.

All
No, let us come in.

Laertes
I pray you give me leave.

All
We will, we will. *Exeunt Laertes' followers*

Laertes
I thank you. Keep the door. O thou vile king. Give me my father! 115

Queen
Calmly, good Laertes.

Laertes
That drop of blood that's calm proclaims me bastard,
Cries cuckold to my father, brands the harlot
Even here between the chaste unsmirched brow

123 fear our person: be afraid for me. (OED obs. usage)

124 such divinity doth hedge: such godliness surrounds ("doth hedge") as a fence or barrier. (OED obs.) King Claudius's hypocrisy would have been ironic for the court audience, since "divinity" did not protect King Hamlet from being murdered by Claudius.

125-6 That treason can but peep . . . his will: that treason can only look on ("but peep") and think about what it would like to do but does "little" to act on it.

129 But not by him.: not by the King.

135 both the worlds . . . negligence: that is, I disregard and am indifferent to it ("negligence" per the OED) for both this world and the next.

137 throughly: fully, completely. (OED archaic)

143 swoopstake . . . and foe: indiscriminately, like one who sweeps up all the stakes on a gambling table. ("swoopstake" OED obs.) The king is asking Laertes if he would seek revenge on innocent and guilty alike.

Of my true mother. 120

King

What is the cause, Laertes,
That thy rebellion looks so giant-like?
Let him go, Gertrude, do not fear our person.
There's such divinity doth hedge a king
That treason can but peep to what it would, 125
Acts little of his will. Tell me, Laertes,
Why thou art thus incensed. Let him go, Gertrude.
Speak, man.

Laertes

Where is my father?

King

Dead.

Queen

But not by him.

King

Let him demand his fill. 130

Laertes

How came he dead? I'll not be juggled with.
To hell, allegiance! Vows, to the blackest devil!
Conscience and grace, to the profoundest pit!
I dare damnation. To this point I stand,
That both the worlds I give to negligence, 135
Let come what comes; only I'll be revenged
Most throughly for my father.

King

Who shall stay you?

Laertes

My will, not all the world's,
And for my means, I'll husband them so well,
They shall go far with little. 140

King

Good Laertes,
If you desire to know the certainty
Of your dear father, is it writ in your revenge
That, swoopstake, you will draw both friend and foe,
Winner and loser?

Laertes

None but his enemies. 145

King

Will you know them then?

148-9 life-rendering pelican . . . blood: alluding to the legend that the pelican fed its young with blood it pecked from its body, even reviving ("life-rendering") them from apparent death.

152 sensibly: consciously and with intense feeling. (OED obs.)

153 level: figuratively, clear and straightforward.

157 virtue: strength, power.

159 our scale turn the beam: that is, tip the bar ("beam") of the scales (of justice).

163-5 Nature . . . loves: probably meaning that fine, natural, human love sends a part of itself ("some precious instance") after the loved one it has lost; thus, Ophelia is losing her mind by sending part of it after her beloved father.

171 A-down, a-down: a common refrain in folk songs.

172 wheel: the refrain, or possibly the wheel of Fortune. Or both.

172-3 false steward . . . daughter: Ophelia continues the thought of a maiden's betrayal by someone "false" to her.

174 This nothing's more than matter.: that is, her apparently trivial and worthless songs ("this nothing") convey more truth than words of some sense and substance ("matter" OED obs.).

175 pray you, love, remember: probably addressing Laertes. Here and in the passage that follows Ophelia gives flowers presumably according to their traditional significance to each of the principal characters.

Laertes
To his good friends thus wide I'll ope my arms,
And like the kind, life-rendering pelican,
Repast them with my blood.
King
Why, now you speak
Like a good child and a true gentleman. 150
That I am guiltless of your father's death,
And am most sensibly in grief for it,
It shall as level to your judgment appear
As day does to your eye. *A noise within*
Let her come in.
Enter Ophelia
Laertes How now, what noise is that? 155
O heat, dry up my brains! tears seven times salt
Burn out the sense and virtue of mine eye!
By heaven, thy madness shall be paid with weight
Till our scale turn the beam. O rose of May!
Dear maid, kind sister, sweet Ophelia! 160
O heavens, is it possible a young maid's wits
Should be as mortal as an old man's life?
Nature is fine in love, and where 'tis fine,
It sends some precious instance of itself
After the thing it loves. 165
Ophelia
[Sings] "They bore him bare-faced on the bier,
And in his grave rained many a tear" —
Fare you well, my dove!
Laertes
Hadst thou thy wits and didst persuade revenge,
It could not move thus. 170
Ophelia
You must sing, "A-down, a-down," and you call him a-down-a. O, how the wheel becomes it. It is the false steward, that stole his master's daughter.
Laertes
This nothing's more than matter.
Ophelia
There's rosemary, that's for remembrance; pray you, love, remember. 175
And there is pansies, that's for thoughts.
Laertes
A document in madness, thoughts and remembrance fitted.

178 fennel for you and columbine.: probably for Gertrude because fennel signifies dissembling/fickelness in love and columbine her infidelity to her first husband, King Hamlet.

178-9 rue for you and here's some for me: Ophelia could give "rue," which signifies regret and repentance, to King Claudius, who should atone for his sins; but the oil of rue was also considered a strong, abortion-inducing drug and keeping some for herself could represent her fear that she may be pregnant by Hamlet, as Anne Cecil (and/or Oxford) no doubt would have feared if they did engage in pre-marital sex.

181-2 They say he made a good end: A deluded and pitiable lament since Polonius did not "make a good end" of his life, dying violently without the opportunity to repent his sins. **"For bonny sweet Robin is all my joy."**: Equally deluded and pitiable, and incongruous, since "Robin" was well-known to the court audience as Queen Elizabeth's nickname for her favorite, Robert Dudley, Earl of Leicester, who rarely brought "joy" to anyone except the queen, who doted on him. Apparently a swipe at Leicester by Oxford.

191 All flaxen was his poll: All white was the hair on his head ("poll")

202 find us touched: find me implicated (using the royal "us").

210 hatchment: a plaque bearing the heraldic insignia of the deceased.

211 formal ostentation: a formal show or display (OED archaic) and not necessarily negative; here a ceremony. For Polonius to be buried in haste without ceremony was an affront to Laertes.

Ophelia

There's fennel for you, and columbines. There's rue for you, and here's some for me; we may call it herb of grace on Sundays. You may wear your rue with a difference. There's a daisy. I would give you some violets, but they withered all when my father died. They say he made a good end—*[Sings]* "For bonny sweet Robin is all my joy." 180

Laertes

Thought and afflictions, passion; hell itself,
She turns to favor and to prettiness.

Ophelia

[Sings] "And will 'a not come again? 185
And will 'a not come again?
No, no, he is dead,
Go to thy death-bed.
He never will come again.
His beard was as white as snow, 190
All flaxen was his poll,
He is gone, he is gone,
And we cast away moan,
God 'a' mercy on his soul."
And of all Christian souls. God buy you. *Exit* 195

Laertes

Do you see this? O God!

King

Laertes, I must commune with your grief,
Or you deny me right. Go but apart,
Make choice of whom your wisest friends you will,
And they shall hear and judge 'twixt you and me. 200
If by direct or by collateral hand
They find us touched, we will our kingdom give,
Our crown, our life, and all that we call ours,
To you in satisfaction; but if not,
Be you content to lend your patience to us, 205
And we shall jointly labor with your soul
To give it due content.

Laertes

Let this be so.
His means of death, his obscure funeral,
No trophy, sword, nor hatchment over his bones, 210
No noble rite nor formal ostentation,
Cry to be heard, as 'twere from heaven to earth,
That I must call it in question.

11 have overlooked this: have looked over and read this letter.

12 some means: some way to have access.

13-17 a pirate . . . . for them.: Oxford had his own encounter with pirates. In April 1576 as he was returning from his Italian tour his ship, like Hamlet's, was attacked in the English Channel. The pirates reportedly plundered his chests of Italian treasures, including rich garments, and stripped him "naked" except for his shirt. There is no piracy episode in the printed sources for *Hamlet*. Oxford probably knew Plutarch's account of pirates in the Mediterranean capturing Julius Caesar for ransom, but Oxford's personal experience with pirates stripping him "naked" is a much more persuasive inspiration for what he describes in his letter to Horatio, especially when he says in his letter to Claudius in the next scene that he was "set naked" on shore.

18 repair thou to me: return to me. (OED obs.)

19-20 make thee dumb: strike you speechless ("dumb").

20 much too light for the bore of the matter: that is, his "words" to Horatio would not do justice ("much too light") to the seriousness of the "matter." The image comes from weaponry where the projectiles of the shot are too small for the size of the cannon's barrel ("the bore") to be fired at high speed and be effective. Another of the many military references and allusions that would come naturally to Oxford, who served in the military but not to Shakspere, who did not.

24 give you way: provide access (to the King).

King
So you shall,
And where the offence is, let the great axe fall.
I pray you go with me. *Exeunt*

Scene 6
Enter Horatio and others

Horatio
What are they that would speak with me?
Gentleman
Sea-faring men, sir. They say they have letters for you.
Horatio
Let them come in. *Exit Gentleman*
I do not know from what part of the world
I should be greeted, if not from Lord Hamlet. 5
Enter Sailors
First Sailor
God bless you, sir.
Horatio
Let Him bless thee too.
First Sailor
He shall, sir, if it please Him. There's a letter for you, sir, it came from the ambassador that was bound for England if your name be Horatio, as I am let to know it is. 10
Horatio
[Reads] "Horatio, when thou shalt have overlooked this, give these fellows some means to the king, they have letters for him. Ere we were two days old at sea, a pirate of very warlike appointment gave us chase. Finding ourselves too slow of sail, we put on a compelled valor, and in the grapple I boarded them. On the instant they got clear of our ship, so I 15 alone became their prisoner. They have dealt with me like thieves of mercy, but they knew what they did; I am to do a good turn for them. Let the king have the letters I have sent, and repair thou to me with as much speed as thou wouldest fly death. I have words to speak in thine ear will make thee dumb, yet are they much too light for the bore of the matter. 20 These good fellows will bring thee where I am. Rosencrantz and Guildenstern hold their course for England. Of them I have much to tell thee. Farewell. He that thou knowest thine. Hamlet."
Come, I will give you way for these your letters,
And do it the speedier that you may direct me 25
To him from whom you brought them. *Exeunt*

1 acquittance: in law, to satisfy a debt or obligation; here, acquit me of any responsibility for Polonius's death.

7 feats: evil acts or crimes. (OED obs.)

10 unsinewed: weak, without sinews of strength.

14 conjunctive: conjoined, united; with an echo of "conjunction," a union in marriage (OED obs.); also the term in astronomy describing two planets that appear to be close together, or even formerly when they were in the same Zodiac sign of astrology, per the OED. The next line continues the allusions to astronomy.

15-16 as the star moves . . . but by her: a simile from Ptolemaic astronomy that just as the "star," the Sun, alluding to Hamlet, "moves" in its own "sphere" around the Earth, so, asserts King Claudius with more than a little exaggeration, his life revolves only around Gertrude.

17 public count: public reckoning or judgment.

18 general gender: common sort of people. (OED obs.)

20 spring . . . stone: Springs in a limestone-rich area can encrust objects like "wood" with a layer of lime, thus appearing to petrify the wood.

21 gyves: shackles; probably metaphorically here for disgraces, faults.

22 slightly timbered: with too light a shaft. **so loud a wind:** so strong a gale (of public emotion and outcry).

28 Stood challenger . . . for her perfections: stood above the rest of the world for all time ("all the age") in her "perfections." The image looks like it's from an ancient tradition in Hungary that a newly crowned king would ride on horseback to the top of an artificial "mount" or hill formed by earth from all parts of his kingdom and brandish his sword as if to challenge anyone questioning his right to the throne--a ceremony that Oxford might well have known about but not Shakspere. See Jenkins' curiously dismissive line note.

Scene 7. A castle room
Enter King and Laertes

King
Now must your conscience my acquittance seal,
And you must put me in your heart for friend,
Sith you have heard, and with a knowing ear,
That he which hath your noble father slain
Pursued my life. 5

Laertes
It well appears. But tell me
Why you proceeded not against these feats
So criminal and so capital in nature,
As by your safety, greatness, wisdom, all things else
You mainly were stirred up.

King
O, for two special reasons,
Which may to you perhaps seem much unsinewed, 10
But yet to me are strong. The queen his mother
Lives almost by his looks, and for myself —
My virtue or my plague, be it either which —
She is so conjunctive to my life and soul,
That, as the star moves not but in his sphere, 15
I could not but by her. The other motive,
Why to a public count I might not go,
Is the great love the general gender bear him,
Who, dipping all his faults in their affection,
Would, like the spring that turneth wood to stone, 20
Convert his gyves to graces, so that my arrows,
Too slightly timbered for so loud a wind,
Would have reverted to my bow again,
But not where I have aimed them.

Laertes
And so have I a noble father lost, 25
A sister driven into desperate terms,
Whose worth, if praises may go back again,
Stood challenger on mount of all the age
For her perfections — but my revenge will come.

King
Break not your sleeps for that. You must not think 30
That we are made of stuff so flat and dull
That we can let our beard be shook with danger
And think it pastime. You shortly shall hear more.
I loved your father, and we love ourself,

39 they say: so they say.

43 I am set naked: Just as the French ambassador to England reported home that Queen Elizabeth was "marvelously angry" that Oxford "was left stark naked ("tout nud" in French)" by pirates, Hamlet writes to Claudius that he was "set naked on your kingdom." The detail from Oxford's personal experience, not something Shakspere would have known, should almost alone be persuasive evidence that Oxford wrote *Hamlet.* (See Anderson and Paul.)

48 abuse: deception. (OED obs.)

50 "Naked.": apparently marveling that Prince Hamlet was stripped naked.

52 Can you devise me?: describe, explain this for me? (OED obs.)

61 to a peace: probably, to ask me to take no action.

63 checking: cutting short.

65 device: planning, devising.

66 he shall not choose but fall: that is, he has no choice but to be killed.

And that, I hope, will teach you to imagine — 35

Enter a Messenger with letters

How now? What news?

Messenger

These to your Majesty, this to the queen.

King

From Hamlet? Who brought them?

Messenger

Sailors, my lord, they say, I saw them not.
They were given me by Claudio. He received them 40
Of him that brought them.

King

Laertes, you shall hear them — Leave us. *Exit Messenger*
[Reads] "High and mighty, You shall know I am set naked on your kingdom. Tomorrow shall I beg leave to see your kingly eyes, when I shall (first asking your pardon thereunto) recount the occasion of my 45 sudden and more strange return. Hamlet."
What should this mean? Are all the rest come back?
Or is it some abuse, and no such thing?

Laertes

Know you the hand?

King

'Tis Hamlet's character. "Naked," 50
And in a postscript here he says "alone."
Can you devise me?

Laertes

I am lost in it, my lord. But let him come,
It warms the very sickness in my heart
That I shall live and tell him to his teeth, 55
"Thus didst thou."

King

If it be so, Laertes —
As how should it be so? How otherwise? —
Will you be ruled by me?

Laertes

Ay, my lord, 60
So you will not overrule me to a peace.

King

To thine own peace. If he be now returned
As checking at his voyage, and that he means
No more to undertake it, I will work him
To an exploit, now ripe in my device, 65
Under the which he shall not choose but fall;

68 uncharge the practice: probably, not accuse us of plotting against Hamlet.

72 organ: means, agent. (OED archaic)

76-9 Your sum of parts . . . unworthiest siege: that is, all your talents and skills ("sum of parts") made "him" (the as-yet unnamed informant) envious, and with "unworthiest" reluctance and feeling under "siege" (from the French expression "d'avoir une mentalité assiegé") he had to admit that he was most envious of one skill in particular, which the King will soon reveal was fencing.

81 the very riband: ribbon. (OED archaic); probably alluding to a decoration that is the finishing touch.

84 weeds: garments denoting rank or profession (per the OED).

85 importing: signifying.

91-2 As had he been incorpsed and demi-natured / With the brave beast: As if he had been incorporated ("incorpsed" OED rare) in the same body as the excellent ("brave" OED obs.) horse and was half its nature (demi-natured), alluding to the half-horse, half-man Centaur of Greek and Roman mythology.

92 topped my thought: exceeded what I imagined he could do.

93 in forgery of shapes and tricks: in imagining ("forgery" OED poetic) figures and feats of horsemanship.

96 Lamord!: "the bite" in French, but as an invented proper name, it probably suggests "the death" ("le mort" in French) since the two words are spelled the same in French except for one letter and are pronounced the same, and especially since he will praise Laertes' skill with a rapier, which will lead to Hamlet's death.

97 brooch: ornament. (OED obs.)

And for his death no wind of blame shall breathe,
But even his mother shall uncharge the practice,
And call it accident.

Laertes

My lord, I will be ruled, 70
The rather if you could devise it so
That I might be the organ.

King

It falls right.
You have been talked of since your travel much,
And that in Hamlet's hearing, for a quality 75
Wherein they say you shine. Your sum of parts
Did not together pluck such envy from him
As did that one, and that, in my regard,
Of the unworthiest siege.

Laertes

What part is that, my lord? 80

King

A very riband in the cap of youth,
Yet needful too, for youth no less becomes
The light and careless livery that it wears
Than settled age his sables and his weeds,
Importing health and graveness. Two months since 85
Here was a gentleman of Normandy—
I have seen myself, and served against, the French,
And they can well on horseback, but this gallant
Had witchcraft in it, he grew unto his seat,
And to such wondrous doing brought his horse, 90
As had he been incorpsed and demi-natured
With the brave beast. So far he topped my thought,
That I in forgery of shapes and tricks
Come short of what he did.

Laertes

A Norman was it?

King

A Norman. 95

Laertes

Upon my life, Lamord!

King

The very same.

Laertes

I know him well. He is the brooch indeed
And gem of all the nation.

99 made confession of you: acknowledged the truth ("confession," from the law) about your skills.

101 in defense: in self-defense in fencing.

104 escrimures: from the French "escrimeurs" for fencers.

108 sudden: immediate. (OED obs.)

109 Now, out of this--: He interrupts himself to get to the point.

116 begun by time: probably, at a point in time.

120 wick or snuff . . . abate it: The snuff is the burned portion of the wick which causes a candle flame to dim; the paradox here is that love is self-consuming by its intensity.

122 a pleurisy: figuratively, an excess or superabundance. (OED obs.)

124 We should . . . would: We ought to act while the will still exists.

128 But to the quick of the ulcer: figuratively, to get to the point. The king cuts short his reflections on decisiveness, which he uses to draw Laertes into his conspiracy and strengthen Laertes' resolve to kill Hamlet.

132 murder sanctuarize: give sanctuary and protection to a murderer, falsely implying that Hamlet committed the premeditated murder of Polonius.

King
He made confession of you
And gave you such a masterly report 100
For art and exercise in your defense,
And for your rapier most especial,
That he cried out 'twould be a sight indeed
If one could match you. The escrimures of their nation
He swore had neither motion, guard, nor eye, 105
If you opposed them. Sir, this report of his
Did Hamlet so envenom with his envy
That he could nothing do but wish and beg
Your sudden coming over to play with you.
Now, out of this —
Laertes
What out of this, my lord? 110
King
Laertes, was your father dear to you?
Or are you like the painting of a sorrow,
A face without a heart?
Laertes
Why ask you this?
King
Not that I think you did not love your father, 115
But that I know love is begun by time,
And that I see, in passages of proof,
Time qualifies the spark and fire of it.
There lives within the very flame of love
A kind of wick or snuff that will abate it, 120
And nothing is at a like goodness still,
For goodness, growing to a pleurisy,
Dies in his own too much. That we would do,
We should do when we would; for this "would" changes,
And hath abatements and delays as many 125
As there are tongues, are hands, are accidents,
And then this "should" is like a spendthrift's sigh,
That hurts by easing. But to the quick of the ulcer:
Hamlet comes back. What would you undertake
To show yourself indeed your father's son 130
More than in words?
Laertes
To cut his throat in the church.
King
No place indeed should murder sanctuarize.

136 put on those: set agents to work.

139 remiss: careless.

143 unbated: not blunted (OED obs.) with a button, as was done with a foil when fencing in sport. **a pass of practice:** a thrust just in practice in the sport of dueling with foils but also with a strong connotation of treachery ("practice" per the OED). The King is setting up Laertes to kill Hamlet in a way that will enable the King to escape any accusation of involvement, just as the Earl of Leicester was able to escape formal accusations in the death of an enemy or someone standing in the way of his ambition by having a henchman do the killing. The parallel between the stratagem of Leicester and that of King Claudius is striking.

148 cataplasm: a poultice, medicinal salve.

149 simples that have virtue: plants with medicinal power. (OED archaic)

155 fit us to our shape.: probably, fit the roles ("shape" OED obs.) that he and Laertes are to perform.

156 that our drift . . . bad performance,: probably, if our plan is revealed through some mistake.

159 If this did blast in proof.: if our plan blows up when we put it in practice.

160 cunnings: skills (OED archaic) in fencing.

161 I have it!: His abrupt exclamation rings a bit hollow, suggesting that he's already planned to use a poisoned drink. Leicester was widely thought to use poison to achieve his ends.

165 for the nonce,: expressly for this purpose. (OED obs.)

166 venomed stuck: poisoned stab.

167 Our purpose may hold there.: that is, we may still achieve ("hold there") our purpose

Revenge should have no bounds. But, good Laertes,
Will you do this? Keep close within your chamber.
Hamlet returned shall know you are come home. 135
We'll put on those shall praise your excellence,
And set a double varnish on the fame
The Frenchman gave you, bring you in fine together,
And wager over your heads. He, being remiss,
Most generous, and free from all contriving, 140
Will not peruse the foils, so that with ease,
Or with a little shuffling, you may choose
A sword unbated, and in a pass of practice
Requite him for your father.

Laertes

I will do it,
And for that purpose I'll anoint my sword. 145
I bought an unction of a mountebank,
So mortal that, but dip a knife in it,
Where it draws blood, no cataplasm so rare,
Collected from all simples that have virtue
Under the moon, can save the thing from death 150
That is but scratched withal. I'll touch my point
With this contagion, that if I gall him slightly,
It may be death.

King

Let's further think of this,
Weigh what convenience both of time and means
May fit us to our shape. If this should fail, 155
And that our drift look through our bad performance,
'Twere better not assayed; therefore this project
Should have a back or second, that might hold
If this did blast in proof. Soft, let me see.
We'll make a solemn wager on your cunnings — 160
I have it!
When in your motion you are hot and dry,
As make your bouts more violent to that end,
And that he calls for drink, I'll have prepared him
A chalice for the nonce, whereon but sipping, 165
If he by chance escape your venomed stuck,
Our purpose may hold there. But stay, what noise?

Enter Queen

Queen

One woe doth tread upon another's heel,
So fast they follow. Your sister's drowned, Laertes.

174-5 long purples . . . a grosser name.: perhaps the *Orchis mascula* which had many nicknames usually based on the testicle-shaped tubers and its purple spike, suggesting a penis.

176 cold: chaste.

177-8 on the pendant . . . to hang: that is, her garland of flowers ("crownet" OED obs.) and clothing ("weeds" OED archaic) catching hold like tendrils ("clambering") on a hanging bough.

178-9 envious sliver broke . . . herself fell: a malicious ("envious" OED obs.) long, thin branch ("sliver") broke, and she "fell" in the brook. Ambiguously, the Queen's apparently second-hand account of Ophelia's drowning is full of details as if she had witnessed it; perhaps it's meant to be from her distraught imagination. She also makes it sound like an accident, although not reporting any struggle against drowning. In the next scene, the gravedigger and his friend will discuss whether it was an accident or suicide.

182 old lauds: old hymns of praise to God.

184 indued . . . that element: able to take in ("indued" OED obs.) and live in the water ("that element"), like a fish.

192 our trick: probably, to fool ourselves.

193 Shame: a feeling of indecorous behavior; here, probably unmanly.

194 The woman will be out: probably, the feminine in me and my tears will be ended.

Laertes
Drowned! O, where? 170
Queen
There is a willow grows aslant the brook,
That shows his hoary leaves in the glassy stream,
Therewith fantastic garlands did she make
Of crow-flowers, nettles, daisies, and long purples
That liberal shepherds give a grosser name, 175
But our cold maids do dead men's fingers call them.
There on the pendant boughs her crownet weeds
Clambering to hang, an envious sliver broke,
When down her weedy trophies and herself
Fell in the weeping brook. Her clothes spread wide, 180
And mermaid-like awhile they bore her up,
Which time she chanted snatches of old lauds,
As one incapable of her own distress,
Or like a creature native and indued
Unto that element. But long it could not be 185
Till that her garments, heavy with their drink,
Pulled the poor wretch from her melodious lay
To muddy death.
Laertes
Alas, then she is drowned?
Queen
Drowned, drowned.

Laertes
Too much of water hast thou, poor Ophelia, 190
And therefore I forbid my tears; but yet
It is our trick--Nature her custom holds.
Let Shame say what it will; when these are gone,
The woman will be out. Adieu, my lord,
I have a speech of fire that fain would blaze, 195
But that this folly drowns it. *Exit*
King
Let's follow, Gertrude.
How much I had to do to calm his rage.
Now fear I this will give it start again,
Therefore let's follow. *Exeunt*

S.d. The play text gives "First Clown" and "Second Clown" for the speakers, but they are not the typical clowns or comedians in the plays or in today's parlance, and for clarity this edition substitutes "Gravedigger" and "His Friend."

1-2 Christian burial . . . own salvation: Suicides were denied a ritual Christian burial in consecrated ground. The Gravedigger must have heard reports that Ophelia killed herself. But "willfully seeks her own salvation" reflects ancient (pagan) Stoic philosophy that allowed suicide for good reason.

3 straight: align it east-west as Christian burial practice required. **crowner:** coroner. (OED obs.)

4 sat on her: sat in judgment on her at the inquest, perhaps with a crude visual pun of "sat on" her.

7 *se offendendo*: a made-up Latin legal phrase created by Oxford, who read law, that translates to hurt oneself, commit an offense against oneself, as when committing suicide. The Gravedigger uses the phrase to mock the contortions of a lawyer arguing an inheritance issue of suicide in a lawsuit. The usual commentary takes the word as an ignorant mistake for *se defendendo*, in self-defense; but Ophelia had no reason to defend herself. Throughout this scene, the Gravedigger is not an ignorant rustic but a knowledgeable, clever and witty jester. Here and in what follows, Oxford is satirizing the logic of the law, notably in the obscure inheritance lawsuit, Hales v. Pettit, in 1560 and its bizarre argument about the suicide of Sir James Pettit. That Will Shakspere would have somehow come across the report of the trial, written in "Law French" and been able to read it is highly unlikely. Oxford knew "Law French" from Gray's Inn law school and had a personal interest in inheritance law. (See Regnier.)

9 argal: supposedly another ignorant mistake, a mishearing of "ergo" from the study of logic, but more likely deliberately alluding to John Argall, a witty lecturer who taught logic at Oxford University, wrote a manual of logic and reputedly was a great actor in plays there. Oxford received an honorary MA degree from the university, knew about Argall and may have heard him lecture. Many in a court audience would recognize the allusion to him. It's doubtful that Shakspere could have heard or read about him. (See Detobel.)

25 first . . . bore arms: Since Adam was the first man, he was the first man with arms, punning on "coat of arms."

Act 5

Scene 1. A graveyard
Enter two Clowns [a Gravedigger and His Friend]

Gravedigger
Is she to be buried in Christian burial when she willfully seeks her own salvation?

His Friend
I tell thee she is, therefore make her grave straight. The crowner hath sat on her, and finds it Christian burial.

Gravedigger
How can that be, unless she drowned herself in her own defense? 5

His Friend
Why, 'tis found so.

Gravedigger
It must be *se offendendo*, it cannot be else. For here lies the point: if I drown myself wittingly, it argues an act, and an act hath three branches — it is to act, to do, to perform; argal, she drowned herself wittingly.

His Friend
Nay, but hear you, goodman delver — 10

Gravedigger
Give me leave. Here lies the water; good. Here stands the man; good. If the man go to this water and drown himself, it is, will he, nill he, he goes, mark you that. But if the water come to him and drown him, he drowns not himself; argal, he that is not guilty of his own death shortens not his own life. 15

His Friend
But is this law?

Gravedigger
Ay, marry, is it — crowner's quest law.

His Friend
Will you have the truth of it? If this had not been a gentlewoman, she should have been buried out of Christian burial.

Gravedigger
Why, there thou say'est, and the more pity that great folk should have 20 countenance in this world to drown or hang themselves, more than their even Christen. Come, my spade. There is no ancient gentlemen but gardeners, ditchers, and grave-makers; they hold up Adam's profession.

His Friend
Was he a gentleman?

Gravedigger
He was the first that ever bore arms. 25

29-30 confess thyself: a shortened version of the saying, "Confess thyself and be hanged."

31 Go to: an expression of impatience and/or disbelief; today's "O come on."

41 unyoke: give up and end your effort; as oxen are free from labor after being unyoked.

45 Cudgel thy brains: literally "beat your brains with a club," figuratively, "think hard." **mend his pace**: improve his pace and speed up.

47 Go, get thee in: presumably into a nearby inn or alehouse.

48 stoup: a tankard or large glass. (OED archaic)

49-52: The Gravedigger's song is recognized as an intentionally corrupted version of the song "The Aged Lover Renounceth Love" by Thomas Lord Vaux, a court poet, as was Oxford. It was published in *Tottel's Miscellany* (1557) the year after he died. Poems by Vaux also appeared in a later poetry collection, *The Paradyse of Daynty Devices* (1576), which included several of Oxford's earliest poems. So Oxford would have been familiar with Vaux's song and might well have known him.

51-52 To contract . . . meet": Presumably, the Gravedigger interrupts his singing with grunts as he works.

His Friend
Why, he had none.
Gravedigger
What, art a heathen? How dost thou understand the Scripture? The Scripture says Adam digged; could he dig without arms? I'll put another question to thee. If thou answerest me not to the purpose, confess thyself— 30
His Friend
Go to.
Gravedigger
What is he that builds stronger than either the mason, the shipwright, or the carpenter?
His Friend
The gallows-maker, for that outlives a thousand tenants. 35
Gravedigger
I like thy wit well, in good faith. The gallows does well; but how does it well? It does well to those that do ill. Now thou dost ill to say the gallows is built stronger than the church; argal, the gallows may do well to thee. To it again, come.
His Friend
Who builds stronger than a mason, a shipwright, or a carpenter? 40
Gravedigger
Ay, tell me that, and unyoke.
His Friend
Marry, now I can tell.
Gravedigger
To it!
His Friend
Mass, I cannot tell.

Enter Hamlet and Horatio afar off

Gravedigger
Cudgel thy brains no more about it, for your dull ass will not mend 45
his pace with beating, and when you are asked this question next, say "a grave-maker." The houses he makes lasts till doomsday. Go, get thee in and fetch me a stoup of liquor.

Exit his friend.

[Sings] " In youth when I did love, did love,
Methought it was very sweet, 50
To contract—O, the time for—a—my behove,
O, methought there—a—was as nothing—a—meet ."
Hamlet
Has this fellow no feeling of his business? He sings in grave-making.

54 easiness: indifference, here to his occupation as a gravedigger.

58 into the land: probably, the land of death.

61 jowls: strikes, slams. (OED archaic)

62 politician: Here, as almost always in Shakespeare, the word is pejorative, meaning one in government who schemes to advance his private cause or ambition.

63 over-reaches: goes beyond (in his scheming) .

67 meant to beg it: to be given the "horse" in return for praising it.

70 my Lady Worm's, chopless,: perhaps, her skull, unsaid but understood, since it is "chopless," that is, without cheeks, and crawling with worms.

70 mazard: head. (OED archaic slang)

71 Here's a fine revolution an we had the trick to see it.: a somewhat obscure line, unless an allusion to astronomy. Copernicus entitled his work *De Revolutionibus*, referring to his theory of the Earth revolving around the Sun (not the Sun revolving around the Earth), and Hamlet may well be saying Copernicus is right if ("an" OED obs.) one has the intelligence ("trick" OED obs.) to recognize it.

73 loggats: an old game with pieces of wood (from "log") thrown at a stake in the ground. (OED obs.)

75 For and: Moreover, per the OED.

79 quiddities: excessive subtleties of argument. **quillities:** quibbles. (OED obs.)

82-8 This fellow . . . no more, ha?: Hamlet in a manic phase delivers a dense and precise parody of legal terminology, reflecting Oxford's knowledge of the law and his life-long involvement with the intricacies of property law. (See Regnier.)

Horatio
Custom hath made it in him a property of easiness.
Hamlet
'Tis even so, the hand of little employment hath the daintier sense. 55
Gravedigger
[Sings] "But age with his stealing steps
Hath clawed me in his clutch,
And hath shipped me into the land,
As if I had never been such." *Throws up a skull*
Hamlet
[To Horatio] That skull had a tongue in it, and could sing once. How 60
the knave jowls it to the ground, as if 'twere Cain's jaw-bone, that
did the first murder. This might be the pate of a politician, which this
ass now over-reaches, one that would circumvent God, might it not?
Horatio
It might, my lord.
Hamlet
Or of a courtier, which could say, "Good morrow, sweet lord. How 65
dost thou, sweet lord?" This might be my lord Such-a-one, that
praised my lord Such-a-one's horse when he meant to beg it, might
it not?
Horatio
Ay, my lord.
Hamlet
Why, even so, and now my Lady Worm's, chopless, and knocked 70
about the mazard with a sexton's spade. Here's fine revolution, an we
had the trick to see it. Did these bones cost no more the breeding but
to play at loggats with them? Mine ache to think on it.
Gravedigger
[Sings] "A pickaxe and a spade, a spade,
For and a shrouding sheet 75
O, a pit of clay for to be made
For such a guest is meet."
Hamlet
There's another. Why may not that be the skull of a lawyer? Where
be his quiddities now, his quillities, his cases, his tenures, and his
tricks? Why does he suffer this mad knave now to knock him about 80
the sconce with a dirty shovel, and will not tell him of his action of
battery? Hum! This fellow might be in his time a great buyer of land,
with his statutes, his recognizances, his fines, his double vouchers, his
recoveries. Is this the fine of his fines, and the recovery of his
recoveries, to have his fine pate full of fine dirt? Will his vouchers 85
vouch him no more of his purchases, and double ones too, than the

89 Not a jot more, my lord.: Horatio, Hamlet's best and most faithful friend, is the voice of reason and common sense, if a rather pedestrian voice, in contrast to Hamlet's episodes of wild manic behavior and when he puts on an "antic disposition" for his own purposes, both of which Horatio accepts with equanimity. One of Oxford's best friends was his cousin Horatio Vere.

93 sheep and calves: fools and simpletons.

93 sirrah: a form of address to inferiors.

94 Mine sir: In the bantering that follows, the Gravedigger shows himself to be a match for Hamlet in quick-witted repartee typical of the court jester in Shakespeare plays who is the truth-teller and voice of the dramatist, Oxford. Here, Oxford, in the character Hamlet, meets his match in his own creation, the Gravedigger.

102 the quick: the living. (OED archaic)

110 How absolute: how perfectly certain, sure of himself. (OED obs.) **speak by the card**: speak to the point, alluding to a mariner's chart and compass, his "card" (OED obs.), for precise navigation; a metaphor reflecting Oxford's experience in sea voyages, which Shakspere lacked. **equivocation:** here, unintended ambiguity.

112-13 the age . . . kibe: a metaphor describing lower-class men, disparagingly "peasants," trying to act and speak like noblemen, and doing it so closely that it irritates them. Hamlet is saying that "the age," that is, these times, has become so overly refined and exquisite ("picked" OED obs. and here sarcastically) that the peasant's toe comes so close on the heel of the courtier that he chafes or irritates ("galls") his sore heel (his "kibe" per the OED). Lord Oxford no doubt was irritated that the "new men" at Queen Elizabeth's court, such as Christopher Hatton, Walter Raleigh and even William Cecil, who were born commoners and were not of the feudal aristocracy, like Oxford, nevertheless rose to significant positions at court and competed for Elizabeth's attention and preference. Notably, for Oxford, these *arrivistes* would have included Robert Dudley, who did not inherit a nobleman's title from his father but was made Earl of Leicester by Queen Elizabeth.

length and breadth of a pair of indentures? The very conveyances of his lands will scarcely lie in this box, and must the inheritor himself have no more, ha?

Horatio

Not a jot more, my lord.

Hamlet

Is not parchment made of sheep-skins? 90

Horatio

Ay, my lord, and of calves'skins too.

Hamlet

They are sheep and calves which seek out assurance in that. I will speak to this fellow. Whose grave's this, sirrah?

Gravedigger

Mine, sir.

[Sings] "O, a pit of clay for to be made 95

For such a guest is meet."

Hamlet

I think it be thine indeed, for thou liest in it.

Gravedigger

You lie out on it, sir, and therefore 'tis not yours; for my part, I do not lie In it, yet it is mine.

Hamlet

Thou dost lie in it, to be in it and say it is thine. 'Tis for the dead, 100
not for the quick; therefore thou liest.

Gravedigger

'Tis a quick lie, sir, 'twill away again from me to you.

Hamlet

What man dost thou dig it for?

Gravedigger

For no man, sir.

Hamlet

What woman then? 105

Gravedigger

For none neither.

Hamlet

Who is to be buried in it?

Gravedigger

One that was a woman, sir, but, rest her soul, she's dead.

Hamlet

How absolute the knave is! We must speak by the card, or 110
equivocation will undo us. By the Lord, Horatio, this three years I have took note of it; the age is grown so picked that the toe of the peasant comes so near the heel of the courtier, he galls his kibe. How

129 Upon what ground?: that is, what are the grounds or reasons for that? But the Gravedigger puns on "ground" meaning the ground we stand on, "here in Denmark."

130-1 sexton . . . thirty years.: Commentators have taken this "thirty years" and other mentions of years and events in the three versions of *Hamlet* to set his age now at thirty, although he was a teenage university student until now. There is perhaps a better analysis at line notes 139 and 149 below.

133 pocky corses: corpses riddled with the pox ("pocky" OED rare) and usually referring to syphilis.

134 scarce hold: that is, barely hold together and not rot away before being buried.

138 whoreson: a term of dislike or contempt but sometimes, probably as here, of joking familiarity. (OED obs.)

long hast thou been grave-maker?

Gravedigger

Of all the days in the year, I came to it that day that our last king Hamlet 115
overcame Fortinbras.

Hamlet

How long is that since?

Gravedigger

Cannot you tell that? Every fool can tell that. It was that very day that
young Hamlet was born — he that is mad, and sent into England.

Hamlet

Ay, marry, why was he sent into England? 120

Gravedigger

Why, because he was mad. He shall recover his wits there, or if he do not,
'tis no great matter there.

Hamlet

Why?

Gravedigger

'Twill not be seen in him there, there the men are as mad as he.

Hamlet

How came he mad? 125

Gravedigger

Very strangely, they say.

Hamlet

How strangely?

Gravedigger

Faith, even with losing his wits.

Hamlet

Upon what ground?

Gravedigger

Why, here in Denmark. I have been sexton here, man and boy, 130
thirty years.

Hamlet

How long will a man lie in the earth ere he rot?

Gravedigger

Faith, if he be not rotten before he die — as we have many pocky
corses nowadays, that will scarce hold the laying in — he will last
you some eight year or nine year. A tanner will last you nine year. 135

Hamlet

Why he more than another?

Gravedigger

Why, sir, his hide is so tanned with his trade that he will keep out water a
great while, and your water is a sore decayer of your whoreson dead body.

139 skull . . . three and twenty years.: Yorick's skull, which lay buried for twenty-three years. See line note 149.

144 Yorick's: an invented name of uncertain origin.

148-9 I knew him . . . bore me on his back: Oxford as a child may well have known a court jester, who, like Yorick, might have carried him piggyback. That would have been Will Somers, the renowned jester at the court of King Henry the Eighth, whose Lord Great Chamberlain was Oxford's father. Somers died when Oxford was ten, and if Oxford knew him, as is likely, his death would have been significant loss for a ten-year-old.

149 bore me on his back: Since Yorick died twenty-three years ago, as the Gravedigger has specified (at line 139), and he gave Hamlet piggyback rides when Hamlet would have been a child of four to six, maybe seven, that would make Hamlet about twenty-eight years old, perhaps thirty, here and to the end of the play. His abrupt aging has caused much debate by commentators. If Oxford had any particular reason to make Hamlet older, it's not known. In his Shakespeare plays, time is sometimes condensed or drawn out for dramatic purposes. It may be simply because he thought of his character Hamlet now acting more mature than even a precocious older teenager.

153 your own grinning: the skull's grinning in a grimace.

154 chapfallen.: with the lower jaw, the "chap" or "chop," hanging down (or missing) because of death (per the OED).

155 to this favor: to this countenance or face, to look like this. (OED archaic)

158 Alexander: Alexander the Great, Greek king of Macedon and a renowned military commander.

163 bunghole: the hole in a barrel or cask that is plugged with a stopper, a "bung."

164 too curiously: too attentively and pryingly. (OED archaic)

Here's a skull now hath lain you in the earth three and twenty years.

Hamlet

Whose was it? 140

Gravedigger

A whoreson mad fellow's it was. Whose do you think it was?

Hamlet

Nay, I know not.

Gravedigger

A pestilence on him for a mad rogue! He poured a flagon of Rhenish
on my head once. This same skull, sir, was, sir, Yorick's skull,
the king's jester. 145

Hamlet

This?

Gravedigger

Even that.

Hamlet

Alas, poor Yorick. I knew him, Horatio, a fellow of infinite jest, of
most excellent fancy. He hath bore me on his back a thousand times,
and now how abhorred in my imagination it is! My gorge rises at it. 150
Here hung those lips that I have kissed I know not how oft. Where
be your gibes now, your gambols, your songs, your flashes of
merriment, that were wont to set the table on a roar? Not one now to
mock your own grinning — quite chapfallen. Now get you to my
lady's chamber, and tell her, let her paint an inch thick, to this favor 155
she must come; make her laugh at that. Prithee, Horatio, tell me one
thing.

Horatio

What's that, my lord?

Hamlet

Dost thou think Alexander looked in this fashion in the earth?

Horatio

Even so.

Hamlet

And smelt so? pah! 160

Horatio

Even so, my lord.

Hamlet

To what base uses we may return, Horatio. Why may not imagination
trace the noble dust of Alexander, till it find it stopping a bunghole?

Horatio

'Twere to consider too curiously, to consider so.

165 modesty: moderation, reasonable consideration.

169-72 Imperious Caesar. . . . winter's flaw.: apparently Hamlet's impromptu summing-up in verse.

174 maimed rites: figuratively, shortened and incomplete funeral rites; deprived of the essentials for a Christian burial. (OED obs.)

176 fordo its own life: kill oneself. (OED obs.) **of some estate:** of some high rank or social standing. (OED archaic)

177 Couch we . . . mark: Let's lie down, hide ourselves ("couch" OED obs.) and observe ("mark").

182 warranty: authorization. **doubtful:** of questionable circumstances, whether her death was suicide or accidental.

183 And but that great command oversways: that is, unless a high legal official ("great command") overrules. ("oversways" OED obs.)

184 in ground unsanctified: a suicide could not be buried in the sanctified ground of a church cemetery, but in Ophelia's case a compromise has been reached because of the uncertainty of the circumstances of her death.

187 crants: garlands.

188 strewments: something strewn (OED rare); here flowers.

194 peace-parted souls: those who died a natural death in peace.

Hamlet

No, faith, not a jot, but to follow him thither with modesty enough 165
and likelihood to lead it. Alexander died, Alexander was buried,
Alexander returneth to dust, the dust is earth, of earth we make
loam; and why of that loam whereto he was converted might they
not stop a beer-barrel? Imperious Caesar, dead and turned to clay,
Might stop a hole to keep the wind away. 170
O that that earth which kept the world in awe
Should patch a wall to expel the winter's flaw.
But soft, but soft awhile, here comes the king.

Enter King, Queen, Laertes, and a priest following a corpse, with lords attendant

The queen, the courtiers. Who is this they follow?
And with such maimed rites? This doth betoken
The corpse they follow did with desperate hand 175
Fordo it own life. 'Twas of some estate.
Couch we a while and mark.

Laertes

What ceremony else?

Hamlet

That is Laertes, a very noble youth. Mark.

Laertes

What ceremony else? 180

Priest

Her obsequies have been as far enlarged
As we have warranty. Her death was doubtful;
And but that great command oversways the order,
She should in ground unsanctified been lodged
Till the last trumpet; for charitable prayers, 185
Shards, flints, and pebbles should be thrown on her.
Yet here she is allowed her virgin crants,
Her maiden strewments, and the bringing home
Of bell and burial.

Laertes

Must there no more be done? 190

Priest

No more be done.
We should profane the service of the dead
To sing a requiem and such rest to her
As to peace-parted souls.

Laertes

Lay her in the earth, 195
And from her fair and unpolluted flesh

199 howling: in hell.

203 decked: adorned or decorated; here with flowers (understood).

206-7 cursed head / Whose wicked deed: referring to Hamlet's slaying of Polonius. **ingenious sense**: intelligence, having good sense (OED obs.), referring to her sanity.

212 Pelion: In Greek mythology, the Titans piled Mount Pelion on top of Mount Ossa to reach the top of Mount Olympus, the highest mountain in Greece and the home of the gods.

213 blue Olympus: This unusual and first such usage of "blue" (per the OED) to describe mountains that appear from a great distance to be a hazy blue is evidence for Oxford as the author of *Hamlet*. During his travels on the Continent, he would have seen distant mountain ranges appearing to have a bluish hue, a very unlikely phenomenon for Shakspere, who never traveled to the Continent, to have seen in the flat terrain around Stratford and London.

216 Conjures: casts a spell on. **the wandering stars:** the planets, which look like fixed stars to the casual observer on any given night but over time are moving relative to the stars and to each other, hence "wandering stars," showing the dramatist's easy grasp of astronomical phenomenon. **makes them stand**: makes the planets stand still in astonishment at Laertes' much embellished expressions of grief.

218 I, Hamlet the Dane: By calling himself "the Dane," Hamlet is claiming to be the preeminent Dane, who should be on the throne.

222 splenative: having a hot or hasty temperament. (OED obs.) The spleen was thought to be the cause of various emotions, chiefly rage.

May violets spring. I tell thee, churlish priest,
A ministering angel shall my sister be
When thou liest howling.

Hamlet

[Aside] What, the fair Ophelia! 200

Queen

Sweets to the sweet, farewell.
I hoped thou should'st have been my Hamlet's wife.
I thought thy bride-bed to have decked, sweet maid,
And not have strewed thy grave.

Laertes

O, treble woe 205
Fall ten times treble on that cursed head
Whose wicked deed thy most ingenious sense
Deprived thee of. Hold off the earth a while,
Till I have caught her once more in mine arms. *Leaps in the grave*
Now pile your dust upon the quick and dead, 210
Till of this flat a mountain you have made
To overtop old Pelion, or the skyish head
Of blue Olympus.

Hamlet

What is he whose grief
Bears such an emphasis, whose phrase of sorrow 215
Conjures the wandering stars and makes them stand
Like wonder-wounded hearers? This is I,
Hamlet the Dane.

Laertes

The devil take thy soul! *Grapples with him*

Hamlet

Thou pray'st not well. 220
I prithee take thy fingers from my throat.
For though I am not splenative and rash,
Yet have I in me something dangerous,
Which let thy wisdom fear. Hold off thy hand!

King

Pluck them asunder. 225

Queen

Hamlet! Hamlet!

All

Gentlemen!

Horatio

Good my lord, be quiet.

229 upon this theme: this matter as a cause for action. (OED obs.)

230 wag: blink or flutter (OED obs.) and thus show the slightest sign of life.

236 forbear him: be patient with him, tolerate him. (OED obs.)

237 'Swounds: short for the strong oath "by God's wounds" when He was on the cross.

239 eisel: vinegar. (OED obs.)

244 our ground: that is, our burial mound.

245 Singeing . . . burning zone,; probably, scorching its summit ("pate" the top of its head, poetically) against the burning Sun in its orbit ("zone").

246 Ossa: the Greek mountain (line note 212 above). **an thou'lt mouth:** if you're going to rave.

251 When that her golden couplets are disclosed: when a pair ("couplets") of newly hatched young doves, covered with "golden" down, are hatched ("disclosed").

256 Hercules: the god of Greek and Roman mythology famous for his strength and courage but also for boasting, apparently alluding to Laertes' elaborate expressions of grief.

257 The cat . . . day.: The cat can't be silenced and the dog won't be denied its chance to succeed, apparently Hamlet's promise that his turn will come.

259 last night's speech: their talk of plotting to kill Hamlet in the duel.

260 present push: to get on with it ("push") right away ("present" OED obs.), and perhaps alluding to the "push" of a sword thrust. (OED obs.)

Hamlet
Why, I will fight with him upon this theme
Until my eyelids will no longer wag. 230
Queen
O my son, what theme?
Hamlet
I loved Ophelia. Forty thousand brothers
Could not with all their quantity of love
Make up my sum. *[to Laertes.]* What wilt thou do for her?
King
O, he is mad, Laertes. 235
Queen
For love of God, forbear him.
Hamlet
'Swounds, show me what thou would do.
Would thou weep, would thou fight, would thou fast, would thou tear thyself?
Would thou drink up eisel, eat a crocodile?
I'll do it. Dost come here to whine? 240
To outface me with leaping in her grave?
Be buried quick with her, and so will I.
And if thou prate of mountains, let them throw
Millions of acres on us, till our ground,
Singeing his pate against the burning zone, 245
Make Ossa like a wart. Nay, an thou'lt mouth,
I'll rant as well as thou.
Queen
This is mere madness,
And thus awhile the fit will work on him.
Anon, as patient as the female dove, 250
When that her golden couplets are disclosed,
His silence will sit drooping.
Hamlet
[to Laertes] Hear you, sir,
What is the reason that you use me thus?
I loved you ever. But it is no matter. 255
Let Hercules himself do what he may,
The cat will mew, and dog will have his day. *Exit Hamlet*
King
I pray thee, good Horatio, wait upon him. *Exit Horatio*
[Aside to Laertes] Strengthen your patience in our last night's speech,
We'll put the matter to the present push-- 260

262 living monument: The "monument" to Ophelia may be her brother Laertes' duel of revenge with Hamlet in which the king expects Hamlet to die and Laertes to emerge still "living."

1 other: what Hamlet did not put in his letter to Horatio (at 4.6.11-23).

3 Remember . . . lord!: that is, how could I forget it.

6 the mutines in the bilboes: the sailors who refuse to obey orders ("mutines" OED obs.) and whose ankles are put in iron shackles joined by long iron bars (bilboes" per the OED) that are locked, confining the sailors together. Oxford's detailed knowledge of such confinements is readily explained by his sea-going travel; no such opportunity is known for Shakspere. **Rashly**: here, impulsively.

9 pall: falter. (OED obs.)

13 scarfed about me: wrapped around me. (OED rare)

14 them: Rosencrantz and Guildenstern.

20 larded: embellished.

21 Importing: citing as significant (OED archaic); no doubt a veiled threat to the king of England's "health" if King' Claudius's "exact command" to kill Hamlet is not carried out.

22 ho, such bugs and goblins in my life: the fears that might be imagined if Hamlet is not killed but continues to live; apparently with some ridicule.

23 on the supervise: upon inspection. (OED obs.) **no leisure bated**: probably, losing no time.

Good Gertrude, set some watch over your son.
This grave shall have a living monument.
An hour of quiet shortly shall we see,
Till then in patience our proceeding be. *Exeunt*

Scene 2. A castle hall
Enter Hamlet and Horatio

Hamlet
So much for this, sir, now shall you see the other —
You do remember all the circumstance?
Horatio
Remember it, my lord!
Hamlet
Sir, in my heart there was a kind of fighting
That would not let me sleep. Methought I lay 5
Worse than the mutines in the bilboes. Rashly —
And praised be rashness for it — let us know
Our indiscretion sometime serves us well
When our deep plots do pall—and that should learn us
There's a divinity that shapes our ends, 10
Rough-hew them how we will.
Horatio
That is most certain.
Hamlet
Up from my cabin,
My sea-gown scarfed about me, in the dark
Groped I to find out them, had my desire,
Fingered their packet; and in fine withdrew 15
To mine own room again, making so bold,
My fears forgetting manners, to unseal
Their grand commission; where I found, Horatio —
Ah, royal knavery! — an exact command,
Larded with many several sorts of reasons, 20
Importing Denmark's health and England's too,
With, ho, such bugs and goblins in my life,
That, on the supervise, no leisure bated,
No, not to stay the grinding of the axe,
My head should be struck off.
Horatio
Is it possible? 25
Hamlet
Here's the commission, read it at more leisure.
But wilt thou hear now how I did proceed?

32 fair: in clear handwriting of a scribe, the newer, clearer Italic script as opposed to the English Secretary hand, still in common use. Oxford's extant letters are in clear, firm Italic handwriting even those he wrote as young student. No texts written by Shakspere have been found.

33 statists: upper-class statesmen (OED archaic); here, as opposed to lower-class scribes.

38 conjuration: a solemn appeal or demand, carrying the possibility of a penalty. (OED obs.)

39-42 As England . . . amities,: In this passage, Hamlet describes how he forged a replacement letter from King Claudius and did it in rhetoric that expresses his disdain for the artificial niceties of diplomats' correspondence. He imitates in paraphrase the ornate, semi-obsequious language of a diplomat who hopes to count on continued friendly relations while calling for a favor he knows must be granted. It's the subtle, specialized rhetoric of aristocratic diplomats that Oxford would readily know about. Hamlet does this perhaps to disguise a bit the brutal fact that his counterfeit letter is intended to cause the hapless Rosencrantz and Guildenstern to be executed.

42 stand a comma . . . amities,: be only a "comma" (the least significant punctuation) in the presumed friendly relations ("amities") of the two countries.

45 Without debatement: without any hesitation or debate. (OED obs.)

47 Not shriving time allowed: no time to confess their sins to a priest and be absolved of them. Claudius was guilty of not allowing Hamlet's father time for confession, nor, as Claudius is planning it, for Hamlet; and here Hamlet, equally guilty, does the same.

48 ordinant: directing, ordering events. (OED obs.)

49 signet: a small seal set in a finger ring.

53 the changeling: a substitute made surreptitiously. (OED obs.)

56 go to it: go to their death, and perhaps in Horatio's view undeservedly.

57 they did make love to this employment.: that is, they were eager to be King Claudius's agents in his plot to have Hamlet out of the way, although they did not know that also meant his execution. Here and in what follows, Hamlet seems to be rationalizing his deadly counterplot, which will have them killed in England.

59 by their own insinuation: by their currying favor with King Claudius and effectively, if indirectly, joining his plot.

60 the baser nature: alluding to Rosencrantz and Guildenstern.

Horatio
I beseech you.
Hamlet
Being thus benetted round with villainies,
Ere I could make a prologue to my brains, 30
They had begun the play. I sat me down,
Devised a new commission, wrote it fair—
I once did hold it, as our statists do,
A baseness to write fair, and labored much
How to forget that learning, but, sir, now 35
It did me yeoman's service—Wilt thou know
The effect of what I wrote?
Horatio
Ay, good my lord.
Hamlet
An earnest conjuration from the king,
As England was his faithful tributary,
As love between them like the palm might flourish, 40
As peace should still her wheaten garland wear
And stand a comma 'tween their amities,
And many such-like as is of great charge,
That on the view and knowing of these contents,
Without debatement further, more or less, 45
He should those bearers put to sudden death,
Not shriving time allowed.
Horatio
How was this sealed?
Hamlet
Why, even in that was heaven ordinant.
I had my father's signet in my purse,
Which was the model of that Danish seal; 50
Folded the writ up in the form of the other,
Subscribed it, gave it the impression, placed it safely,
The changeling never known. Now the next day
Was our sea-fight, and what to this was sequent
Thou knowest already. 55
Horatio
So Guildenstern and Rosencrantz go to it.
Hamlet
Why, man, they did make love to this employment.
They are not near my conscience. Their defeat
Does by their own insinuation grow.
'Tis dangerous when the baser nature comes 60

61 Between the pass and fell incensed points: between a foil thrust ("pass" from fencing just in sport) and deadly ("fell"), angry ("incensed") foil "points" when using fencing to kill one's adversary.

63 stand me now upon?: become incumbent on me?

65 Popped in between the election: between the election of Hamlet as king of Denmark in the normal process of senior noblemen confirming by "election" an heir as the successor king, and the election (before the play begins) that Claudius probably manipulated, taking advantage of Hamlet being underage and away at the university in Germany.

66 angle: fish hook. (OED archaic)

67 with such cozenage: with such deception and trickery.

68 To quit him: to get rid of him (OED obs.) with a connotation of pay-back.

74 a man's life . . . "one.": a human's life is as short as counting to "one."

79 bravery: courage, but also bravado, boasting. (OED obs.)

84 water-fly: an aquatic insect that skims the water's surface, like the multi-colored dragonfly; hence figuratively and derisively for Osric as a superficial, gaudy insect. This portrait of Osric as a "water-fly" here and in what follows is a satire on rural land-owners trying to succeed in Queen Elizabeth's court by imitating the dress, manners and wit of born-and-raised aristocrats, like Oxford.

86 gracious: fortunate. (OED obs.)

87-88 let a beast . . . king's mess: If you let a lower-class creature, "a beast," like Osric, be lord over barnyard animals, his "beasts," then his dinner table, "his crib," a manger for feeding animals, will be set alongside the king's dinner table.

88-89 chough . . . . dirt: literally a crow, but also a boorish, ill-bred countryman, a "chuff," the two words being pronounced the same. Also, a "chough" or crow was considered an avian chatterer that reputedly could imitate words it hears. **spacious . . . dirt**: that is, owns a lot of mere "dirt."

Between the pass and fell incensed points
Of mighty opposites.

Horatio

Why, what a king is this!

Hamlet

Does it not, think thee, stand me now upon?
He that hath killed my king and whored my mother,
Popped in between the election and my hopes, 65
Thrown out his angle for my proper life,
And with such cozenage. Is it not perfect conscience
To quit him with this arm? And is it not to be damned,
To let this canker of our nature come
In further evil? 70

Horatio

It must be shortly known to him from England
What is the issue of the business there.

Hamlet

It will be short; the interim's mine,
And a man's life's no more than to say "one."
But I am very sorry, good Horatio, 75
That to Laertes I forgot myself,
For by the image of my cause I see
The portraiture of his. I'll court his favors.
But sure the bravery of his grief did put me
Into a towering passion. 80

Horatio

Peace, who comes here?

Enter young Osric, a courtier

Osric

Your lordship is right welcome back to Denmark.

Hamlet

I humbly thank you, sir.
[Aside] Dost know this water-fly?

Horatio

[Aside] No, my good lord. 85

Hamlet

[Aside] Thy state is the more gracious, for 'tis a vice to know him. He hath much land, and fertile; let a beast be lord of beasts, and his crib shall stand at the king's mess. 'Tis a chough, but, as I say, spacious in the possession of dirt.

Osric

Sweet lord, if your lordship were at leisure, I should impart a thing to you 90 from His Majesty.

96 indifferent cold: rather cold but neither too cold nor too hot.

101 for my complexion: for my body or constitution. (OED obs.)

106 for my ease: that is, I would feel better not wearing my hat in your presence.

108 very soft society: probably his way of saying "very good, genteel manners."

109 card or calendar: chart or directory, both obsolete usages per the OED.

110 continent: content or capacity (OED obs.), hence embodiment.

111-116 Sir, his definement . . . . nothing more.: In this speech and the dialogue that follows, Hamlet mocks Osric with hollow rhetoric and made-up words verging on nonsense.

121 Is it not . . . really.: Speaking to Osric, Horatio asks him to speak in a plainer language ("another tongue") rather than in his ridiculously affected speech.

Hamlet
I will receive it, sir, with all diligence of spirit. Put your bonnet to his right use, 'tis for the head.
Osric
I thank your lordship, it is very hot.
Hamlet
No, believe me, 'tis very cold, the wind is northerly. 95
Osric
It is indifferent cold, my lord, indeed.
Hamlet
But yet methinks it is very sultry and hot 100
for my complexion.
Osric
Exceedingly, my lord, it is very sultry — as 'twere — I cannot tell how. My lord, His Majesty bade me signify to you that he has laid a great wager on your head. Sir, this is the matter —
Hamlet
I beseech you remember. *Hamlet signals him to put on his hat* 105
Osric
Nay, good my lord, for my ease, in good faith. Sir, here is newly come to court Laertes, believe me, an absolute gentleman, full of most excellent differences, of very soft society, and great showing; indeed, to speak feelingly of him, he is the card or calendar of gentry; for you shall find in him the continent of what part a gentleman would see. 110
Hamlet
Sir, his definement suffers no perdition in you, though I know to divide him inventorially would dozy the arithmetic of memory, and yet but yaw neither, in respect of his quick sail; but in the verity of extolment, I take him to be a soul of great article, and his infusion of such dearth and rareness as, to make true diction of him, his semblable is his mirror, and 115 who else would trace him, his umbrage, nothing more.
Osric
Your lordship speaks most infallibly of him.

Hamlet
The concernancy, sir. Why do we wrap the gentleman in our more rawer breath?
Osric
Sir? 120
Horatio
Is it not possible to understand in another tongue? You will to it, sir, really.
Hamlet
What imports the nomination of this gentleman?

124 His purse: Osric's supply of fancy rhetoric.

127 not much approve me: little commend me (because of Osric's lack of judgment).

130 I dare . . . excellence,: With courteous modesty, Hamlet declines to compare himself to Laertes in excellence.

31 know a man well . . . himself.: to know another well, one must first know oneself.

132 imputation: the attribution of a fault or crime to someone. Osric probably confuses it with reputation, a mistake with unfortunate results.

133 in his meed he's unfellowed: in his merit (OED obs.) he is without an equal fellow.

137 Barbary horses: a highly valued North African breed, prized by royalty and aristocratic horse-owners in Elizabethan England for their speed.

138 impawned: pledged as security, but Osric must mean wagered.

138-141 with their assigns . . . liberal conceit.: Assigns are agents or those to whom property has been assigned (OED), but Osric must mean accessories or appurtenances. The "girdle" was a belt from which one or two decorated straps served as sword "hangers," which Osric goes on to say in his pretentious way, are fanciful, matched to the swords, carefully shaped with ingenuity.

143 you must be edified by the margent: Hamlet would require explanations ("be edified" OED obs.) for Osric's nonsense, as explanations are sometimes made in the margins ("margent" OED obs.) of a book.

144 carriages . . . hangers: But hangers are not called "carriages" even though they "carry" swords. Cannons, however, are carried on carriages, as Hamlet will point out.

Osric
Of Laertes?
Horatio
His purse is empty already, all his golden words are spent.
Hamlet
Of him, sir. 125
Osric
I know you are not ignorant—
Hamlet
I would you did, sir, yet, in faith, if you did, it would not much approve me. Well, sir?
Osric
You are not ignorant of what excellence Laertes is.
Hamlet
I dare not confess that, lest I should compare with him in excellence, but 130 to know a man well were to know himself.
Osric
I mean, sir, for his weapon, but in the imputation laid on him by them, in his meed he's unfellowed.
Hamlet
What's his weapon?
Osric
Rapier and dagger. 135
Hamlet
That's two of his weapons — but well.
Osric
The king, sir, hath wagered with him six Barbary horses, against the which he has impawned, as I take it, six French rapiers and poniards, with their assigns, as girdle, hangers, and so. Three of the carriages, in faith, are very 140
dear to fancy, very responsive to the hilts, most delicate carriages, and of very liberal conceit.
Hamlet
What call you the carriages?
Horatio
I knew you must be edified by the margent ere you had done.
Osric
The carriages, sir, are the hangers.
Hamlet
The phrase would be more germane to the matter if we could carry a 145 cannon by our sides; I would it might be hangers till then. But on six Barbary horses against six French swords, their "assigns," and three liberal-conceited carriages; that's the French bet against the Danish. Why is this all impawned, as you call it?

150 dozen passes . . . for nine: The King is betting on Hamlet, but the odds given by the king, as Osric describes them, have long puzzled commentators and mathematicians. It may well be that Osric has simply confused what the king told him and made nonsense of the odds. In any case, even this credible scrambling of the odds reflects knowledge of the earliest thinking about probability theory, knowledge Oxford would have had, but not Shakspere. (See Saunders.)

156 breathing time: probably, the time for exercise to stimulate breathing.

164 for his turn: to serve his turn; no one to commend him but himself.

165 This lapwing . . . his head: Osric puts his hat back on his head as he leaves, reminding Horatio of a newly hatched "lapwing," a ground-nesting bird, that was thought to run around with part of its shell still on its "head" (per the OED).

166 comply . . . dug: deferentially and politely approach or "address" someone ("comply" OED obs.) like a hungry new-born baby looking forward eagerly to its mother's or nurse's nipple.

167 drossy age: worthless, shoddy times.

168 the tune of the time: the fashionable language of the day.

169 yeasty collection: a frothy, superficial collection (of their affected mannerisms and ways of speaking.)

170 opinions: that are expressed in conversations.

171 bubbles are out.: probably, their hollow, weightless, trivial comments ("bubbles") are exposed ("out") as such.

175-7 If his fitness . . . ready.: Hamlet seems to say that if the King thinks it proper and convenient ("if his fitness speaks" OED obs.), that he, Hamlet, is physically fit and "ready" for the duel.

Osric
The king, sir, hath laid, sir, that in a dozen passes between yourself 150
and him, he shall not exceed you three hits; he hath laid on twelve for
nine; and it would come to immediate trial, if your lordship would
vouchsafe the answer.
Hamlet
How if I answer no?
Osric
I mean, my lord, the opposition of your person in trial. 155
Hamlet
Sir, I will walk here in the hall. If it please His Majesty, it is the breathing
time of day with me. Let the foils be brought, the gentleman willing, and
the king hold his purpose, I will win for him and I can; if not, I will gain
nothing but my shame and the odd hits.
Osric
Shall I deliver you so? 160
Hamlet
To this effect, sir — after what flourish your nature will.
Osric
I commend my duty to your lordship.
Hamlet
Yours. *Exit Osric*
He does well to commend it himself, there are no tongues else for his turn.
Horatio
This lapwing runs away with the shell on his head. 165
Hamlet
He did comply, sir, with his dug before he sucked it. Thus has he, and
many more of the same breed that I know the drossy age dotes on,
only got the tune of the time, and out of an habit of encounter, a kind
of yeasty collection, which carries them through and through the most
profound and winnowed opinions, and do but blow them to their trial, 170
the bubbles are out.

Enter a lord

Lord
My lord, his Majesty commended him to you by young Osric, who brings
back to him that you attend him in the hall. He sends to know if your
pleasure hold to play with Laertes, or that you will take longer time.
Hamlet
I am constant to my purposes, they follow the king's pleasure. If his 175
fitness speaks, mine is ready; now or whensoever, provided I be
so able as now.
Lord
The king and queen and all are coming down.

179 In happy time.: fortuitously, just at the right time. (OED obs.)

180 use some gentle entertainment: that is, treat Laertes ("use . . . entertainment" OED obs.) gently and greet him with some courtesy as the gentleman you are. Gertrude anticipates antipathy between the two, especially given Laertes' desire to avenge his father's death.

183 You will lose, my lord.: an unexpected and odd prediction for Horatio to make, unless he means Hamlet may better Laertes in the dueling itself but "lose" the wager as the King has set it up.

185-6 how ill . . . my heart: how much evil (the original and now obsolete meaning of "ill" per the OED), and thus hostility Hamlet has in his "heart," no doubt for the King.

188 foolery: being foolish. **gaingiving:** giving in return. (OED obs.); here probably getting revenge.

192 defy augury: reject trying to predict the future

195 to leave betimes?: to leave early, here to die young.

196 this hand: Laertes' hand, which the King puts into Hamlet's.

199-210 This presence knows. . . . Hamlet's enemy: In this passage, Oxford as Hamlet acknowledges his mental disorder, his antic disposition, his periodic manic highs, his "madness;" notwithstanding his deliberately putting on an antic disposition at times to serve his purposes. (See the Introduction.)

199 This presence: This royal assembly (per the OED), and by extension the Elizabethan court audience watching the play.

200 I am punished with a sore distraction: that is, I am made to suffer from a serious ("sore") form of madness ("distraction." (OED obs.)

202 exception: disapproval. (OED obs.)

Hamlet
In happy time.
Lord
The queen desires you to use some gentle entertainment to Laertes before you fall to play. 180
Hamlet
She well instructs me. *Exit Lord*
Horatio
You will lose, my lord.
Hamlet
I do not think so; since he went into France I have been in continual practice. I shall win at the odds. Thou wouldst not think how ill all's here about my heart — but it is no matter. 185
Horatio
Nay, good my lord —
Hamlet
It is but foolery, but it is such a kind of gaingiving, as would perhaps trouble a woman.
Horatio
If your mind dislike anything, obey it. I will forestall their repair hither, and say you are not fit. 190
Hamlet
Not a whit, we defy augury. There is special providence in the fall of a sparrow. If it be now, 'tis not to come; if it be not to come, it will be now; if it be not now, yet it will come. The readiness is all. Since no man knows aught of what he leaves, what is it to leave betimes? Let be. 195

A table prepared with flagons of wine on it.
Enter Trumpets, Drums, and Officers with cushions, foils, daggers;
King, Queen, Laertes, Osric, and all the state

King
Come, Hamlet, come, and take this hand from me.
Hamlet
[to Laertes] Give me your pardon, sir. I have done you wrong,
But pardon it as you are a gentleman.
This presence knows, and you must needs have heard,
How I am punished with a sore distraction. 200
What I have done
That might your nature, honor, and exception
Roughly awake, I here proclaim was madness.
Was it Hamlet wronged Laertes? Never Hamlet!
If Hamlet from himself be taken away, 205

211 in this audience: before the full court assembled by the King to watch the duel, and also the play's aristocratic audience who would see Prince Hamlet as Lord Oxford.

215 my brother: figuratively, Laertes, who would have become Hamlet's brother-in-law if Hamlet had married Ophelia, as she and Gertrude had hoped. Laertes, the son of Polonius, probably represents Thomas Cecil, the elder son of William Cecil Lord Burghley, who is Polonius in the play. Thomas Cecil became Oxford's brother-in-law when Oxford married his sister, Anne. (See the Introduction.)

216-222 I am satisfied . . . ungored.: Disingenuously, Laertes says in his usual oblique manner that he will suspend his natural impulse to seek "revenge" (for his father's death by Hamlet's sword) but that his "honor" does not allow "reconcilement" until someone in authority proclaims that his reputation is not wounded ("ungored") by his failing to seek proper revenge.

228 mine ignorance: my lack of knowledge of or skill in fencing.

231 Cousin: a general term of polite address among aristocrats, most of whom were related however distantly, and often for a nephew or niece. (OED obs.) Not strictly for the son or daughter of one's uncle or aunt in the modern sense.

233 weaker side.: that is, favoring Hamlet, who is being modest about his fencing skills.

And when he's not himself does wrong Laertes,
Then Hamlet does it not, Hamlet denies it.
Who does it then? His madness. If it be so,
Hamlet is of the faction that is wronged,
His madness is poor Hamlet's enemy. 210
Sir, in this audience,
Let my disclaiming from a purposed evil
Free me so far in your most generous thoughts,
That I have shot my arrow over the house
And hurt my brother. 215

Laertes
I am satisfied in nature,
Whose motive in this case should stir me most
To my revenge, but in my terms of honor
I stand aloof, and will no reconcilement
Till by some elder masters of known honor 220
I have a voice and precedent of peace
To keep my name ungored. But till that time
I do receive your offered love like love,
And will not wrong it.

Hamlet
I embrace it freely,
And will this brothers' wager frankly play. 225
Give us the foils.

Laertes
Come, one for me.

Hamlet
I'll be your foil, Laertes. In mine ignorance
Your skill shall like a star in the darkest night
Stick fiery off indeed.

Laertes
You mock me, sir.

Hamlet
No, by this hand. 230

King
Give them the foils, young Osric. Cousin Hamlet,
You know the wager?

Hamlet
Very well, my lord.
Your grace has laid the odds on the weaker side.

King
I do not fear it, I have seen you both;

235 he is bettered: probably, Laertes has become "better" at the sport of fencing by training in France.

236 let me see another.: choose another foil; this is Laertes' opportunity to select the foil with its sharp tip not protected by a button, as was done for fencing in sport; and here with its tip poisoned.

237 a length?: the same length? Hamlet does not notice that one of the foils, which Laertes selected, does not have a button on its tip.

241-2 If Hamlet . . . exchange,: Stratfordian commentators have debated the king's meaning of the terms of the wager, but an Oxfordian mathematician offers a solution. (See Saunders, and Jenkins' Long Note v.ii.162-4.)

243 union: a large, valuable pearl, (OED archaic), perhaps so-called originally from "onion" (per the OED), which is large, round and white.

246 the cups: tankards or "stoups" of wine, probably four of them for the principals in this scene.

251 judges: courtiers as the referees, although Osric seems to be the lead referee.

257 very palpable: very easily felt or perceived, very obvious. Osric probably asserts this so strongly because he's uncertain about his judgment and does not want it questioned.

259-60 this pearl is thine, ... the cup.: The King drops the pearl in the poisoned cup. **to thy health**!: a lie and deeply ironic since the poisoned cup is intended to kill Hamlet **Give him the cup:** the cup with the poison that the King has put in it. Like the Earl of Leicester, King Claudius avoids giving the poison himself to his intended victim; here a servant will offer the poisoned cup to Hamlet, which he declines.

But since he is bettered, we have therefore odds. 235

Laertes

This is too heavy; let me see another.

Hamlet

This likes me well. These foils have all a length?

Osric

Ay, my good lord.

King

Set me the stoups of wine upon that table.
If Hamlet give the first or second hit, 240
Or quit in answer of the third exchange,
Let all the battlements their ordnance fire.
The king shall drink to Hamlet's better breath,
And in the cup an union shall he throw
Richer than that which four successive kings 245
In Denmark's crown have worn. Give me the cups,
And let the kettle to the trumpet speak,
The trumpet to the cannoneer without,
The cannons to the heavens, the heaven to earth,
Now the king drinks to Hamlet. Come, begin. 250

Trumpets the while

And you, the judges, bear a wary eye.

Hamlet

Come on, sir. *They begin to fence*

Laertes

Come, my lord.

Hamlet

Onc!

Laertes

No! 255

Hamlet

Judgment?

Osric

A hit, a very palpable hit.

Laertes

Well, again.

King

Stay, give me drink. Hamlet, this pearl is thine,
Here's to thy health! Give him the cup. 260

Drum, trumpets, and shot. Flourish. A piece goes off

Hamlet

I'll play this bout first, set it by a while.

265 Our son: no doubt deeply offensive to Hamlet, who rejected the King's calling him his "son" in Hamlet's first words in the play (1.2.67).

266 fat: sweaty or out of condition, or both. Gertrude seems to be reaching for reasons to express her motherly concern.

268 carouses: drinks deeply. (OED obs.)

269 Good madam: a polite "thank you." Or perhaps an expression of approval, ("Good"), which would be dramatic irony for play's Elizabethan audience, who know the cup is poisoned. Or both.

272 it is too late: But the King and Queen would be sitting next to each other, and it is probably not too late for the King to move quickly and stop her from drinking from the poisoned cup. He apparently, for unstated reasons of his own, may in a split second have decided to let her die or he may have chosen not to stop her because it might betray his knowledge that the cup was poisoned. Or both. His motives and actions are ambiguous, as are those of all the principal characters in this final scene.

279 pass: in fencing, to make a thrust. **best violence**: with greatest force, strongest effort.

280 a wanton: a child spoiled with leniency. (OED obs.)

283 Have at you now!: Violating the rules of fencing in sport, Laertes suddenly lunges at Hamlet ("now!"), catching him off-guard and wounding him fatally with the poisoned tip of his foil. Laertes has avenged his father's death, not in cold-blooded revenge but by impulsively cheating. Just seconds later he will call it a "foul practice" (line 301) and then will ask Hamlet's forgiveness (lines 314-16). His desire for revenge has been deeply ambiguous.

S.d.*: *Hamlet seizes Laerte's foil: In some manner not explained in the play text, they have exchanged foils. Commentators speculate how this might have happened, perhaps after dropping their foils in a scuffle, which seems unlikely, or by some clever stratagem by Hamlet. If the latter, the fencing duel would have fascinated a court audience, particularly courtiers trained in the aristocratic sport of fencing. (See John Dover Wilson for one possible stratagem.)

Come. *They resume fencing*
Another hit; what say you?

Laertes
A touch, a touch, I do confess it.

King
Our son shall win. 265

Queen
He's fat, and scant of breath.
Here, Hamlet, take my napkin, rub thy brows.
The queen carouses to thy fortune, Hamlet.

Hamlet
Good madam.

King
Gertrude, do not drink. 270

Queen
I will, my lord, I pray you pardon me.

King
(Aside) It is the poisoned cup; it is too late.

Hamlet
I dare not drink yet, madam; by and by.

Queen
Come, let me wipe thy face.

Laertes
[Aside to the king] My lord, I'll hit him now. 275

King
[Aside to Laertes] I do not think it.

Laertes
*[Aside]*And yet it is almost against my conscience.

Hamlet
Come, for the third, Laertes, you do but dally.
I pray you pass with your best violence;
I am sure you make a wanton of me. 280

Laertes
Say you so? Come on.

Osric
Nothing, neither way.

Laertes
Have at you now!

Wounded, Hamlet seizes Laertes' foil

King
Part them, they are incensed.

Hamlet
Nay. Come again. 285

Hamlet wounds Laertes

289 as a woodcock to mine own springe: caught in my own snare ("springe") like a "woodcock," which was thought to be stupid and easy to trap. (OED obs. for the simile)

292 She sounds: swoons, faints (per the (OED). But the King is lying; he knows she is dying from the poisoned cup and tries to deflect attention from it.

301 unbated and envenomed: with the tip uncovered and poisoned.

310 Drink of this potion!: the poisoned wine ("potion"), which the King himself devised. **union**: the pearl and probably metaphorically for Gertrude's "union" in marriage with Claudius, which Hamlet deplored with such vehemence in the closet scene with her. Hamlet nominally gets revenge for his father's death by killing the King but he does so only impulsively, not in cold-blooded revenge as directed by feudal custom. His revenge is ambiguous.

311 Follow my mother!: Hamlet's immediate intent here is to avenge the murder of his mother, not his father, although that is what he has been contemplating throughout the play. (See the Introduction.)

313 tempered: guided, directed. (OED obs.)

Osric
Look to the queen there. Ho!
Horatio
They bleed on both sides. How is it, my lord?
Osric
How is it, Laertes?
Laertes
Why, as a woodcock to mine own springe, Osric.
I am justly killed with mine own treachery. 290
Hamlet
How does the queen?
King
She sounds to see them bleed.
Queen
No, no, the drink, the drink — O my dear Hamlet —
The drink, the drink! I am poisoned. *The queen dies*
Hamlet
O villainy! Ho, let the door be locked! 295
Treachery! Seek it out!. *Osric exits, Laertes falls*
Laertes
It is here, Hamlet. Hamlet, thou art slain.
No medicine in the world can do thee good;
In thee there is not half an hour's life.
The treacherous instrument is in thy hand, 300
Unbated and envenomed. The foul practice
Hath turned itself on me. Lo, here I lie,
Never to rise again. Thy mother's poisoned.
I can no more — the king, the king's to blame.
Hamlet
The point envenomed, too? 305
Then, venom, to thy work. *Hurts the king*
All
Treason! Treason!
King
O, yet defend me, friends, I am but hurt.
Hamlet
Here, thou incestuous, murderous, damned Dane,
Drink of this potion! Is thy union here? 310
Follow my mother! *The king dies*
Laertes
He is justly served,
It is a poison tempered by himself.
Exchange forgiveness with me, noble Hamlet.

315 come not upon thee: not be judged against you. Although he could claim revenge for his father's death, Laertes absolves Hamlet of any guilt and asks his forgiveness.

318 Wretched queen: miserable; unhappy queen that you were. Dying, Hamlet's final thoughts are about the murder of his mother; again not a word about avenging the murder of his father by Claudius.

320 mutes . . . to this act: silent, speechless witnesses.

323-4 Report . . . unsatisfied: Hamlet enlists Horatio to explain what he has been trying to do, his purpose and his reasons. ("cause" OED obs.) Given the personal, "autobiographical" nature of the play it is hard to escape concluding that this is also a symbolic plea by Oxford, aging and aware that he must die, for his cousin Horatio Vere to "report" his "cause," what he has been trying to say about himself, to future audiences and readers who might be "unsatisfied," unless they know how he put into *Hamlet* the truth of his life, his deepest concerns, his conflicted anger with his mother and his despair at the corruption of Elizabeth's court, especially that of the Earl of Leicester.

326 an antique Roman: who prefers suicide to life without honor, as did ancient Romans; here, one who prefers to follow an honorable leader, Hamlet, in death.

330 wounded name: Hamlet and Oxford both led lives that in the common and unknowing view "wounded" their reputations.

341 overcrows: overcomes (per the OED), perhaps alluding to the crowing of a rooster after his triumph in a cockfight.

343-344 I do prophesy the election lights on Fortinbras: Since neither the King nor Hamlet left sons and heirs, Denmark's most influential noblemen will chose the next king, not by formal vote or balloting but by a generally understood consensus among them, called an "election," and absent any challengers; and Hamlet predicts that Fortinbras will be chosen. Moreover, Fortinbras's army is at the front gate. In like manner, Queen Elizabeth left no heir to the Crown of England, and (the year before Oxford died) Robert Cecil, younger son of the late Lord Burghley and her principal adviser, engineered an unchallenged consensus of the English nobility that King James VI of Scotland should succeed her as King of England, as well.

344 my dying voice: Hamlet's support for Fortinbras as the next King of Denmark. As the hereditary king, albeit for only a few minutes, his support would carry great weight in choosing his successor.

345 occurrents more and less . . . solicited-- : events ("occurrents" OED obs.) major and minor; thus, all that has happened, which has moved or persuaded ("solicited" per the OED) Hamlet to support Fortinbras.

Mine and my father's death come not upon thee, 315
Nor thine on me. *Laertes dies*

Hamlet

Heaven make thee free of it. I follow thee.
I am dead, Horatio. Wretched queen, adieu.
You that look pale, and tremble at this chance,
That are but mutes or audience to this act, 320
Had I but time — as this fell sergeant, Death,
Is strict in his arrest — O, I could tell you —
But let it be. Horatio, I am dead,
Thou livest. Report me and my cause aright
To the unsatisfied.

Horatio

Never believe it; 325
I am more an antique Roman than a Dane.
Here's yet some liquor left.

Hamlet

As thou art a man,
Give me the cup. Let go! By heaven, I'll have it!
O God, Horatio, what a wounded name, 330
Things standing thus unknown, shall I leave behind me.
If thou didst ever hold me in thy heart,
Absent thee from felicity a while,
And in this harsh world draw thy breath in pain
To tell my story. *A march afar off and a shot* 335
What warlike noise is this?

Enter Osric

Osric

Young Fortinbras with conquest come from Poland,
To the ambassadors of England gives
This warlike volley.

Hamlet

O, I die, Horatio, 340
The potent poison quite overcrows my spirit.
I cannot live to hear the news from England,
But I do prophesy the election lights
On Fortinbras, he has my dying voice.
So tell him, with the occurrents more and less 345
Which have solicited— The rest is silence. *Hamlet dies*

Horatio

Now cracks a noble heart. Good night, sweet prince,
And flights of angels sing thee to thy rest. *March within*
Why does the drum come hither?

351 wonder: astonishing disaster. (OED obs.)

352 This quarry cries on havoc: This pile of the dead, like game killed in sport and piled up after the hunt ("quarry" OED obs.), solemnly evokes ("cries on" OED obs.) devastation like that caused by soldiers' pillaging. ("havoc" OED obs.) A concise, double allusion that would come easily to Oxford, an aristocrat allowed to hunt on game preserves, including royal preserves, and who twice was a military officer who would have known about the shouted command, "Havoc!" ordering troops to pillage the enemy, slaughter and create chaos. Commoners, like Shakspere, were not allowed to hunt wild game; nor did he serve in the military.

352-3 Death, What feast is toward: what a feast for you is coming ("toward" OED obs.). Death, personified, was sometimes thought of as devouring the deceased, not a very complimentary image by Fortinbras for the dead Danish nobility in this final scene.

356 *First Ambassador*: of England to Denmark. In his only appearance in the play, this character could represent a cameo of Oxford's brother-in-law, Lord Willoughby, Queen Elizabeth's ambassador to Denmark and Oxford's brother-in-law; and perhaps a passing acknowledgment of his contribution to Oxford's knowledge of Denmark's court and especially about the names Rosencrantz and Guildenstern.

364 He never . . . their death.: But Hamlet's forgery of the King's letter did command the King of England to have Rosencrantz and Guildenstern summarily executed. Horatio may judge it proper to lie about it in order to cover for Hamlet and preserve his reputation. Still, it shows how even he, and anyone (and even Hamlet), can be drawn into the corrupt ways of a corrupt monarch's court.

365 But since so jump upon . . . question: since you, Fortinbras, and you the ambassadors from England, arrive so precisely and unexpectedly ("so jump upon"), possibly alluding to the as yet undecided or possibly disputed issue ("question" OED obs.), no doubt of succession.

372 casual: by chance, unintended (the earliest meaning per the OED).

380 some rights of memory in this kingdom: some still-remembered rights to land that Fortinbras' late father had lost to the late King Hamlet in trial by single combat and that Fortinbras had planned to re-take until his uncle Norway stopped him at the behest of King Claudius.

Enter Fortinbras with the English Ambassadors
with Drum, Colors, and Attendants.

Fortinbras
Where is this sight?
Horatio
What is it you would see? 350
If aught of woe or wonder, cease your search.
Fortinbras
This quarry cries on havoc. O proud Death,
What feast is toward in thine eternal cell,
That thou so many princes at a shot
So bloodily hast struck? 355
First Ambassador
The sight is dismal,
And our affairs from England come too late.
The ears are senseless that should give us hearing,
To tell him his commandment is fulfilled,
That Rosencrantz and Guildenstern are dead. 360
Where should we have our thanks?
Horatio
Not from his mouth,
Had it the ability of life to thank you.
He never gave commandment for their death.
But since so jump upon this bloody question, 365
You from the Polack wars, and you from England,
Are here arrived, give order that these bodies
High on a stage be placed to the view,
And let me speak to the yet unknowing world
How these things came about. So shall you hear 370
Of carnal, bloody, and unnatural acts,
Of accidental judgments, casual slaughters,
Of deaths put on by cunning and forced cause,
And in this upshot, purposes mistook
Fallen on the inventors' heads: all this can I 375
Truly deliver.
Fortinbras
Let us haste to hear it,
And call the noblest to the audience.
For me, with sorrow I embrace my fortune.
I have some rights of memory in this kingdom, 380
Which now to claim my vantage doth invite me.
Horatio
Of that I shall have also cause to speak,

387 stage: probably a raised platform; also alluding to the theater stage.

390 soldiers' music . . . war: Hamlet, never a military commander, is given a military funeral procession. The seventeenth Earl of Oxford, the Lord Great Chamberlain of England, who did serve in the military but sought in vain a significant command, died, probably a suicide, without any recorded funeral rites or ceremony. (See Detobel.)

393 Becomes the field . . . much amiss.: would be expected and fitting ("becomes") for a "field" of battle but is not right ("much amiss") here in the monarch's castle, the capitol of Denmark.

And from his mouth whose voice will draw no more.
But let this same be presently performed
Even while men's minds are wild, lest more mischance 385
On plots and errors happen.

Fortinbras

Let four captains
Bear Hamlet like a soldier to the stage,
For he was likely, had he been put on,
To have proved most royal; and for his passage,
The soldiers' music and the rite of war 390
Speak loudly for him.
Take up the bodies. Such a sight as this
Becomes the field, but here shows much amiss.
Go bid the soldiers shoot.

Exeunt marching; after the which
a peal of ordinance is shot off

Hamlet's Sources, Influences, and Its 'Forerunners' by Oxford

The primary sources of *Hamlet* were both personal and literary, as are the sources of the creative writings of recognized artistic genius. The personal sources are found in the turbulent, troubled life of the mercurial dramatist, Edward de Vere, the seventeenth Earl of Oxford. The literary sources, which are the subject of this research paper, were primarily the ancient Danish legend of the hero Amlethus first published in Latin and later re-told in French by Francois de Belleforest in a free translation. And the most important influence on the play was probably the story of the Greek hero Orestes.

But that's not all. This survey of the literary sources and influences also suggests how difficult, if not impossible, it would have been for Will Shakspere of Stratford to have seen them—a problem for Stratfordian commentators—whereas the Earl of Oxford had them close at hand.

In addition, this survey presents evidence indicating that Oxford was the author of three plays, the first when he was seventeen, that Stratfordian scholars have considered sources for *Hamlet* or influences on it. For Stratfordians, the authorship of these three plays is not entirely clear, but they may well have been "forerunners" by Oxford of what would become his final version of *Hamlet* just before he died.

To begin at the beginning, the Danish legend of Amlethus, written in Latin by Saxo Grammaticus (c. 1150-1220), appeared in a multi-volume history of Denmark, published in Paris in 1514. Belleforest's much embellished translation of Saxo's story into French and set in a Renaissance court was published in a multi-volume set of books, in 1572, also in Paris.

The parallels in *Hamlet* to the Saxo/Belleforest story of Amleth are quite clear. Amleth (Gallicized by Belleforest from Saxo's "Amlethus") was Prince of Denmark, a troubled young man who found himself entangled in the intrigues of court power politics, as is Hamlet, Prince of Denmark (whose name is Anglicized by anagram from "Amleth").

Amleth was the son of King Horwendil (old King Hamlet) who was murdered by his brother Fengo (Claudius) to become the sole ruler and who married his brother's widow, Amleth's mother (Gertrude). Fearing that he might suffer the same fate as his father, Amleth feigned madness and talked in riddles and doublespeak to turn aside suspicions (as does "antic" Hamlet). Fengo tried to trap Amleth by entangling him with his foster-sister (Ophelia), by putting an eavesdropper in his mother's bedchamber (Polonius) and by sending him to the English king with two henchmen (Rosencrantz and Guilderstern) carrying instructions to the king to have him killed. Amleth, however, changed the instructions to have the two henchmen killed (as in *Hamlet*). In the end, to avenge his father's death, Amleth killed Fengo with Fengo's own sword. (Analogously, Hamlet kills Claudius with the poison-tipped foil that Claudius intended for Hamlet's death in his duel with Laertes.)

Details that are in Belleforest but not in Saxo give Belleforest an advantage as the more important source for *Hamlet*, although Oxford probably read both. For example, Belleforest adds the "incest" and adultery of Amleth's uncle, as in *Hamlet*. In Belleforest, Amleth's character traits include melancholy and conscience qualms, as are Hamlet's, while Saxo's Amleth was stalwart, confident, cunning and ruthless. In Belleforest, but not in Saxo, the young woman enlisted to seduce Amleth is said to be in love with him, as was Ophelia. Belleforest has Amleth twice mentioning *ombres*, French for "shades" in the afterlife, or ghosts. One mention referred to the appearance of the ghost of Amleth's murdered father the king when Amleth berates his mother in her bedroom (as does the Ghost in *Hamlet*). There was no ghost in Saxo. (See Jolly.)

It must be emphasized that Oxford would not have mechanically copied plot elements and character traits from Saxo and Belleforest. He certainly read widely (including Greek drama) and when he began to draft what would become his *Hamlet* he would naturally remember from his readings parallels to his own life and concerns, drawing from his readings for what he intended to say in his personal story of himself as Hamlet. The same would be true for other Shakespeare plays, but *Hamlet* in particular came from the depths of his being. Finding and analyzing "sources" and "influences" is legitimate and important, but over-emphasizing them risks trivializing what Oxford brought to his plays, how he selected and adapted what he would use in his own plotting and character development. And perhaps not incidentally, his so-called "borrowings" would provide cover, if needed, for the expression of his personal concerns and problems and especially his satires of prominent, contemporary figures.

Establishment Shakespeare scholars recognize that somehow the story of Amlethus in Saxo and then as Amleth in Belleforest was the primary literary source for *Hamlet*. Significantly, however, they can only speculate tentatively about how that happened. They steer clear of addressing whether Will Shakspere acquired or read either of them. They use qualifiers such as "may possibly," and "seems to have read," "directly or indirectly," but without any supporting detail.

The problem for Stratfordians is that both Saxo and Belleforest were multi-volume sets of books published on the Continent. There was no single-volume edition entitled something like "Amleth's Story," as Stratfordian commentary might lead one to believe. The Amlethus story in Saxo's long narrative history of Scandinavia, *Gesta Danorum*, begins in the middle of volume three of the sixteen volumes, but without a chapter title, and ends in the middle of volume four. In Belleforest's *Histoires Tragics*, written in French, the Amleth story is the fifth of twelve stories in volume five of seven volumes that were not published in English until 1894. Even if Will Shakspere had the opportunity and time to see Belleforest's seven volumes and notice the Amleth story, there's no historical evidence that he had an opportunity to learn French; it was not taught in the Stratford grammar school.

These two multi-volume sets of expensive, imported books were not likely to have been sold in the book stalls at St. Paul's churchyard where Will Shakspere was supposed to have browsed to read what he is supposed to have read. In England they were rare and very valuable sets of books, typically purchased on the Continent for a few wealthy collectors for their libraries. One of the most active book collectors was William Cecil Lord Burghley, Oxford's guardian during his teenage years.

Even if Will Shakspere somehow gained access to them somewhere it's very doubtful that he would have had the time to plow through the multi-volume sets and notice the Amleth story amid scores of other legends, myths and historical accounts. In the Stratfordian view he was not only a busy actor memorizing his roles, rehearsing and performing but also a real estate investor with properties, and his family, a three-day journey away in Stratford, and the author of at least thirty-nine plays, two long narrative poems and 154 sonnets. None of the research and reading could have been begun before he was twenty-one when he was still in Stratford and his twins were born. It's all very improbable, and *Hamlet*'s editors have struggled with the problem.

The most significant influence on *Hamlet*, if not a direct source, was probably Greek drama, especially the *Oresteia* trilogy. Surprisingly, modern-day editors of *Hamlet* have overlooked it or chosen to ignore it. The story of Orestes is found mainly in the *Oresteia* by Aeschylus and in versions by Euripides and Sophocles, which were written in Greece in the fifth century BCE. Nicholas Rowe, the first editor of the Shakespeare plays, was the first to notice the influence of the Orestes story. In his attempt in 1709 at a biography of Will Shakspere he wrote that *Hamlet* was founded on Sophocles' version of the Orestes story in his *Electra*. Sixty-five years later, the Shakespeare editor George Steevens would note the influence of Greek drama in the original Greek. He wrote that a plea for proper funeral rites in *Titus Andronicus* convinced him that its author "was conversant with the Greek tragedies in their original language." He called the passage a clear allusion to Sophocles' *Ajax* "of which no translation was extant in the time of Shakespeare." Since then, Shakespeare scholars have paid almost no attention to the influence of Greek drama on *Hamlet*, while scholars of Greek language and literature have found numerous, clear similarities in *Hamlet* to the Greek plays.

Hamlet's Sources and Influences

To cite a few of the more striking similarities in *Hamlet* to the story of Orestes in Greek drama, as described by Earl Showerman in "Orestes and Hamlet" in *The Oxfordian 2004*:

Both Orestes and Hamlet revered their fathers, Agamemnon and Hamlet senior, who were honorable men and successful warriors. Agamemnon led the victorious Greek forces at the siege of Troy. Hamlet senior, king and leader of the Danish military, was challenged to single combat by the Norwegian king and leader of his army, the elder Fortinbras, and killed him in their sword fight, winning the Norwegian's lands and averting a battle between the two armies.

Orestes and Hamlet were away from their homes when their fathers were murdered by close relatives at their homes. Agamemnon was stabbed in his bath by his wife; Hamlet senior was poisoned by his brother while napping in his garden.

Both Orestes and Hamlet suspected that the otherworldly apparitions who call on them to seek revenge for the murder of their fathers might be evil, deceiving spirits, the Furies for Orestes and the Ghost of Hamlet's father. Both young men take on the responsibility to seek revenge.

Orestes and his sister Electra are scandalized that their murdered father, Agamemnon, was buried without public mourning or suitable funeral rites. For the Greeks, this was considered intolerable. In *Hamlet*, the Ghost of Hamlet's father laments that he was murdered before he could confess his sins and avoid Purgatory: "O horrible. O horrible. Most horrible." (1.5.80) And later Laertes complains that his father Polonius (like Agamemnon) had an unhonored "obscure burial" (3.4.209) without public acknowledgment that Hamlet killed him and without a funeral procession or noble rites of mourning.

In addition, Orestes and Hamlet each have a trusted friend, Pylades and Horatio. Both Orestes and Hamlet see phantoms that no one else sees when they are in their mothers' bedchambers, Orestes the Furies and Hamlet the ghost of his father, Gertrude's first husband. Importantly, their strange madness is a major characteristic of both distraught Orestes and "antic" Hamlet.

The opening scenes are both very similar. In the *Oresteia* trilogy, a watchman on the roof of a Greek castle just before dawn eagerly awaits news of the siege of Troy by the Greeks led by Agamemnon. In the opening scene of *Hamlet*, sentinels on the ramparts of Elsinore castle at night nervously await the arrival of Horatio to verify the appearance of the ghost of Hamlet's father.

The closing scenes of the *Oresteia* and *Hamlet*, however, could hardly be more different. In the *Oresteia,* Orestes is on trial for killing his mother to avenge his father, whom she murdered. In a secret vote, the ballots of the chorus are evenly split. The goddess Athena casts the deciding vote and

Orestes is acquitted. Although the prosecuting chorus bitterly denounces the verdict, Athena mollifies them by reminding them of their split vote and assuring them that Athens will have a peaceful, glorious future. Through a jury trial, justice is served, however imperfectly. *Hamlet* ends in a stark and no doubt deliberate contrast. Hamlet, Claudius and Laertes die in a violent melee, the result of Claudius's corruption and his murderous poisonings gone awry. The poisoned Hamlet dies, and young Fortinbras arrives at the head of his army and asserts his claim to the vacant throne of Denmark.

If the *Oresteia* was not a primary source for *Hamlet*, it was almost certainly a significant influence, as were other Greek and Roman classics. Once again, however, it is problematic how Will Shakspere might have found and read the Greek plays. There is no evidence that he could read the ancient Greek language, which is much more difficult than Latin, or that he attended a university where it was taught. Even in Latin translations published on the Continent, the plays were rare and expensive books in England.

Oxford, however, had the Greek and Roman classics close at hand in the libraries of William Cecil Lord Burghley at Cecil House where Oxford lived during in youth. And what may have been the only copy in London of Aeschylus' *Oresteia*, the most significant influence on *Hamlet*, was in the library of Mildred Cooke Cecil, William Cecil's wife. She had a leading role in the education of their own children and probably influenced that of her husband's wards as well.

She and her siblings had been brought up and educated in a household that valued intellectual achievement, especially in the classics. Her father, Sir Anthony Cooke, renowned for his learning and for his teaching skills, was a tutor of the young King Edward VI, along with the more famous John Cheke and with Roger Asham, who was also a tutor of the future Queen Elizabeth.

At Cecil House, Mildred Cecil built her own library of books and was reputed for her skill in writing and speaking Latin and especially ancient Greek. Caroline Bowden cites John Strype quoting Roger Asham as saying that she understood and spoke Greek as easily as she spoke English. She could have influenced Oxford's reading and also been the first to foster in the mother-less teenager an appreciation of intelligent, educated, strong-willed women, often depicted in his Shakespeare plays. One of her biographers suggests that she was also involved in the translation of the Geneva Bible, which Shakespeare scholars consider to have been the principal biblical source for the author of Shakespeare's works. Oxford owned a copy, now in the Folger Shakespeare Library in Washington D. C.

For scholars of the Greek classics, the influence of Aeschylus's *Oresteia* trilogy on the writing of *Hamlet* has been both too strong to ignore and a problem to explain. Two early twentieth century scholars of the Greek language and literature explored in considerable detail what they saw as the significant influence of Greek drama on the Shakespeare plays, especially the

Oresteia on *Hamlet*. J. Churlton Collins and Gilbert Murray both found many similarities that they considered remarkable, even extraordinary; but they had to resort to conjectures and hypotheses to try to explain how Will Shakspere could have read the *Oresteia.*

Collins found scores of parallels of language and incident, some stronger than others, between Greek drama and Shakespeare plays, including *Hamlet*. His purpose was "to establish a probability that reminiscences, more or less unconscious perhaps, of classical reading not in English translations but in Latin and possibly in Greek, were constantly occurring to Shakespeare's memory [that is, Shakspere's]. They could not be ignored. And cumulatively they are remarkable." The title of the first chapter of his collected *Studies in Shakespeare* (1904) is

"Shakespeare as a Classical Scholar." A graduate of Oxford, where he studied the classics, Collins was professor of English literature at Birmingham University.

Collins makes a strong case for "Shakespeare as a Classical Scholar" with the ability to read Greek with facility and understanding. (There's no evidence that Shakspere knew Greek; it was not in the elementary school curriculum.) Although he initially suggests that the parallels he will describe could have been commonplace sayings or coincidences of language, he then cites with great admiration more than seventy-five passages in Greek drama that correspond closely to passages in Shakespeare plays, including a dozen in *Hamlet*. He often adds comments such as "exactly Aeschylus," "exactly Sophocles," "a remarkable parallel," "an admirable paraphrase," "nothing could be more purely Greek," and again with admiration "how exactly does he [Shakspere] recall the speech of Agamemnon."

Will Shakspere, he contends, gained a remarkably extensive, in-depth knowledge of Greek drama and its diction through Latin translations. He says that "it is indeed in the extraordinary analogies--analogies in sources, in particularity of detail and point, and in the relative frequency of employment--presented by his metaphors of the Attic tragedians that we find the most convincing testimony of his familiarity with their writings."

"It is not likely" he continues, "that Shakespeare [that is, Shakspere] could read the Greek language with facility, but if he possessed enough of it to follow the original Latin version, as he probably did, he would not only be able to enrich his diction with its idioms and phraseology but would acquire that *timbre* in style of which I have given illustrations." *Timbre*, from the French, describes distinctive overtones, as in music, and a characteristic "color" or style of writing--for Collins the *timbre* of the ancient Greek writing even when translated into Latin. That kind of in-depth understanding and appreciation of a Greek poet's diction, however, could realistically only be acquired by being able to read and absorb the ancient Greek language with facility, not through Latin translations. As the Italians warn: *Traduttore, traditore*. Moreover, his examples of parallels are not from the Latin translations that Shakspere is supposed to have read. They are in the original Greek, with his own translations into English.

Toward the end of his chapter, Collins hedges his enthusiasm: "I do not, as I have already said, cite them [the many parallels] as positive proofs of imitation or reminiscences on the part of Shakespeare. They may be mere coincidences. But if on the other hand further and more satisfactory evidence of Shakespeare's acquaintance [that is, Shakspere's] with the Greek dramatists can be adduced [not so far], then surely such parallels will not be without importance as corroborative testimony." Collins makes an excellent case for the author of the Shakespeare canon as his "Classical Scholar" but is conflicted about the validity of his conjectures since it's so difficult to see how Will Shakspere could have done it.

Then there still remains the problem of where Shakspere would have had access to the Latin versions of the Greek plays. Published on the Continent, many of them were ornately decorated, beautiful books according to Collins and others. Some included the Greek on facing pages. Typically, they would be printed in limited editions. Wealthy English aristocrats and nobility who had an interest in literature and education would have their agents on the Continent purchase these valuable editions for their libraries. For commoners in England they would have been hard to find and very expensive to buy.

Collins implicitly recognizes their rarity but conjectures that Shakspere could have had access to them through the Earl of Southampton, in the private libraries of the wealthy, and in other private libraries such as those of Ben Jonson, the historian William Camden and even the Archbishop of Canterbury and Queen Elizabeth. This astonishing ease of access would have been quite unusual, if not impossible, for a commoner from an illiterate Stratford family and an actor. Actors were officially branded "rogues and vagabonds." Moreover, it's almost impossible to conceive that he could have had the time to secure access to these private libraries, read through their holdings and come across the Greek plays in Latin, immersing himself in them to such an extent that they would influence him, as Collins suggests, in the writing of *Hamlet.*

Five years later, William Theobald, a Baconian, noted Collins' work, and in *The Classical Element in the Shakespeare Plays* (1909) he provided a long list of references and allusions to Greek and Roman authors in Shakespeare, including many in *Hamlet*. Theobald's purpose was to support the proposition that Sir Francis Bacon, the philosopher/scientist and statesman, was the author of the Shakespeare canon. Bacon, however, left no poetic, imaginative writings that would qualify him as the author of the Shakespeare works.

The classicist Gilbert Murray also recognized what he called the many "extraordinary" similarities between ancient Greek drama and Shakespeare plays, especially between the heroes Orestes and Hamlet. Murray was professor of Greek at Glasgow University and then at the University of Oxford. He published translations of several Greek plays.

In chapter 8, "Hamlet and Orestes," of his *Classical Tradition in Poetry* (1927), he describes in detail how "the points of similarity, some fundamental and some perhaps superficial, between these two tragic heroes are rather extraordinary." He notes, for example, that both heroes are sons of kings who are murdered by kinsmen who succeed to the throne. The widows of the kings marry the murderers, and the heroes undertake to avenge their fathers. Some forms of madness and disguise characterize the heroes, who act as Fools or gross Jesters to hide their intentions. Both are prone to soliloquies and to hesitating before acting. Both go on sea voyages. And more.

To try to explain how Will Shakspere could have created the hero of *Hamlet* whose story resembles so closely the story of Orestes, Murray proposes that independently of Greek drama (and presumably Saxo/Belleforest) Shakspere drew on a collective, unconscious "tradition" of myths and legends, including the Amleth story, that existed before Saxo first wrote them down. They became essentially an ingrained, unconscious memory of a prehistoric, mythical hero who surfaced in the collective minds of writers as both Orestes in the fifth century BCE and Hamlet more than a thousand years later.

In his concluding paragraph, Murray describes his suspicion that Shakspere experienced "a strange, unanalyzed vibration below the surface, an undercurrent of desires, fears and passions, long slumbering yet eternally familiar, which have for thousands of years lain near the root of our most intimate emotions and been wrought into the fabric of our most magical dreams." Thus, according to Murray, did Shakspere create *Hamlet*, without having to read the Saxo/Belleforest story of Amleth or the Greek plays in ancient Greek or in Latin translations, although he allows that Shakspere's university friends, whom he does not identify, might have told him about the Greek plays, a rather desperate conjecture.

Gilbert Highet, a famous professor of Greek and Latin at Columbia, came to the same conclusion as Murray but without mentioning him and in a simpler form. In *The Classical Tradition: Greek and Roman Influences on Western Literature* (1949), he wrote: "We can be sure that he [Shakspere] had not read Aeschylus. Yet what can we say when we find some of Aeschylus's thoughts appearing in Shakespeare's plays? The only explanation is that great poets in times and countries distant from each other often have similar thoughts and express them similarly." He then adds conjectures that Shakspere might have heard the Greek plays discussed or seen adaptations of them in the works of his contemporaries, but without citing examples or any evidence for that. In any case, he concludes, "we must make the widest possible allowance for his power of assimilating classical ideas from the classical atmosphere that surrounded him." Highet and Murray were driven to conjure up a sort of mystical, cerebral osmosis to explain what they saw as the significant Greek influence on the Shakespeare plays.

Colin Burrow of Cambridge University offered yet another unusual explanation. In *Shakespeare and Classical Antiquity* (2013), he says: "Shakespeare [that is, Shakspere] almost certainly never read Sophocles or Euripides (let alone the much more difficult Aeschylus) in Greek, yet he managed to write tragedies that invite comparison with those authors. . . . Having 'less Greek' could therefore have enabled him to appear to understand more about Greek tragedy [through Plutarch] than if he had been able to read Aeschylus and Euripides in the original Greek." This trick of seeming to know more about Greek tragedy by knowing less received the implied endorsement of leading establishment Shakespeareans Peter Holland and Stanley Wells, who included Burrow's book in their series "Shakespeare Topics."

Modern-day editors of *Hamlet* are unaccountably silent on its significant parallels to Greek drama despite the enthusiasm for its influence by respected classical scholars like Collins, Murray and Highet. Perhaps the editors have understood how unlikely it is that Shakspere could have read ancient Greek or had access to Greek plays in Latin translations.

Scholars hunting for sources for *Hamlet* and influences on it have proposed a wide variety of possibilities, and three of them stand out for their significance by virtue of the historical and internal evidence. They are the court interlude *Horestes* (1567), the anonymous *Spanish Tragedy* (c. 1584-92) and the so-called "Ur-Hamlet" (c.1588). Close examination of the evidence, however, suggests that these three plays were not just sources for *Hamlet* but were Oxford's early and quite different versions of his final Shakespeare play, published in 1604. And some Stratfordian scholarship supports this view, albeit unintentionally.

HORESTES

The seventeen-year-old Earl of Oxford might well have been the author of *Horestes*, a short play that has prompted comparisons to his *Hamlet*. It was published in 1567 as by a "John Pickeryng" and was performed at court as "Orestes" during the Christmas season of 1567-8, but scholars have been puzzled about the author's identity. There is no record of it being performed in a public theater, again at court or anywhere else. Nor was it reprinted, or even mentioned, as far as can be determined, in any contemporary records—all indications that the unusual play by such a young, aristocratic author was probably controversial.

Horestes was the first revenge play in English drama, and scholars have admired its fluid, innovative writing. It re-tells the tragic Greek story of Orestes (here "Horestes") but adds from the English medieval morality plays the comic villain Vice and other allegorical characters, such as Revenge and Truth. Slapstick scenes with rustics, horseplay with the audience and the low comedy of the devious but entertaining Vice character alternate with appalling scenes of the hero Horestes' grave moral crises, including the execution on stage of Clytemnestra's lover and co-conspirator by hanging. Especially unusual for the time are four songs sung to popular tunes, prefiguring Ophelia's songs, plus drumming at crucial plot points. The hybrid play appears to be the exuberant and daring work of a young and as yet unpolished genius.

Some scholars of *Horestes* pair it with *Hamlet* in a way that suggests that it was a forerunner of the Shakespeare play. L.-A. George of the University of Dundee, Scotland, says *Horestes* "keenly anticipates" *Hamlet* and finds "striking" similarities at times between Hamlet's situation and that of Horestes. Robert S. Knapp of Reed College calls *Horestes* the first revenge play of the English Renaissance and makes several thematic comparisons with *Hamlet.* Shakespeare scholar and editor John Kerrigan linked the two names in a book chapter title, "'Remember Me!': Horestes, Hieronimo and Hamlet," a study of revenge memories. "Remember me!" are the words of the Ghost in *Hamlet.* (Hieronimo is the hero of *The Spanish Tragedy*, also a forerunner of *Hamlet.*) The Shakespeare scholar Tucker Brooke of Yale put *Horestes* at the pinnacle of the traditional "interlude" as drama. Interludes were short plays and other entertainments written to be performed for Queen Elizabeth and her court.

The editor of *Horestes*, Daniel Seltzer, cited it as having the first, if imperfect, example of the Shakespearean soliloquy in its purest form, the expression, moment by moment, of the evolving, inner thoughts and feelings of a character such as Hamlet, and several other Shakespearean heroes. In his article in *Shakespeare Survey 30* (1977) Seltzer also expresses twice in the opening paragraph some uncertainly about the identity of the author, first "probably" John Pickeryng, even though that's the name on the title page, and then "John Pickerying, whoever he was." Seltzer was a professor of English at Harvard and then Princeton.

Two Oxfordian researchers argued in the late 1980s that Oxford was the author of *Horestes* and several other dramatic works that were also not attributed to him. Elizabeth Sears and Stephanie Caruana noted in their self-published, 99-page,"draft' booklet, "Oxford's Revenge: Shakespeare's Dramatic Development from Agamemnon to Hamlet" (1989) the dramatic themes, such as the guilty mother (Gertrude), that appear in both works, rare words in *Horestes* that also appear in Shakespeare as well as the use of the soliloquy and the mingling of tragedy and comedy in both works. The "draft" booklet is out of print. (See Boyle.)

Horestes has also been seen as a political allegory supporting calls for the execution of Mary Queen of Scots. She was Queen Elizabeth's close cousin and fellow monarch but also a rival for her throne. Mary was widely believed, although without proof, to have been an accomplice in the murder of her husband-consort in Scotland in 1567, the year *Horestes* was published. Soon after, she married the man believed to have arranged the assassination. She was deposed and imprisoned but escaped and fled to England where she was put under rural house arrest as a threat to Elizabeth, who would have her executed two decades later.

In 1567, Oxford was living in Cecil House, where he would have heard about the sensational developments that year in Scotland and might have even seen reports of them that William Cecil was receiving almost weekly. *Horestes* would be Oxford's first use of drama to comment on current events.

Oxford was only seventeen when *Horestes* was published and performed at court. That he was capable of such an achievement at that age is witnessed by Arthur Golding, his uncle and a scholar-translator who lived in Cecil House where Oxford was a ward of the Crown. Golding saw great literary promise in him. In the dedication to Oxford in one of his books three years earlier Golding had written that he and others noted Oxford's eagerness already at age fourteen to read the classics and follow current political events, as well as his mature judgment. Golding noted Oxford's ingrained "earnest desire . . . to read, peruse and communicate with others as well, the histories of ancient times, and things done long ago, as also of the present state of things in our days, and that not without a certain pregnancy of wit and ripeness of understanding." (See Green.) He added that everyone expected great things of him.

The title page of *Horestes* gives the author as "John Pickeryng," not a name associated with plays or any other imaginative works. At least two Stratfordian scholars suggest that he was a young John Puckering, who decades later would serve as speaker of the House of Commons and be an ardent foe of Mary Queen of Scots. John Puckering, however, never published any other plays or imaginative works, quite unusual for the author of such an innovative, accomplished and topical interlude.

Oxford might well have used "John Pickeryng" as a pseudonym to deflect attention from himself, a teenage, titled nobleman, as the author of such a daring play that managed to be performed at court. He may have impishly taken the pseudonym from the surname of William Pickering, a career diplomat, retired ambassador to France and a colorful, eccentric courtier, who would have caught young Oxford's attention as a kindred spirit. As a leading courtier-diplomat, Pickeringe would have been a familiar at Cecil House. Rowdy in his youth, he studied Greek at Cambridge, was mentioned as a possible husband for Queen Elizabeth, and was briefly involved (perhaps as a spy?) in the Throckmorton conspiracy to assassinate her and put Mary Queen of Scots on the throne, but he was never accused of disloyalty to Elizabeth. As it happens, he also bought books in Paris for Cecil. (See the DNB for Pickering.)

The full title of the play in its 1567 printing was *A New Interlude of Vice Containing the History of Horestes with the Cruel Revengement of His Father's Death Upon His One Natural Mother.* Worth noting are the similarities of the title's wording to Hamlet's anger at his mother's re-marriage in act 3 scene 4 and to Oxford's apparent estrangement from his mother. For Oxford, the hero Horestes might naturally have represented himself, and much later been Hamlet, who exacted "cruel revengement" when he berates his "natural mother," Gertrude, for her hasty re-marriage after "his father's death." The son's metaphorical revenge on his mother in both *Horestes* and *Hamlet* suggests that the teenage Oxford may have had an angry encounter with his mother after his father's death and her re-marriage soon after to a man he thought much inferior to his father, the sixteenth Earl of Oxford.

On balance, the precocious Earl of Oxford, ambitious to be a dramatist and see his first play performed at court, might well be the best candidate as the author of *Horestes*, especially given his authorship of *Hamlet*, which would have many thematic similarities to it.

THE SPANISH TRAGEDY

Often cited by Stratfordians as a source for *Hamlet* or influence on it is *The Spanish Tragedy, or Hieronimo Is Mad Again,* the title page of which gave neither the author's name nor a publication date. The consensus for a date of composition is between 1584 and 1592, perhaps1587 (when Oxford was thirty-seven). Today the anonymous play is routinely attributed to Thomas Kyd but on shaky evidence not embraced until the eighteenth century.

The revenge play is set in the royal courts of Spain and Portugal. Just a few years earlier Spain had defeated Portugal at the battle of Alcantara in 1580-81. A long, fictionalized account of the battle opens *The Spanish Tragedy.* Two years later, a Spanish fleet of a hundred ships captured Terceira, the island capital of the Portuguese Azores, after a sea battle. Terceira is mentioned in *The Spanish Tragedy* in act 1 scene 3, and a knowledgeable court audience would recognize the references to Spain becoming a major naval power and potential threat to England. The Spanish Armada would try to attack England in 1588. The play demonstrates an in-depth and insightful knowledge of the international religio-politics of the time, as detailed by Eric J. Griffin in his *English Renaissance Drama and the Specter of Spain: Ethnopoetics and Empire.*

The many parallels and similarities in *Hamlet* to *The Spanish Tragedy* have struck commentators as quite obvious, although they avoid calling it a source. Both plays are typical revenge plays whose heroes are torn apart by whether it is right to obey an instinctive impulse to avenge the murder of a close relative by killing the murderer. Both Hieronimo and Hamlet feign madness (as did Amleth in Saxo/Belleforest) to deflect suspicion about their intent to seek revenge. In both plays, it is left unclear whether the heroes feigned madness or were having episodes of neurotic madness under great emotional stress.

Several features of *Hamlet* are found in *The Spanish Tragedy* and sometimes *Horestes* but nowhere else. For example, all three plays weave comedy into the tragic plot, which was unusual at the time for an Elizabethan tragedy. *The Spanish Tragedy* has a ghost commenting on the action of the play in its conversation with a Revenge character from the morality plays. The hero Hieronimo seeks revenge for the murder of a family member, as will Hamlet. Hieronimo distrusts a letter that reveals the murderer, just as Hamlet suspects the Ghost's call for revenge. Hieronimo pledges to avenge the murder of his son, Horatio, just as Hamlet and Laertes both pledge to avenge their fathers, respectively King Hamlet and Polonius. Both Hieronimo and Hamlet ponder revenge in soliloquy.

Hieronimo reproaches himself for his delay, as does Hamlet. Both have thoughts of suicide. Both arrange for a play-within-the play that is crucial to the plot. Both plays have dumb shows. Both have a major character named Horatio, who is a trusted friend of the heroes. In both, a brother kills the lover of his sister. In *The Spanish Tragedy* Bel-Imperia's suicide foreshadows Ophelia's. And there are more of lesser significance. (See Jenkins, Thompson-Taylor, Stoll.)

Leading Stratfordian scholars have noted the significant resemblances in *Hamlet* to *The Spanish Tragedy*. The first was Frederick Boas, in1901, who cited in the first critical edition of the play its many parallels in *Hamlet*, calling it a "forerunner." David Bevington says that the "extensive similarities" of Hieronimo's dilemma to Hamlet's underscore the dramatist's debt to *The Spanish Tragedy*. Philip Edwards says in his edition of *Hamlet* that the relationship between the two plays is "profoundly important." Kenneth Muir says *Hamlet* "was clearly influenced" by *The Spanish Tragedy* and provided a model for the Shakespeare play. And significantly the editors of the Arden 2006 edition of *Hamlet* say that *The Spanish Tragedy* has "many similarities" to *Hamlet* that are not in Saco/Belleforest, listing a few of the more important.

E. K. Chambers found clear resemblances of dramatic technique and noted several echoes of *The Spanish Tragedy* in *Hamlet*. *The Reader's Encyclopedia* called it a "remarkable counterpoint" to *Hamlet*. William Empson in his 1994 essay said "Hieronimo is just like Hamlet in being both mad and not mad, both wise and foolish, and so forth." T.S. Eliot went even farther, writing that "there are verbal parallels so close to *The Spanish Tragedy* as to leave no doubt that in places Shakespeare [that is, Shakspere] was merely *revising* the text of Kyd" (his emphasis). It would seem more likely that these revisions and the extensive similarities were the result of Oxford's adapting and reshaping passages in his *Spanish Tragedy* for his *Hamlet*, not plagiarizing it.

None of these editors and commentators considers the possibility that *The Spanish Tragedy* was its author's forerunner to his *Hamlet*. Instead, they struggle to find a way to attribute it to Thomas Kyd, but the only evidence for that attribution before the late eighteenth century was an elusive allusion by Thomas Nashe, a brief, off-hand mention in a book and a misspelling in a mid-seventeenth- century book catalog. Nothing firmly direct. The book catalog even listed Shakespeare as the author, along with a "Kyte" spelling for Kyd. Shakespeare scholars have nothing to say about the possible significance of this tantalizing mention of Shakespeare.

The earliest potential attribution to Kyd, in1589, was allusive at best and probably not intended. Thomas Nashe wrote in a long passage criticizing inept translators that Seneca provides "whole Hamlets, I should say, handfuls of tragical speeches." (This was the first mention in the records of a Hamlet play.) A dozen lines later Nashe castigated Seneca's inept followers who "imitate the Kidde in Aesop" by taking up work for which they are not qualified, translating literary works. But the reference to a young goat, a kid, in Aesop has no direct connection to "whole Hamlets." It seems merely illustrative of unqualified translators. Another problem with the suggestion that the "Kidde" in Nashe indicates that he thought Kyd wrote this early version of *Hamlet* is undermined by more than a dozen references to the offending translators in the plural, not just one. (See Nashe and Erne.)

The next supposed attribution of the play to Kyd was in 1612, almost two decades after he died. The playwright/actor Thomas Heywood wrote that "therefore M. Kid, in *The Spanish Tragedy*, upon occasion presenting itself, thus writes," followed by three lines from the play. That's all. No elaboration or indication of his source. This off-hand mention, perhaps prompted by the vague "Kidde" connection in Nashe, went unnoticed.

Then four decades later, a book catalog attributed *The Spanish Tragedy* to "Thos. Kyte," but surprisingly also attributed *Jeronimo* (another title for *The Spanish Tragedy, Or Hieronimo Is Mad Again*) to "Will. Shakespeare," by now the famous spelling of the famous dramatist, and Oxford's pen name. Stratfordian scholars give some weight to the "Kyte" attribution but none to the "Shakespeare" attribution. There may well have been some unspoken suspicion that the author of *Hamlet* wrote *The Spanish Tragedy.* (See Erne.)

Finally, in 1773, when still no one had found direct evidence for Kyd, a book on the origins of English drama elevated to hard evidence Heywood's off-hand mention in 1612 of "M. Kid, in *The Spanish Tragedy,*" to assert that Kyd was the author. Until then, his name had not been on the title page of any of the many editions. Nevertheless, ever since, scholars of Kyd and Shakespeare have routinely accepted Kyd as the author of the play.

Thomas Kyd never claimed nor received credit for the very popular play. The ten reprints of it up to 1633 were anonymous. It was performed almost thirty times in its first five years, but Kyd's contemporaries never left word that he wrote it nor other plays that would later be cautiously attributed to him, also on slight evidence. In the 184 years since Nashe's reference to Aesop's Kidde no one had stated that Kyd wrote the well-known, popular *Spanish Tragedy*. Little is known about Kyd's life, and in sum the evidence for Kyd is woefully inadequate.

It is much more likely that the author of *The Spanish Tragedy* was the Earl of Oxford, a successful dramatist as Shakespeare and a courtier in his late thirties who was close to England's leaders, especially William Cecil, the queen's principal adviser, and who no doubt was immersed in the international religio-politics of the day involving England, Spain and France.

In 1952, Oxfordians Dorothy and Charlton Ogburn (parents of Charlton) noted a "pervasive connection . . . between *The Spanish Tragedy* and *Hamlet*" and later in a footnote "a hundred instances [of] the unmistakable mark of Shakespeare's hand" in *The Spanish Tragedy* but without elaborating. (No one suggests that Will Shakspere wrote it; he was in his early twenties, too young to have written this highly sophisticated, topical play.)

THE UR-HAMLET

The third of the three plays that arguably were early versions of the Hamlet story, and which Oxford probably wrote, was the lost, anonymous play dubbed the "Ur-Hamlet." No manuscript has been found, nor any evidence for its publication, nor any direct evidence for its author, but that it really existed in 1589 or earlier is not in doubt. In that year Thomas Nashe alluded to "whole Hamlets . . . of tragical speeches." It was acted on stage at Newington Butts, south of London, in 1594, and mentioned in 1596 by Thomas Lodge, who referred to a "ghost which cried so miserably at the Theatre, like an oyster-wife, Hamlet, revenge."

The Stratfordian consensus is that the Ur-Hamlet was not written by Will Shakspere but perhaps by Thomas Kyd, and they include it among the possible sources for *Hamlet*. They probably resist attributing the Ur-Hamlet to Shakspere because he was too young to have written it in time for publication, performance and the published comment by Nashe in 1589. He was only in his early twenties and not mature enough to have written even an early version of *Hamlet*, whose composition they date around 1600, more than ten years later.

Some go so far as to suggest, indeed imagine, certain characters and plot elements in the phantom Ur-Hamlet that prefigured characters and situations in the final *Hamlet* despite the fact that no text of the Ur-Hamlet exists. Those conjectured elements, they suggest, came from various sources and even, retrospectively, from the final *Hamlet*. In effect, they conjecture a skeletal, phantom Ur-Hamlet prefiguring *Hamlet*. Much of their conjecturing amounts to a form of circular reasoning. Unsaid but implied is that Will Shakspere somehow saw the lost Ur-Hamlet manuscript and used it as a source. It's all very improbable.

The theory of the Ur-Hamlet as a source or influence has been adopted to a greater or lesser extent by most editors of *Hamlet*. For example, Philip Edwards, editor of the New Cambridge edition (1985-2012), concludes that *Hamlet* was influenced by the Ur-Hamlet as well as by *The Spanish Tragedy*. The Ur-Hamlet is "the immediate source" of *Hamlet* for the co-editor of *The Reader's Encyclopedia of Shakespeare*.

A few commentators, however, argue that the author of *Hamlet* was the author of the Ur-Hamlet. In *Hamlet Studies* (1988), Eric Sams critiqued at length the debates and disagreements among his fellow Stratfordians and described the "mare's nest and wild goose chase" they created trying to situate the Ur-Hamlet as a source or influence and assigning it to Kyd. He argued that scholars have found so many similarities in the Ur-Hamlet that "either Shakespeare was a great dramatist who wrote U [the Ur-Hamlet in his parlance] or he was a gross plagiarist who abused it." Sams concluded that the Ur-Hamlet "is logically connected through Q1 to Q2 [of *Hamlet*], which are plainly announced on both their title pages as Shakespeare's successive versions of his own play. All these roads lead straight to the expression U---->Q1. Only a dizzying U-turn can avoid it."

Back in 1936, the Stratfordian scholar A. S. Cairncross included a discussion of *The Spanish Tragedy* and the Ur-Hamlet in *The Problem of Hamlet, a Solution*. He concluded that the second and final quarto of *Hamlet* in 1604 was the play mentioned by Thomas Nashe in 1589 that became known as the Ur-Hamlet (probably an early version.) Neither Sams nor Cairncross have won the support of editors of *Hamlet* probably because Will Shakspere was too young to have written the Ur-Hamlet.

The Ur-Hamlet and *The Spanish Tragedy*, and their relationship to each other, to the first quarto of *Hamlet* and to the final *Hamlet* of 1604, have generated endless debate among Stratfordian scholars. To cite a recent example of the uncertainty of it all: The editors of the 2006 Arden edition conclude that "perhaps Shakespeare's play [the 1604 *Hamlet*] draws on Kyd's play [*The Spanish Tragedy*], but perhaps both plays draw on the Ur-Hamlet." Uncertainty, speculation and disagreements pervade the Stratfordians' debates about the sources for *Hamlet* and influences on it. With Oxford as the author of *Hamlet* and the Shakespeare canon, he almost certainly was the author of the Ur-Hamlet, the earliest version of the play, written when he was in his late thirties and first mentioned in 1589 by Thomas Nashe.

A PROPOSED SCENARIO

A more realistic and much simpler scenario would explain why Stratfordian commentators struggle to identify the authors of the three plays, which instead make more sense as forerunners of *Hamlet* by the author of *Hamlet*.

In this scenario, when Oxford was seventeen he wrote the *Horestes* interlude, a court entertainment mixing brash comedy with grim tragedy and a serious, topical theme. In his early thirties, no doubt inspired in part by the concerns in Queen Elizabeth's court about the threat to England of the growing Spanish naval power, he wrote *The Spanish Tragedy,* setting it the courts of Spain and Portugal, with Spain conquering Portugal in land and sea battles. In his late thirties he wrote the first version of his *Hamlet,* which was performed and mentioned by Thomas Nashe and Thomas Lodge but not published. This version became known much later as the anonymous, lost Ur-Hamlet, and for Stratfordians a supposed source for *Hamlet*.

In 1603 *Hamlet* first appeared in print as "By William Shakespeare," Oxford's pen name, and notably "as it has been diverse times been acted," according to its title page. This so-called "bad" quarto was arguably a pirated version created by an actor who had memorized an "acted" performance, written it down and sold it to the publisher. Meanwhile, Oxford, now in his early fifties had no doubt been continuing to write and re-write his *Hamlet*, and just a year after the flawed "bad" quarto appeared he finished his *Hamlet* (perhaps with some speed in order to replace the pirated version) and had it published in 1604 with the title page stating that it was "newly imprinted and enlarged to almost as much again as it was according to the true and perfect copy." It was twice as long as the pirated text of the "acted" play and it was a "true" copy set in type from the author's manuscript. Most scholars consider it the best text, even including the posthumous text in the First Folio of 1623, the collected Shakespeare plays.

Thus Oxford wrote and rewrote from age seventeen to his early fifties just before he died the bitterly comic tragedy that was his most personal play and the closest to his lifelong concerns and experiences, a revenge play about the dilemma of whether it's right to kill to avenge the murder of a close relative, as was traditionally believed. It drew originally on the Danish Amleth story and the Greek Orestes story and for the final scene in *Hamlet* probably on the death of Beowulf in the ancient Anglo-Saxon epic poem. All based on his experience of the corruption in Queen Elizabeth's court, the loss of his inheritance to the Earl of Leicester (Claudius in the play) and his conflicted feelings about revenge stemming from his suspicions about Leicester's rumored strategic poisonings, including that of Oxford's father, and their rivalry for the queen's favor. More textual and historical research and analysis might well confirm this scenario.

Hamlet's Sources and Influences

Unlike Shakspere, Oxford was perfectly placed to see the printed sources for *Hamlet* and influences on it. During his pre-teen and teenage years, he lived in households with scholars of Greek and Latin and had ready access to their libraries of the classics, among the largest at the time.

As was customary for sons of high ranking noblemen, Oxford at a very early age was sent to live with and be educated by Sir Thomas Smith, a leading scholar of Greek, who brought him up until age twelve. Smith had been the head of Eton, the boarding school for boys, and a professor at Cambridge University, where he taught the Greek language and literature. An experienced educator of boys, he began the education of Oxford, no doubt including Greek. He also hired Thomas Fowler, a graduate of Cambridge, as a tutor for a short time. Smith had one of the largest libraries in England. Based on his inventory, he owned at least four hundred books, nearly all in Latin, Greek, French and Italian (only 21 in English). They included Saxo Grammaticus in Latin and plays by Euripides and Sophocles in the original Greek and in Latin translations. (See Hughes.)

When Oxford was twelve, he became a ward of the Crown during his minority. He was sent to live with William Cecil, later Lord Burghley, and Cecil's wife, Mildred, in their London mansion. Cecil was Queen Elizabeth's Secretary of State, her most influential adviser, and later Lord Treasurer. He recognized the importance of education in the classics for young noblemen like Oxford, and as the queen's master of the wards, sons of deceased noblemen, he arranged for their education. He was also an avid book collector and had friends and associates on the Continent buy books for his library. His library included many classics, including Saxo Grammaticus and Francois Belleforest as well as Euripides and Sophocles with their treatments of the Orestes story. His library held about a thousand books when Oxford lived in the Cecil household. (See Jolly and Bowden.)

Historians have called Cecil House the best school for boys being groomed to become statesmen. It is also thought to have been an unrivaled meeting place for intellectuals. The guidance of tutors may have been important, but the teenage Edward may well have achieved a largely self-directed education, living as he did in close proximity to the riches of the Cecil House libraries, where he almost certainly read the epic poem *Beowulf*.

BEOWULF

The dying words and death of the hero Beowulf evidently inspired the way Hamlet died by poison and his dying words to Horatio. The only text of *Beowulf* was a manuscript at Cecil House in the hands of Laurence Nowell, Oxford's tutor. Nowell, who lived at Cecil House while tutoring Oxford, was the foremost scholar of Anglo-Saxon literature; he compiled the first Anglo-Saxon/English dictionary. The anonymous manuscript, written in Anglo-

Saxon (Old English), is dated around 1000 AD. It was not transcribed and printed until the nineteenth century. (Will Shakspere could not have seen it.)

The similarities between *Beowulf* and *Hamlet* are striking. One of the monarch's two sons killed the other unintentionally with an arrow that went wide of its mark. When Hamlet apologizes to Laertes for killing his father, he says he did not intend it and asks Laertes to "Free me so far in your generous thoughts / That I have shot my arrow over the house / And hurt my brother." (5.2.213-15) If Hamlet and Ophelia had married, Hamlet and Laertes would have been brothers-in-law. (Oxford would probably have also noted that like himself Beowulf also became a ward of the monarch when a pre-teen.)

Just as the villainous dragon in *Beowulf* had stolen the people's treasure of jewels and gold, the villain Claudius in *Hamlet* by usurping Denmark's throne stole its crown jewels and treasury. And in Oxford's view the villainous Earl of Leicester had managed to steal by appropriation much of Oxford's inheritance during his minority.

At the climax of *Beowulf* the hero Beowulf, leader of his people and called a prince, battles a fifty-foot dragon that guards treasure it stole from the people by terrorizing them. The dragon bites Beowulf on the neck with its poisoned fangs, but Beowulf, before dying and with the help of his loyal comrade Wiglaf, kills the dragon with his dagger and ends its tyranny.

Poison as the cause of death figures prominently in *Beowulf* and *Hamlet* (and Leicester's reputation). The dragon's poisoned fangs kill Beowulf, and in the play the hero Hamlet is fatally poisoned by Laertes' foil in their fencing match, the poisoned foil tip having been Claudius's idea. Before the poison takes effect, however, Hamlet kills Claudius with the same poisoned foil. Claudius's use of poison reflects Leicester's reputation for strategic poisonings by henchmen, including as Oxford probably suspected the sudden, unexpected death of his father.

Both Beowulf and Hamlet live long enough to speak their dying thoughts, which are quite similar. Beowulf tells his loyal friend Wiglaf that he is dying, that the dragon's treasure should be used for the needs of his people and that he wants Wiglaf to build a monument over his grave and call it Beowulf's Barrow, his burial mound, so that his name and achievements will be remembered. In his dying words, Hamlet says to his loyal friend: "Horatio, I am dead. . . . Report me and my cause aright. . . . tell my story." (5.2.323-4, 335) If Hamlet is the voice of his creator, his "cause" or purpose (OED obs.) and his "story" can be interpreted as Oxford's monument, the treasure he leaves for posterity, that is, the plays and poems that appeared as by William Shakespeare, his pseudonym. Hamlet's dying words are powerfully evocative of (if not totally parallel to) Beowulf's dying words.

Both Beowulf and Hamlet leave no heirs, and their kingdoms will go to foreigners. Both have had the support of their people and are solicitous for them. Beowulf tells his friend Wiglaf that he wants the dragon's stolen treasure to go to his people, but soon it's clear that without their leader a foreign power will conquer them. Hamlet, now the direct heir apparent to the Crown of Denmark but himself without an heir, tells his friend Horatio that he gives his dying voice to the foreigner Fortinbras to take the vacant throne of Denmark.

It's hard to imagine any Elizabethan youth who aspired to be a writer enjoying a richer literary environment than young Oxford, brought up by the scholar-diplomat-book collector Sir Thomas Smith and living and reading during the most formative years of his life in the highly educated Cecil household with its library of many hundreds of books. Reading the classics and coming across the stories of the heroes Amleth and Orestes, and of Beowulf in manuscript, Oxford no doubt saw the parallels in them to his own life experience, his deepest concerns and his mercurial, "antic" temperament and was driven to combine them into his most intensely personal and autobiographical play, *The Tragedy of Hamlet, Prince of Denmark.*

Selected Works Consulted for this Essay

Of the many annotated, Stratfordian editions of *Hamlet*, the following are of special interest for their line notes and commentaries on *Hamlet's* sources and influences and its forerunners by Oxford:

Edwards, Philip, ed. *Hamlet*. Cambridge UP, 1985, 2003. Esp. for *The Spanish Tragedy* and the Ur-Hamlet (2-4).

Hibbard, G. R., ed. *Hamlet.* Oxford UP, 1987. In his section on sources (5-14) he calls Belleforest the most likely source, oddly omitting mention of *The Spanish Tragedy.*

Jenkins, Harold, ed. *Hamlet* in the Arden Shakespeare Series. London: Methuen, 1982. For its analogies to *The Spanish Tragedy* (97-8).

Thompson, Ann and Neil Taylor, eds. *Hamlet* in the Arden Shakespeare Series. London: Thomson Learning, 2006, 2016. For the difficulties in sourcing and dating *Hamlet* (43-59), the similarities to *The Spanish Tragedy*, the uncertainty about the Ur-Hamlet (4-7,70) and for the academic phenomenon of "source-hunting" (59-74). Theirs is the only modern-day edition to even mention Greek drama as a possible source or influence (63-4), citing the 1990 article by Louise Schleiner. Their revised edition of 2016 with "Additions and Reconsiderations," includes mention of a book by the Oxfordian Margrethe Jolly on Q1 and Q2.

Among the most pertinent works of research and commentary for this article are the following:

Anderson, Mark. *Shakespeare by Another Name: The Life of Edward de Vere, the Earl of Oxford, the Man Who Was Shakespeare*. New York: Penguin, 2005. For his education (6-9, 20-35; for Rosencrantz and Guildenstern (191-2), esp. the end notes for those pages.

Beowulf (anon.) c. 1000. Translation from the Anglo-Saxon (Old English) manuscript by Seamus Heaney. New York: Norton, 2000. See esp. pp. 165-213. Translations vary considerably. Cf. Francis Barton Gummere's (1910), Albert W. Haley's (1978), Burton Raffle's (1963). See also Ignoto.

Berney, C.V. "Who Wrote *The Spanish Tragedy?* in *Shakespeare Matters* (winter 2005); "Hidden Allusions in Oxford's *Spanish Tragedy"* in *Shakespeare Matters* (summer 2005); Óxford's *Spanish Tragedy:* More Hidden Allusions" in *The Shakespeare Oxford Newsletter* (spring 2015).

Bevington, David, ed. *The Spanish Tragedy / Thomas Kyd.* Manchester UP, 1996. Esp. p. 11.

Boas, Frederick S. *The Works of Thomas Kyd*. Oxford: Clarendon Press, 1901. He notes that by the turn of the century there was "a growing conviction that Kyd was a forerunner of Shakespeare in dramatizing the story of Hamlet."(vii)

Bowden, Caroline. "The Library of Mildred Cooke Cecil, Lady Burghley" in *The Library* (March 2005). For her knowledge of Latin and Greek and her library, which included the seven extant plays of Aeschylus, notably the *Oresteia*, as well as those of Euripides and Sophocles.

Boyle, Bill. Letter to the Editor re the Sears-Caruana draft booklet "Oxford's Revenge." In *The Shakespeare Oxford Newsletter* (spring 2018) 28. See also the letter to the editor from Tom Goff on the same page.

Brooke, Tucker. *The Tudor Drama.* Boston: Houghton Mifflin, 1911. For *Horestes*' importance. (139)

Cairncross, A. S. *The Problem of Hamlet, a Solution*. New York: Macmillan, 1936, 1978. For the Ur-Hamlet and *The Spanish Tragedy*. (103-6) See also Ogburn, Charlton; and Harold Bloom's *Shakespeare: The Invention of the Human*. New York: Riverhead, 1998, for the assessment by the Yale professor and Shakespeare scholar that the Ur-Hamlet was written by the author of *Hamlet*. (xiii, 383)

Chambers, E. K. *William Shakespeare, a Study of Facts and Problems*. Oxford: Clarendon Press, 1930. For resemblances of *Hamlet* to *The Spanish Tragedy*. (1:424)

Collins, J. Churlton. "Shakespeare as a Classical Scholar" in *Studies in Shakespeare.* New York: Dutton, 1904.

Eliot, T.S. "Hamlet and His Problems." *The Sacred Wood* (1920). New York: Barnes & Noble, 1928. For *The Spanish Tragedy.* (64)

Emerson, Kathy Lynn. *Who's Who of Tudor Women* on line at kateemersonhistoricals.com/TudorWomen. For Mildred Cecil and her children's education "as well as that of the various wards her husband was responsible for, including the Earl of Essex and the Earl of Oxford."

Erne, Lucas. *Beyond* The Spanish Tragedy: *a Study of the Works of Thomas Kyd.* For *Hamlet* analogues to it (5); for the authorship problem, Heywood, the bookseller's catalog and Hawkins. (47-8); and for the play as a "comitragedy." (84-7)

George, L.-A. "'A pestelaunce on the crabyd queane': The Hybrid Nature of John Pickerying's *Horestes.*" Sederi 14 (2004).

Golding, Arthur. For his dedication to Oxford in one of his books, www. Oxford-Shakespeare.org > Documents, 1564, STC 24290. One of hundreds of valuable transcriptions pertaining to the Oxfordian proposition on Nina Green's website.

Hamill, John. "The Ten Restless Ghosts of Mantua: Part 2" in *The Shakespeare Oxford Newsletter* (autumn 2003). For "The Murder of Gonzago." See also Magri.

Hannas, Andrew. See Ignoto, a pseudonym.

Heywood, Thomas. *An Apology for Actors.* London: Oakes, 1612. For the mention of "Kyd . . . Spanish Tragedy" in this pamphlet.

Horestes. See Pickering.

Hughes, Stephanie Hopkins. "Shakespeare's Tutor: Sir Thomas Smith (1513-1577)." *The Oxfordian* (2000). See also her website, politicworm.com, for Oxford's education, his tutors, the Smith and Cecil libraries, and the section on "Hamlet and Hieronimo."

____. "Oxford's Childhood: The First Four Years with Smith, Part I." *Shakespeare Oxford Newsletter* (winter 2006).

____. "Oxford's Childhood: The First Four Years, Part II." *The Shakespeare Oxford Newsletter* (Fall 2006).

Hume, Martin A. S. *The Great Lord Burghley.* London: Nisbet, 1898. For Sir Thomas Smith (9), and for Burghley as an "insatiable book buyer." (48-9)

Ignoto (Andrew Hannas). "Beowulf, Hamlet and Edward de Vere." *The Shakespeare Oxford Newsletter* (Spring 1990). Hannas was the first to note the parallels in *Hamlet* to Beowulf's dying words and death.

Jolly, Eddi (Margrethe). "Shakespeare and Burghley's Library" in *The Oxfordian* (2000). For the size of William Cecil's library and its holdings of sources for *Hamlet.* Her estimate of 1,700 titles (including some in multi-volume editions) in his library is based on her analysis of a 1687 book sale catalog, which probably included books purchased up to his death in 1598. This suggests an estimate of about a thousand books when Oxford was living in Cecil House the 1560s.

____. "*Hamlet* and the French Connection: The Relationship of Q1 and Q2 *Hamlet* and the Evidence of Belleforest's *Histoires Tragiques*" in *Parergon* 29.1 (2012). For a detailed list of the borrowings from Belleforest in Q1 and Q2.

____. *The First Two Quartos of* Hamlet: A *New View of the Origins and relationships of the Texts.* Jefferson NC: McFarland, 2014. An exhaustive review of the extensive Stratfordian debate and analysis of who wrote what and when. In brief, she concludes that the author of *Hamlet* wrote the first quarto, against the theory that it was a memorial reconstruction by an actor. The revised Arden edition of *Hamlet* (2016) cites her book.

Kerrigan, John. " 'Remember Me!': Horestes, Hieronimo and Hamlet," a chapter title in his *Revenge Tragedy: Aeschylus to Armageddon.* Oxford: Clarendon Press, 1998.

Knapp, Robert S. "The Uses of Revenge" in the *ELH* journal: Johns Hopkins UP (summer 1973). He also finds that "ultimately, and also like *Hamlet, Horestes* is a drama of the fallen world . . . in which justice and mercy are sometimes fearfully and mysteriously incompatible." (218-19)

Lodge, Thomas. *Wits Miserie and the Worlds Madness*. London: 1597. For his "Hamlet, revenge."

Magri, Noemi. "*Hamlet*'s 'The Murder of Gonzago' in Contemporary Documents" in *The De Vere Society Newsletter* (June 2009)

Miola, Robert S., ed. *Hamlet, a Norton Critical Edition.* New York: Norton, 2011. In his introduction, "Imagining *Hamlet,*" he says that Shakspere "probably knew some mediated version of Belleforest and a lost play, probably by Thomas Kyd, known as the *Ur-Hamlet";* and that "Orestes prefigures Hamlet." (xiii) See also excerpts from Nicholas Rowe and Margreta de Grazia.

Muir, Kenneth. *The Sources of Shakespeare's Plays*. London: Methuen, 1977. Reprint Routledge, 2014. In chapter 24, he calls the Ur-Hamlet the main source for *Hamlet*, but uncertainty is pervasive as he speculates about whether it was written perhaps by Shakspere or someone else, how that might have happened and how Saxo, Belleforest, *The Spanish Tragedy* and Thomas Nashe fit into his subtle and complex scenario of intertwined influences and borrowings, all mostly speculative and tentative. Although he acknowledges that there is "no certain knowledge of the Ur-Hamlet" he deduces what might have been in it from other Hamlet stories and concludes that with the Ur-Hamlet as the main source "echoes of books published before 1589 may have been present before Shakespeare took a hand."

Murray, Gilbert. *Hamlet* and *Orestes*. Oxford UP, 1914; reprinted as chap 8 in his *Classical Tradition in Poetry*, Harvard UP, 1927.

Nashe, Thomas. Preface to *Menaphon* by Robert Greene. London: Sampson Clarke, 1589. For "Whole Hamlets" and the passage re Aesop's Kidde.

Neill, Michael. ed. *The Spanish Tragedy*, a Norton Critical Edition. New York: Norton, 2014. For Kyd's reputation and the popularity of the play in performance and in print.

Nelson, Alan. *Monstrous Adversary: the Life of Edward de Vere, 17th Earl of Oxford.* Liverpool UP, 2003. For Edward de Vere's tutors.

Nichols, John Gough, ed. *Literary Remains of King Edward the Sixth, Edited from His Autograph Manuscripts, with Historical Notes and a Biographical Memoir.* London: J. B. Nichols and Sons, 1857. For the educational accomplishments of Mildred Cecil's father. (xlix-li)

Ogburn, Charlton . *The Mysterious William Shakespeare: The Myth and the Reality*. McLean Va.: EPM Publications, 1984. Second edition 1992. For Cairncross and *The Spanish Tragedy.* (387)

Ogburn, Dorothy and Charlton Ogburn (Sr.). *This Star of England*. New York: Coward-McCann, 1952. For *The Spanish Tragedy.* (428, 1014 fn)

Phillips, James E. "A Revaluation of *Horestes* (1567)" in *The Huntington Library Quarterly*. Univ. of Pennsylvania Press, May 1955. For historians of English drama baffled as to the identity of the author of *Horestes* and his argument that it was probably John Puckering.

Pickerying, John (?). *A New Interlude of Vice Containing the Historye of Horestes*. London: William Griffith, 1567. Reprinted as *The Interlude of Vice (*Horestes*)*, ed. Daniel Seltzer for the Malone Society reprint series. OUP, 1962. For a modern-day, online transcription with original spelling, see Flues, Barboura and Robert Brazil, at elizabethanauthors.org/Horestes. See also the DNB for William Pickering.

Rowe, Nicholas. "Some Account of the Life Etc. of Mr. William Shakespeare [that is, Shakspere] in his *Works of Mr. William Shakespeare*. London: Tonson, 1709.

Sams, Eric. "Taboo or Not Taboo, the Text, Dating and Authorship of *Hamlet*." *Hamlet Studies* (1988). 10:12-46. The article is on-line but without page numbers.

Saxo Grammaticus. *Gesta Danorum*. (c. 1150-1220). For the story of Amlethus. First publication, in Latin, in 1514 in Paris; first English translation by Oliver Elton in 1894, included in *The Nine Books of the Danish History: Gesta Danorum,* ed. Mark

Ludwig Stinson. CreateSpace (2012), pp. 126 ff. See also "Amleth, Prince of Denmark," ed. D.L. Ashliman, an English text by Elton, and online at www. Pitt.edu/~dash/Amleth.html.

Schleiner, Louise. "Latinized Greek Drama in Shakespeare's Writing of *Hamlet*" in *Shakespeare Quarterly* (41-1 spring 1990). She says she was "convinced that at least some passages of Euripides' *Orestes* and Aeschylus' *Oresteia* . . . by some means influenced *Hamlet*" and conjectures that Will Shakspere might have read Latin translations of Aeschylus and might have seen performances of two anonymous, lost English plays about the Orestes story or could have heard about them from friends. (29-48)

Showerman, Earl. "Orestes and Hamlet: From Myth to Masterpiece." *The Oxfordian* 7 (2004). A wealth of parallels and arguments for Aeschylus's *Oresteia* trilogy as an important influence or even a source for *Hamlet*. He compiles and analyzes the "astonishing variety of Greek and Roman sources in *Hamlet*" (104) that must have been well-known to the author of *Hamlet*, including notably Homer, whose *Odyssey* was not put into English until 1616. For more of his important, detailed work on the influence of Greek drama and epics on Shakespeare's works, see his article, "Shakespeare's Greater Greek: *Macbeth* and Aeschylus' *Oresteia*" in *Brief Chronicles III* (2011-12).

____ "*Horestes* and *Hamlet*." *The Shakespeare Oxford Newsletter* (spring 2008). For his report of an early Oxfordian suggestion that *Horestes* was Oxford juvenilia.

____ "The Rediscovery of Shakespeare's Greater Greek" in *The Oxfordian 17* (2015).

Steevens, George and Samuel Johnson. *The Plays of William Shakespeare*, vol. 8. London: C. Bathurst, 1773. For Steeven's signed footnote that he was convinced that the dramatist was conversant with the original Greek language. (417)

Stoll, Elmer Edgar. "*Hamlet* and *The Spanish Tragedy*," Quartos I and II: a Protest" in *Modern Philology* (August 1932). Stoll found many "striking resemblances" in *Hamlet* to "the stage devices and details of the story of *The Spanish Tragedy*, in the phrasing and the rhythm peculiar to Q1 [of *Hamlet*] . . . practically the same story turned around." That is, a father's revenge for his son's murder and a son's revenge for his father's murder.

This article and its bibliography first appeared in a slightly different form in the Winter 2018 edition of The Shakespeare Oxford Newsletter.

Astronomy in *Hamlet*

The extraordinary number of references and allusions to astronomy in *Hamlet* testify to Oxford's authorship of it. Significantly, mentions of them are missing from Stratfordian editions of the play, perhaps for that very reason. Peter Usher, emeritus professor of astronomy and astrophysics at Pennsylvania State University, describes them in several books and many articles. Many of the references and allusions reflect the nascent awareness among the few scientist-mathematician-astronomer-astrologers in England that the Ptolemaic and Roman Catholic, Earth-centered conception of God's universe was erroneous and that the Sun was the center of the solar system in an infinite universe of stars and planets. It was a revolutionary—and dangerously heretical—idea that overturned the prevailing belief in a limited universe that God created with the Earth, and mankind, at the center of it.

The most striking of the play's allusions to astronomy occurs in act 2. Bantering maniacally with Rosencrantz and Guildenstern, and apropos of nothing, Hamlet exclaims: "O God, I could be bounded in a nutshell, and count myself a king of infinite space—were it not that I have bad dreams." (2.2.237-8) Stratfordian editors of the play do not gloss the line, which otherwise seems quite enigmatic.

The juxtaposition of "nutshell" and "infinite space," strongly suggests a contrast of the old Ptolemaic astronomy to the emerging, new Copernican model. The nutshell would be the relatively small shell of stars encircling the Earth of Ptolemy's universe. "Infinite space" would be the revolutionary and even heretical idea that the universe has no finite boundary, first proposed by Thomas Digges, one of the earliest supporters of Copernicus's sun-centered model of the solar system.

A few minutes later, Hamlet refers to the heavens of Claudius Ptolemy's universe as having a fixed "roof" of stars: "this canopy . . . this brave overhanging firmament, this majestical roof," but he then immediately rejects this Ptolemaic "roof" of stars, condemning it—and by extension Ptolemy's namesake King Claudius—as a "foul and pestilent congregation of vapors." (2.2.269-72) Oxford was the first to give the usurping king in the Amlethus/Amleth/Hamlet story the name "Claudius," identifying him with the discredited astronomy of Claudius Ptolemy.

Both passages reflect the dramatist's knowledge of the revolutionary but as yet not widely known Copernican challenge to the widely accepted but erroneous Ptolemaic notion of an Earth-centered planetary system, as well as radical new proposal of an infinite universe. Both were revolutionary challenges to the long-standing notion that Earth was center of a finite universe, postulated by Ptolemy, which had the Sun and planets revolving around the Earth, the center of God's universe and mankind. It was embraced by the Church and was a fundamental premise of many centuries of science, philosophy and literature.

Copernicus, a Polish mathematician, published his new theory of the universe in 1543 in Nuremberg just before he died. His book, *De Revolutionibus*, however, was largely ignored for decades. It was written in the technical lingo of astronomers, of which there was as yet only a handful in England. Thomas Digges, the mathematician/astronomer, praised Copernicus and added his own proposal of a universe that was infinite. Effectively however, he hid his controversial conclusions, which would later be condemned by the church as heretical, as an appendix to an edition of his late father's almanac. Neither the Copernican theory nor Digges's infinite universe would likely have been known beyond the small circle of mathematician-scientists who were also interested in astronomy.

In act 1, King Claudius tells Hamlet that contrary to Hamlet's plan to return to the university at Wittenberg, Germany, he wants him to stay in England. He says that Hamlet's plan is "most retrograde to our desire." (1.2.116) The passage contains two allusions to astronomy. The earliest meaning of "retrograde" described the motion of certain planets that appear at times to move contrary to that of the other planets in the Ptolemaic system. Significantly, Wittenberg was the first university where scholars considered the Copernican model of the universe. In the play, Hamlet agrees with Copernicus, while Claudius is associated with Ptolemaic astronomy, which will be discredited and replaced by the Copernican.

In his research, Usher found a significant sub-text of *Hamlet* as an allegory of Copernicus's challenge to the long-standing Ptolemaic theory. He also describes an extraordinary number of references and allusions to astronomy in *Hamlet* and other Shakespeare plays in two books, primarily in *Hamlet's Universe* (2006, 2007) and also in *Shakespeare and the Dawn of Modern Science* (2010), and in a dozen scholarly articles in astronomy journals and Oxfordian publications. Usher also suggests that several allusions in *Hamlet* to features of the Sun and Moon indicate that its author used an early, rudimentary version of the telescopic, built by Thomas Digges' father. Usher's ingenious and insightful studies have also convinced him that the astronomy of Tycho Brahe, a Danish nobleman, was a significant influence on *Hamlet* and other Shakespeare plays.

Oxford certainly knew about the coming Copernican revolution. His tutor Sir Thomas Smith, a leading humanities scholar and amateur astronomer/astrologer, owned a copy of Copernicus's book, as did Oxford's guardian William Cecil. At Cecil House, his three courses of academic study at one point were Latin, French and Cosmography, the study of the Earth and the universe. Astronomy was no doubt an occasional topic of discussion among educated visitors at Cecil house when Oxford was living there during his teenage years. He was probably among the first to know about and embrace the revolutionary astronomy of Copernicus and Digges.

In 1572 (when Oxford was twenty-two) Cecil asked Digges for his opinion about the sudden appearance of a new and very bright star that the sentinel Bernardo would describe in act 1 of *Hamlet* as "westward from the pole [the North Pole] . . . where now it burns." (1.1.38-40) This was the supernova of 1572, an exploding star that burned brightly for about a year and then began to fade and finally disappear. In his report to Cecil on the supernova, Digges also mentioned his admiration for Copernicus, and four years later he would publish his *Perfit Description,* a translation of part of Copernicus's book, adding his own equally revolutionary proposal of an infinite universe. He got his ideas into print for the laymen but hid them in an appendix to a reprint of his father's almanac, apparently in an attempt to escape persecution for heresy, which succeeded. Initially, his ideas were largely unknown beyond his small circle of fellow astronomers and admirers.

It's most unlikely that Will Shakspere would have known about the work of Copernicus or Tycho Brahe or Thomas Digges. Their books were rare, expensive and written principally for fellow astronomers who would understand the mathematics and significance of their findings. Stratfordian commentary on *Hamlet* routinely ignores or denies the existence or any importance of astronomy in the play, but the evidence from the history of the science of astronomy indicates the contrary. (See Usher in the Bibliography.)

Selected, Annotated Bibliography

Of the many Stratfordian editions of *Hamlet*, four are of special interest for their glosses and commentaries reflecting decades of scholarship and for their occasional insights that touch on its authorship:

Edwards, Philip, ed. *Hamlet*. Cambridge UP, 1985, 2003.

Hibbard, G. R., ed. *Hamlet.* Oxford UP, 1987.

Jenkins, Harold, ed. *Hamlet* in the Arden Shakespeare Series. London: Methuen, 1982. For its perceptive interpretations, extensive line notes and esp. his Longer Notes at the back, e.g. on the significance of Ophelia's flowers, Polonius's "precepts" for Laertes, and Hales v. Pettit. (547)

Thompson, Ann and Neil Taylor, eds. *Hamlet* in the Arden Shakespeare Series. London: Thomson Learning, 2006, 2016. See esp. 1-2 and 132-7 for "The Continuing Mystery of *Hamlet.*"

So much has been written about *Hamlet* that this annotated bibliography can only include a small fraction and must necessarily be very selective, as are page citations. Most of the works, however, include generous references to additional publications the reader might also consult.

Anderson, Mark. "*Shakespeare" by Another Name: The Life of Edward de Vere, Earl of Oxford, the Man Who Was Shakespeare*. New York: Gotham Books, 2005. The most recent of the authoritative, Oxfordian biographies. For Oxford's education (chap 2); for Oxford and pirates (112-13), the Earl of Leicester (17, 116, 193-7,167-8), the Earl of Sussex (193-7), the First Folio and the two earls (369-78), *Beowulf* as a source (23), for Ophelia as Anne Cecil (49-51, 67, 78, 116-120), and for Anne Cecil's pregnancy, see Anderson's "Ophelia's 'difference,' or 'To catch the conscience of the counselor'" in *The Shakespeare Oxford Newsletter* (Winter 2000). See also Christopher Paul and Alan Nelson for Oxford and the pirates.

Anonymous. *Leicester's Commonwealth*. See Peck.

Brandes, Georg. *William Shakespeare, a Critical Study*. 2 vols. London: Heineman, 1898. For Claudius as Leicester (2:347).

Bullough, Geoffrey. "The Murder of Gonzago" in *The Modern Language Review* (v. 30 no. 4 Oct. 1935). A detailed account by a Stratfordian scholar of the murder of the Duke of Urbino by poison as the probable source for details of the murder of King Hamlet by poison and of the play-within-the play. See also Hamill.

Cavalli, Sigismondo di, Venetian ambassador to London. *Calendar of State Papers . . . Relating to English Affairs.* For his dispatch to the Signory of Venice 31 August 1573 regarding Leicester being detested but having great influence on Queen Elizabeth .

Cecil, William, Lord Burghley. *Ten Precepts* [to his] *Son Robert,* in *English Prose*, ed. Henry Craik. London: Macmillan, 1907, vol. 1. Also in Bartleby .com. The question arises whether Laertes, Polonius's son, who must listen to his father's now-famous "precepts" before leaving for Paris, represents Robert Cecil, the addressee of his father's *Ten Precepts*, or whether Laertes represents Cecil's older son, the wayward Thomas. William Cecil probably wrote them in the 1580s when Robert was in his late teens and early twenties and beginning to show great promise for politics that Cecil would have wanted to encourage and aid with sound, if shallow, advice. Robert would succeed his father as chief minister to Queen Elizabeth and then to her successor, King James. It may be that Oxford wrote Polonius's "precepts" for Laertes after seeing the manuscript of Cecil's *Precepts* for Robert (not published until 1618.) Or perhaps more likely, Oxford based them simply on his long experience as a teenager in the Cecil household hearing the verbose William Cecil hold forth time and again with rather pompous and shallow advice to his young sons and his aristocratic wards on how to behave. It was Thomas Cecil, however, who most likely was the model for the brash, impulsive, over-exuberant Laertes, who was sent to Paris to further his education. Thomas was sent to Paris (in 1560) to further his education; Robert was not. In Paris, Thomas gained a reputation for his extravagant and irresponsible life-style. The teenage Oxford may have looked up to him as a kindred spirit. Thomas did not show much promise for statecraft or much ambition to be an influential statesman. Like many aristocrats, he was in the military and was a public official, but mainly by virtue of being Burghley's elder son and inheriting his title as Baron Burghley. His father seems to have given up on him as having potential for major accomplishments. Conceivably, publication of Cecil's *Ten Precepts* in 1618 might have been intended as a posthumous tribute to the father, who had died two decades earlier, and also to his son Robert, who had died six years earlier. (See W. H. Charlton *Burghley: the Life of William Cecil* London: Langley, 1847, for biographies of Thomas and Robert Cecil at 110-123, 259-60).

_____. Memorandum to himself, in Calendar of State Papers, in *Collection of State Papers . . . William Cecil*, eds. Haynes & Murdin. London: Bowyer, 1709. For Cecil's note that Leicester was hated by many. (1-444)

Chambers, E. K. *William Shakespeare: a Study of Facts and Problems.* Oxford UP, 1930. For Cecil as Polonius, Cecil's *Ten Precepts* and Thomas Cecil as Laertes (1:418).

Chapman, George. *Bussy d'Ambois and The Revenge of Bussy d'Ambois*, ed. Frederick S. Boas. London: Heath, 1905. See 3.4.83-122 in *Revenge* for Chapman's description of Oxford as a difficult, mercurial, unpredictable nobleman and a writer. Chapman (c. 1559-1634) was a contemporary playwright and a decade younger than Oxford. See also Whalen "On Looking."

Charlton, William Henry. See Cecil

Clark, Eva Turner. *Shakespeare's Plays in the Order of Their Writing.* London: Cecil Palmer, 1930, and New York: Payson, 1931 as *Hidden Allusions in Shakespeare's Plays.* Reprinted in 1974 by Minos Publishing, Jennings LA, in an edition by Ruth Loyd Miller that included her introduction, notes and essays and essays by others. For Clark's chapter on *Hamlet,* and esp. for Miller's essay on Burghley/Polonius as a fishmonger, "Hamlet's Fish Days." (673-77)

Collier, John Payne. *The History of English Dramatic Poetry in the Time of Shakespeare* (1879). Chestnut Hill MA: Adamant Media, 2010. For "writ" and "liberty" at 2.2.348-9. See also Whalen *"Commedia del Arte* in *Othello."*

Cutting, Bonner Miller. "Evermore in Subjection: Edward de Vere and Wardship in Early Modern England" in *The Oxfordian 18* (2016). See also Green.

Declaration of Reasonable Doubt About William Shakespeare's Identity: www. DoubtAboutWill.org. Founder/Editor John M. Shahan, chairman of the Shakespeare Authorship Coalition web site, which includes the declaration, a running total of signatories, notable signatories, news and other matters.

Detobel, Robert. "'To Be or Not to Be,' The Suicide Hypothesis" in *The Oxfordian* 7 (2004). For the evidence that Oxford was probably a suicide, and for the gravedigger's witty word play on *se offendendo* and "argal" at the start of 5.1.

____. "An Overlooked Allusion to *Hamlet* in One of Oxford's Letters" in *The Shakespeare Oxford Newsletter.* (summer 2014) For Cecil's servant Reymondo/Polonius's servant Reynaldo.

Eliot, T. S. "Hamlet and His Problems" in *The Sacred Wood.* New York: Knopf, 1921.

Encyclopedia Britannica, 11th ed. 1910. Entry for "Robert Dudley, Earl of Leicester (c.1531-1588), 8: 636, by the editor, Sidney Lee. Esp. for Leicester's character and reputation.

Feldman, Bronson. *Hamlet Himself.* Philadelphia: Lovelore Press, 1977. Reprint New York: iUniverse, 2010. A thoroughly researched, in-depth study of Hamlet's personality by a scholar of English literature with a PhD from the University of Pennsylvania, who later became a practicing psychoanalyst.

French, George Russell. *Shakespeareana Genealogica*. London: Macmillan, 1869. For the earliest identification of Cecil and his son and daughter as Polonius and his son and daughter. (301)

Gristwood, Sarah, *Elizabeth & Leicester*. New York: Viking Penguin, 2007. For a benign description of Leicester and for the circumstances of his death. (334)

Gurr, Andrew. *The Elizabethan Stage, 1574-1642*. 4th edition. Cambridge UP, 2009. For the rivalry between the acting companies of Oxford and Leicester. (40)

Hamill, John. "The Ten Restless Ghosts of Mantua" in *The Shakespeare Oxford Newsletter* (autumn 2003). Section 8 "The Ghost of the Titian Portrait." For Titian's painting of the Duke of Urbino in armor as an inspiration for the Ghost's armor. See also Bullough.

Hume, Martin A. S. *The Great Lord Burghley: A Study in Elizabethan Statecraft*. London: Nisbet 1898. Reprint New York: Haskell House, 1968. For "the unprincipled influence of Dudley" (99) and for Burghley's network of spies (127, 130, 136, 184, 210, 224, 346, 391 and esp. 467).

Hurstfield, Joel. "Lord Burghley as Master of the Court of Wards: 1561-98" in *Transactions of the Royal Historical Society* (1949); reprinted in *The Oxfordian 3* (2000). An historian's important analysis of the wardship system under Burghley and his careful management of the great wealth it brought him and the queen through a mostly corrupt exploitation of his wards' inherited estates.

____. *The Queen's Wards: Wardship and Marriage Under Elizabeth I*. London: Longmans, Green. 1958. For Burghley's *Ten* Precepts as the voice of Polonius. (257)

Jamison, Kay Redfield. *Touched With Fire: Manic-Depressive Illness and the Artistic Temperament*. New York: Simon & Schuster (Free Press), 1994. She holds a doctorate in psychology from UCLA and is a professor of psychiatry at Johns Hopkins medical school. See esp. 47, 53-6, 63-71, 98, 102, 237, 267-70, 283-92; for Leonardo, see Walter Isaacson *Leonardo da Vinci,* New York: Simon and Schuster, 2017. (p. 8), See also Whalen "On Looking."

Jenkins, Elizabeth. *Elizabeth and Leicester*. London: Phoenix Press, 1961, 2002. For Leicester as a deceitful smiler (141, 279); the circumstances of his death. (360-1)

Jolly, Eddi. "Dating the Plays: *Hamlet,*" chapter 19 in *Great Oxford: Essays on the Life and Work of Edward de Vere, 17th Earl of Oxford 1550-1604,* ed. Richard Malim. Tunbridge Wells: Parapress, 2004. She concludes that the first version of *Hamlet* was written in the 1580s, and gives many of the arguments for Oxford as the author; also chapter 20, "The Writing of *Hamlet,*" which includes Titian's picture of the Duke of Urbino in feudal armor as the likely inspiration for the full armor of the Ghost. (184)

Kneale, William and Martha. *The Development of Logic.* OUP, 1985. For the gravedigger's pun on the surname of John Argall, the logician. (299-300) See also the DNB for Argall citing Anthony Wood on his being a great actor.

Lee, Sidney. See *Encyclopedia Britannica.*

Londré, Felicia Hardison. "*Hamlet* as Autobiography: An Oxfordian Analysis." At www. Shakespeareoxfordfellowship.org/hamlet-as-autobiography. A reprint from *The Bulletin of the Faculty of Letters,* #39-1993, Hosei University, Tokyo. A detailed examination of the evidence by Dr. Londré, curator's professor of theatre at the University of Missouri, Kansas City.

Magri, Noemi. "Hamlet's 'The Murder of Gonzago' in contemporary documents" in *The De Vere Society Newsletter* (June 2009).

Messia, Marco Antonio. His letter 27 August 1588 to King Philip of Spain regarding Leicester's death. In the *Calendar of State Papers Relating to English Affairs, Simancas 1558-1603* vol. 4 pp 411-31.

Miller, J. Valcour."Corambis, Polonius and the Great Lord Burghley in *Hamlet,*" chap, XXI in *Shakespeare Identified*, vol. 2, ed. Ruth Loyd Miller. Jennings LA: Minos Publishing, 1975.

Naunton, Sir Robert. *Fragmenta Regalia, or Observations on the Late Queen Elizabeth, Her Times and Favorites.* London: 1641. Leicester is the first of twenty-two courtiers in Naunton's memoir, available at Archive.com and in an edition from HardPress.net (2016). Naunton (1563-1635), a familiar in Elizabeth's court, was twenty-five when Leicester died. He says Leicester in appearance was "a very goodly person, tall and singularly well-featured [and] of a sweet aspect" but had a reputation as a poisoner. (47) He also says that Leicester showed great "cunning and dexterity" in the power plays among the courtiers in Queen Elizabeth's court and was continually opposed to the Earl of Sussex, the Queen's Lord Chamberlain" [and Oxford's close friend]. (48) Naunton became secretary of state under King James and Master of the Court of Wards.

Nelson, Alan. *Monstrous Adversary, the Life of Edward de Vere, 17th Earl of Oxford.* Liverpool UP, 2003. For his many, valuable transcriptions of important documents (despite his consistently anti-Oxford interpretations), including Oxford and the pirates (135-7), and Leicester. (316-18)

Ogburn, Charlton. *The Mysterious William Shakespeare: The Myth and the Reality*. McLean VA: EPM Publications, 1992. For Oxford's education.(chap 21); for *Hamlet* 359-372; Oxford's character 398; Leicester 370, 433-4, 666-7, 695-7; and for feudalism 252, 476

Oxford, seventeenth Earl of. *Letters and Poems of Edward, Earl of Oxford*, ed. Katherine Chiljan. San Francisco: Horatio Society, 1998. For letters on Burghley's informers, pp. 16, 32, 36; esp. for his last extant letter, dated, June 19, 1603. (83)

Pointon, A. J. *The Man Who Was Never Shakespeare*. Tunbridge Wells, Kent: Parapress, 2011. For Shakspere vs. Shakespeare (24) and throughout for evidence that Shakspere was not Shakespeare. See also Whalen "Shakspere/Shakespeare Spelling.

Paul, Christopher. "Oxford, *Hamlet* and the Pirates: The Naked Truth," in *The Shakespeare Oxford Newsletter* (winter 2004), for the significance of the word "naked."

Peck, D. C., ed. *Leicester's Commonwealth.* Ohio UP, 1985. A comprehensive, scholarly edition of the anonymous tract of 1584. Its authorship has so far not been firmly established, but Peck and others suggest that the author was chiefly Charles Arundell aided by other Roman Catholics in exile. See esp. pp. viii, ix, 1, 15, 21, 25-45, 41-2. Its title, added to manuscripts of it two years after its first appearance, might have been a sarcastic allusion to Leicester's self-serving, ruthless control of much of England's government (commonwealth.)

Read, Conyers. *Lord Burghley and Queen Elizabeth.* New York: Knopf, 1960. For Catholic/Protestant factions, 11; for Burghley's verbosity, 24, 32, 136; for Leicester as "king" 31, his reputation and death 435-6; for "fishmonger" Burghley, 304. A history professor at the University of Pennsylvania, Read devoted most of chapter 9 to a biography of Oxford based on primary sources. Writing in the 1950s before more modern Oxfordian scholarship, he noted that Oxford was "put forth seriously" as Shakespeare (125) but that he himself (a Stratfordian) took no position, except in an end note angrily dismissing "the most pretentious of the various advocates for Oxford" and Ogburn and Ogburn, whose idea of valid historical evidence "is widely at variance with mine own." (556)

Regnier, Thomas. "The Law in *Hamlet*" in *Brief Chronicles III* (2011), on-line at www. ShakespeareOxfordFellowship.org/BriefChronicles. A comprehensive analysis and appreciation of the law in *Hamlet* showing how unlikely it is that Will Shakspere wrote it and how the legal knowledge in the play supports the case for Oxford as Shakespeare. Regnier's law degree is from the University of Miami, and he has a master of laws degree from Columbia University. See esp. sections on ecclesiastical law and Ophelia's funeral, on the law of homicide re Claudius and Hamlet, and on property law re Hamlet's and Oxford's lost inheritance. See also Anderson (33-35), and Jenkins' Longer Note on the dramatist's knowledge of the lawsuit Hales v. Pettit and on Jenkins' uncertainty about how Will Shakspere could have seen it. (547).

Rye, Walter, ed. *The Norfolk Antiquarian Miscellany*, vol. 3 issue 1. Norwich: Agas H. Goose, 1887. "Appendix XV, The Queen's Gifts and Grants to Leicester," 327-332. Rye lists almost seventy-five, including several castles, e.g. Kenilworth and the licensing of Windsor and its forests, and many manors, wardships, and licenses, e.g. to export wool and timber. His thorough examination of the relations between Leicester and Queen Elizabeth, including "The Murder of Amy Robsart," is based on his transcriptions of many primary source documents. In his introduction to it, he notes "the wave of whitewash, which has of late years, swept over English history," including the reputations of Leicester and the queen "[which] covers a very paltry woman, made up of meanness, caprice and lechery." (251) That "whitewash" continues even to today. He argues that Leicester arranged the murder of Amy Robsart.

Saunders, Sam. "Could Shakespeare Have Calculated the Odds in Hamlet's Wager?" in *The Oxfordian 10* (2007. A detailed analysis of the king's wager at 5.2.240-1 on the duel between Hamlet and Laertes, the meaning of which has caused much debate by Stratfordian commentators. Saunders, a retired mathematics professor at Washington State University, uses logic and algebraic equations to demonstrate the meaning of the wager. He also cites *Liber de Ludo Aleae* ("On Games of Chance") by the Italian mathematician/physician/gambler Girolamo Cardano (1501-1576), the first systematic work on probability. As it happens, Cardano also wrote *De Consolatione,* the book that Stratfordians have long suggested is the book Hamlet is reading in 2.2. Oxford sponsored the publication in 1573 of the first translation of it into English as *Cardanus Comforte*. Cardano's slim volume on games of chances was not published until 1663, and whether and how Oxford might have learned of his work has not been determined. In any case, Saunders concludes that Oxford was correct in the passage on the king's wager and that Cardano's work influenced it. See also Stritmatter.

Shahan, John M. See *Declaration*.

Spurgeon, Caroline. *Shakespeare's Imagery: And What It Tells Us*. Cambridge UP, 1905. She argues with examples that the underlying metaphor in *Hamlet* is that of a "foul tumor [Claudius], rottenness and corruption." (79). See also pp. 316-19, where she suggests that the play's dominating thought is "rottenness, disease and corruption," which poisons the body politic of Denmark. (318)

Stritmatter, Roger. "The Biblical Origin of Edward de Vere's Dedicatory Poem in Cardan's *Comforte"* in *The Oxfordian 1* (1998). For the significance of the book that Hamlet is reading in act 2 scene 2 and of the poem and prose preface Oxford contributed to Cardan's book. See also Saunders.

Talbot, Gilbert. Letter to his father 11 May 1573. For Oxford's "fickle head."

Usher, Peter D. "Astronomy and Shakespeare's *Hamlet*" in *Bulletin of the American Astronomical Society* vol. 28 (May 1996).

____. "Hamlet's Transformation" in *The Elizabethan Review.* (Spring 1999) See esp. pp. 49, 50, 54.

____. "Shakespeare's Support for the New Astronomy" in *The Oxfordian 5* (2002). See esp. pp 142-3.

____. "Hamlet's Love Letter and the New Philosophy" in *The Oxfordian 8* (2005).

____. *Hamlet's Universe*. San Diego CA: Aventine Press, 2006, 2007. His principal work on the astronomy in *Hamlet*.

Ward, B. M. *The Seventeenth Earl of Oxford 1550-1604 from Contemporary Documents*. London: Murray 1928. For Oxford's education (16-27); for William Cecil's assessment of Oxford's personality (68); for Oxford's contempt for Tyrell (80); and for Horatio Vere, Oxford's favorite cousin, along with Horatio's brother, Francis "the Fighting Veres" (126-7).

Waugh, Alexander. "The True Meaning of Ben Jonson's Phrase 'Sweet Swan of Avon' in *The Oxfordian 16* (2014) as "Waugh on Jonson's "Sweet Swan of Avon." Waugh also notes that the earliest local historian (or antiquary), John Leland (c.1503-1552) wrote "Swan Song" (1545), a Latin poem in which Leland in the guise of a swan swims down the Thames from Oxford to Greenwich, describes the topography of its banks and calls Hampton Court "Avona" five times.

Weir, Alison. *The Life of Elizabeth I.* New York: Ballantine, 1998. For Leicester's reputation as poisoner (291) and throughout.

Whalen, Richard F. "On Looking into Chapman's Oxford: A Personality Profile of the Seventeenth Earl of Oxford" in *The Oxfordian 5* (2002). See esp. pp. 125-9.

____. "The Stratford Bust: a Monumental Fraud" in *The Oxfordian 8* (2005). Reprinted in *"Report My Cause Aright": Fiftieth Anniversary Anthology, the Shakespeare Oxford Society* (2007).

____. "A Dozen Shakespeare Plays Written After Oxford Died? Not Proven!" in *The Oxfordian 10* (2007).

____. "*Commedia dell'Arte in Othello*" in *Brief Chronicles III* (2011)

____. "Ambiguity in the First Folio" in *Shakespeare Matters*.(Summer 2011).

____. "Shakspere/Shakespeare Spelling" in *Brief Chronicles* (Summer 2015). See also Pointon.

Wilson, Derek. *Sweet Robin, a Biography of Robert Dudley, Earl of Leicester 1533-1588*. London: Allison & Busby, 1997; reprint London: Hamish Hamilton, 1981. An admittedly deliberate rehabilitation of Leicester's reputation, while briefly recognizing "all the unsavory stories of adulteries, murders and intrigues." Wilson gives little credence to the rumors, reported widely, about Leicester as a villainous poisoner for political and personal gain and the circumstantial evidence supporting the rumors. (x)

Wilson, John Dover. *The Essential Shakespeare*. Cambridge UP, 1932. For Polonius as Burghley (104).

____. *What Happens in Hamlet*. Cambridge University Press, 1951 (3rd edition). For his many perceptive insights and esp. the most credible solutions to the problems of the dumb-show (144-60, 183-97) and the fencing match (277-90). See also pp 200-201 for how *Hamlet* would be especially appreciated by statesmen and courtiers.

Whittemore, Hank. "Methinks I Have Astronomy," #61 in *100 Reasons Shake-speare Was the Earl of Oxford.* Somerville MA. Forever Press, 2016.

Acknowledgements

First and foremost, I must acknowledge that my greatest debt is to my associate in the *Hamlet* project, Brig. Gen. Jack Shuttleworth (USAF ret.), who was head of the English department at the U.S. Air Force Academy for two decades before his retirement in 1999. His PhD in English literature is from the University of Denver. For this Oxfordian edition of *Hamlet* he prepared the text of the play, based on the 1604 second quarto, resolving the many textual issues and judiciously modernizing the spellings and punctuation (as is done for all the Shakespeare plays). He also wrote a draft of the line notes and began a draft of the introduction before he had to leave the *Hamlet* project for personal reasons. Jack also deserves great credit and our thanks for inspiring and encouraging the Oxfordian Shakespeare Series with his scholarly paper "Prolegomena for the Oxfordian Shakespeare," delivered at the De Vere Studies Conference at Concordia University, Portland, Oregon, in April 1998, and published in *The Oxfordian 2* in 1999.

It should go without saying that I owe a tremendous debt to the many Oxfordian scholars and others whose research in the Shakespeare authorship issue, interpretations of *Hamlet* and analysis of the evidence for Oxford's authorship of it have been invaluable. It would be impossible to name them all, but many are in the suggested readings and the bibliographies. In particular, I want to thank Alex McNeil for his corrections, comments and suggestions for improvements for the draft Introduction and Bibliography and Nina Green for her editorial assistance with the sections in the Introduction on the Earl of Leicester.

Peter D. Usher, professor emeritus of astronomy and astrophysics at Pennsylvania State University, provided extensive guidance for the essay on the astronomy in *Hamlet.* Always close at hand have been Mark Anderson's *Shakespeare by Another Name* with its extensive and valuable end notes and Charlton Ogburn's *The Mysterious William Shakespeare.*

I am of course fully aware that this first Oxfordian edition of *Hamlet* is just that, a first attempt. The hope is that it will inspire more research into the evidence and more interpretations that point to Oxford as the author for an even greater appreciation of the genius of his accomplishment. Oxfordian scholars in the years to come will undoubtedly find more parallels to Oxford's life and concerns and will have more and better insights into this richly "autobiographical" Shakespeare play.

Made in the USA
Columbia, SC
08 October 2018